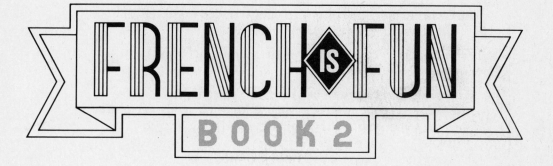

FRENCH IS FUN

BOOK 2

Cassettes

The Cassette program comprises six two-sided cassettes. The voices are those of native speakers of French.

Each of the twenty lessons in the textbook includes the following cassette materials:

Oral exercises (from the *Teacher's Manual* and textbook) in four-phased sequences: cue—pause for student response—correct response by native speaker—pause for student repetition.

The narrative or playlet at normal listening speed.

Questions based on the narrative or playlet in four-phased sequences.

The dialog with model responses at normal speed, then again by phrases with pauses for student repetition.

In addition, the final cassette includes the listening-comprehension passages in the Proficiency Test.

The Cassettes (Ordering Code N 560 C) are available separately from the publisher. A complete cassette script is included.

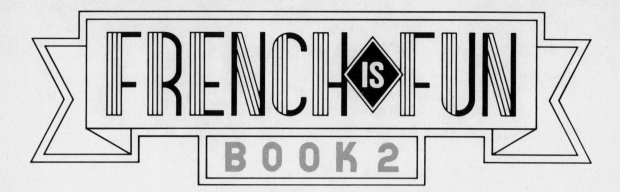

FRENCH IS FUN
BOOK 2

Lively lessons for advancing students

Gail Stein

Foreign Language Department
Martin Van Buren High School
New York City

When ordering this book, please specify *either* **R 560 S**
or FRENCH IS FUN, BOOK 2, SOFTBOUND EDITION

Dedicated to serving

AMSCO

our nation's youth

AMSCO SCHOOL PUBLICATIONS, INC.
315 Hudson Street/New York, N.Y. 10013

ISBN 0-87720-029-7

Printed in the United States of America

1 2 3 4 5 6 7 8 9 10   99 98 97 96 95 94 93 92

With love. . .
   To Doug, Eric and Michael,
      and to my parents,
         Sara and Jack Bernstein

Finally, Tome II, MBF. Thanks for all your support,
   inspiration, and help. I couldn't have done it without you!
      Love always,
         Gail

Preface

If French is fun, more French is more fun. That is the premise on which this book is based.

FRENCH IS FUN, BOOK 2 continues the natural, personalized, enjoyable, and rewarding program of language acquisition begun in the first course. BOOK 2 provides all the elements for a full second course and prepares students for their first formal proficiency testing.

FRENCH IS FUN, BOOK 2 is designed to broaden the student's level of achievement in basic skills, with special emphasis on communication. Through the topical contexts, students will also expand their acquisition of vocabulary, their control of structure, and their ability to communicate about their daily lives, express their opinions, and supply real information.

FRENCH IS FUN, BOOK 2 consists of four parts. Each part contains five lessons followed by a *Révision* unit, in which structure and vocabulary are recapitulated and practiced through various *activités*. These *activités* include games and puzzles as well as more conventional exercises. A concluding Proficiency Test provides an opportunity for evaluating student performance in speaking, listening comprehension, reading comprehension, and writing.

Each lesson includes a step-by-step sequence of learning elements designed to make the materials directly accessible to students:

Vocabulary

Each lesson begins by presenting the topical and thematically related vocabulary through sets of drawings that convey the meanings of new words and expressions in French without recourse to English. This device, sometimes in individual vignettes, sometimes in composite scenes, enables students to make a direct and vivid association between the French terms and their meanings. The *activités* that follow directly also use pictures to help students practice words and expressions.

Structure

FRENCH IS FUN, BOOK 2 introduces new structural elements in small learning components—one at a time, followed directly by appropriate *activités*, many of them personalized and presented in a communicative framework. By following this simple, straightforward, guided presentation, students make their own discoveries and formulate their own conclusion and in the process gain a feeling of accomplishment and success.

Conversation

To encourage students to use French for communication and self-expression, each lesson includes a dialog exercise designed to stimulate creative speaking. All dialogs are illustrated in cartoon-strip fashion, with students completing empty "balloons" with appropriate bits of original dialog. Students should have fun with these dramatizations.

Reading

Each lesson contains a short narrative or playlet that features the new structures and vocabulary and reinforces previously acquired vocabulary. Each reading selection not only is a vehicle for the presentation of these elements but also deals with a topic of intrisic interest related to the real, everyday experiences of today's students: social relationships, humorous science-fiction, school experiences, human-interest material, and so on. Cognates and near-cognates are used extensively to permit a much greater range of vocabulary.

Personal Information

A major goal of the entire program is to enable students to personalize language by relating the situation in the lesson to their own lives. In this activity, students are asked easy-to-answer, open-ended questions that require them to respond with information from their own experiences.

Composition

Guided writing practice affords students the opportunity to express themselves creatively about a variety of situations related to the theme and topic of the lesson.

Culture

Each lesson is followed by an *Intervalle culturel*. These twenty *intervalles*, most of them illustrated, offer students a picturesque view of the vast mosaic of French culture.

Cahier d'exercices

FRENCH IS FUN, BOOK 2 has a companion workbook, CAHIER D'EXERCICES, which features additional writing practice and stimulating puzzles to supplement the textbook exercises.

Teacher's Manual and Key; Testing

A separate *Teacher's Manual and Key* provides suggestions for teaching all elements in the book, additional oral practice materials, and a complete Key to all exercises and puzzles.

The *Manual* also includes a Quiz for each lesson, a Unit Test for each part, and two Achievement Tests. These tests are designed to be simple in order to give all students a sense of accomplishment. The tests use a variety of techniques through which mastery of structure and vocabulary as well as comprehension may be evaluated. Teachers may use these tests as they appear or modify them to fit particular needs. Keys are provided for all test materials.

The author wishes to express special thanks to her consultant, Roger Herz, for his professional help and for supplying much of the authentic backup materials used in this book.

G.S.

Contents

Troisième Partie

Quatrième Partie

Première Partie

1 À la fête française

The Verb **servir**;
Irregular **-ir** Verbs;
Interrogative **quel**

1 Vocabulaire

**RESTAURANT
À LA FÊTE FRANÇAISE
PLATS DU JOUR
(Dishes of the day)**

VIANDES

Gigot d'agneau (Leg of lamb)
Rosbif froid (Cold roast beef)
Rôti de bœuf (Roast beef)
Canard à l'orange (Duck baked with oranges)
Saucisses grillées (Grilled sausages)
Ragoût de veau (Veal stew)

SPÉCIALITÉS

Crevettes à la mayonnaise (Shrimp cocktail)
Salade de maïs et saumon (Corn and salmon salad)
Pâtes fraîches (Fresh pasta)
Omelette aux champignons (Mushroom omelet)

DESSERTS

Riz au lait (Rice pudding)
Tarte aux pommes (Apple pie)

__ ACTIVITÉ _____

A. Anne and Janine are at the French food festival at their school. What dishes do they eat?

EXAMPLE:

Elles mangent du poulet.

1. (f.) _____

2. (f. pl.) _____

3. (f. pl.) _____

4. (m.) _____

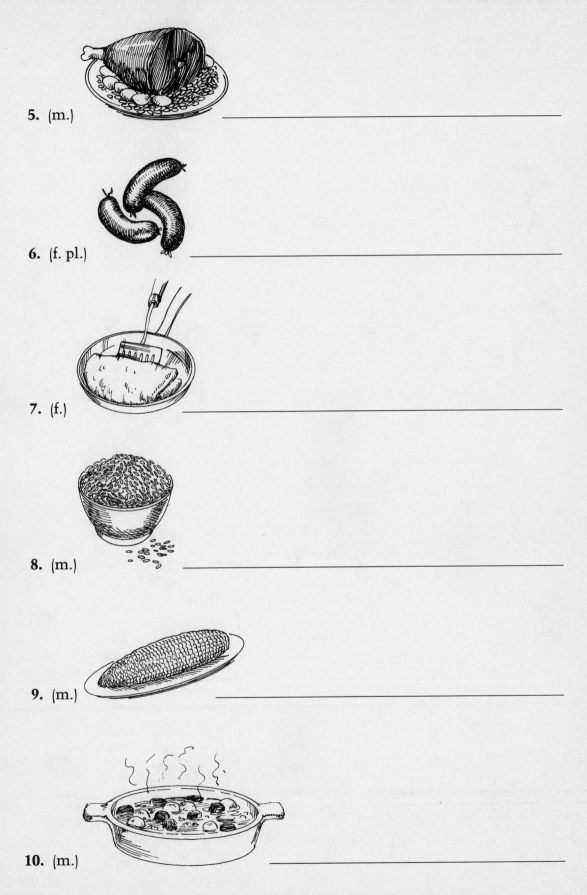

5. (m.) _____

6. (f. pl.) _____

7. (f.) _____

8. (m.) _____

9. (m.) _____

10. (m.) _____

2 What are the students in Mme Dupont's French class serving at the food festival? Read the dialog and see if you can find all the forms of the verb **servir** (*to serve*):

Now fill in all the forms of the verb **servir** from the dialog:

je _____   nous _____

tu _____   vous _____

il _____   ils _____

elle _____   elles _____

3   Look carefully at the singular column. Which letters were dropped from the infinitive to form the verb stem? _____ Which ending was added for **je**? _____; **tu**? _____; **il**? _____; **elle**? _____.

Now look carefully at the plural column. Which letters were dropped from the infinitive to form the verb stem? _____ Which ending was added for **nous**? _____; **vous**? _____; **ils**? _____; **elles**? _____.

Other verbs conjugated like **servir** are **dormir** (*to sleep*), **partir** (*to leave*), **sentir** (*to feel, to smell*), and **sortir** (*to go out*).

Now see if you can fill in all the forms for these verbs:

	dormir	partir	sentir	sortir
je	_____	_____	_____	_____
tu	_____	_____	_____	_____
il	_____	_____	_____	_____
elle	_____	_____	_____	_____
nous	_____	_____	_____	_____
vous	_____	_____	_____	_____
ils	_____	_____	_____	_____
elles	_____	_____	_____	_____

__ ACTIVITÉS _____

B. Fill in the correct form of the verb:

1. (dormir) Tu _____ beaucoup.

2. (partir) Ils _____ avant le dîner.

3. (sortir) Avec qui _____-elle?

4. (servir) Que _____-elles?

5. (sentir) Les filles _____ les fleurs.

6. (dormir) Nous _____ chez nous.

7. (partir) Je _____ à 6 heures.

8. (sortir) Ils _____ de la maison.

9. (servir) Paul _____ le déjeuner.

10. (sentir) Le chien _____ un danger.

C. Tell how each of the following prepares for the food festival:

1. Je ne _____ pas longtemps.

2. Les garçons _____ pour le festival.

3. Marie _____ les plats français.

4. Tu _____ le gâteau du réfrigérateur.

5. Ils _____ les tartes.

6. Nous _____ jusqu'à dix heures.

7. Vous _____ les hors-d'œuvre.

8. Il _____ le ragoût.

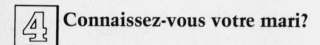

4 Connaissez-vous votre mari?

Connaissez *know*
mari *husband*

You know how to ask questions in French that require a yes or no answer. But if you want to ask for specific information, you need special question words: **quel** is such a question word. Let's read about a special game played for entertainment at the food festival. Watch especially for the various forms of **quel**:

MAÎTRE DE CÉRÉMONIE: Bonsoir, chers spectateurs. Je suis François Bavard, le maître de cérémonie. Soyez les bienvenus à notre jeu: «Connaissez-vous votre mari?» Les règles sont simples. Nous posons cinq questions à l'épouse mais nous connaissons déjà les réponses de son mari. Le couple gagne cent dollars pour chaque réponse correcte de l'épouse, jusqu'à un total de cinq cents dollars. Et maintenant, notre première compétitrice. Bonsoir. Quel est votre nom?

LA COMPÉTITRICE: Marie.

M. DE C.: Eh bien bonne chance, Marie. Tout de suite la première question: il est évident que votre mari aime manger, quelle cuisine préfère-t-il?

MARIE: Il préfère la cuisine de sa mère! Ha, ha! Non, il préfère la cuisine française.

chers *dear*

soyez les bienvenus
   welcome
   jeu *game*
les règles *rules*
   posons *ask*
l'épouse *wife*
déjà *already*
chaque *each*

cuisine *cooking*

M. DE C.: Quels légumes mange-t-il?

MARIE: Il est comme les enfants, il ne mange pas de légumes.

M. DE C.: Quel restaurant fréquente-t-il?

MARIE: Son restaurant favori est «Le Versailles».

M. DE C.: Quelles pâtisseries aime-t-il?

MARIE: Regardez mon mari. Il aime toutes les pâtis-series!

M. DE C.: Quel est son plat préféré?

MARIE: Le ragoût d'agneau.

M. DE C.: Mesdames, mesdemoiselles, messieurs, quel mariage parfait! Applaudissons Marie. Cinq réponses correctes! Félicitations, Marie, vous connaissez bien votre mari, Martin Renard.

MARIE: Quoi? Quel mari? Quel Martin? Quelle histoire sensationnelle! Martin Renard n'est pas mon mari: c'est le mari de l'autre compétitrice!

pâtisseries *pastries*

___ ACTIVITÉ _____

D. Répondez aux questions:

1. Quel est le nom du jeu?

_____

2. Qui est la première compétitrice?

_____

3. Combien d'argent est-ce que le couple peut gagner?

_____

4. Quelle cuisine le mari préfère-t-il?

_____

5. Quels légumes est-ce qu'il mange?

_____

6. Quel restaurant fréquente-t-il?

_____

7. Quelles pâtisseries aime-t-il?

_____

8. Quel est son plat préféré?

_____

9. Combien de réponses correctes a Marie?

_____

10. Quelle est la surprise à la fin de l'histoire?

_____

---

5 Let's take a closer look at the question word **quel**:

> *Quel* restaurant fréquente-t-il?   *Quels* légumes mange-t-il?
> *Quelle* cuisine préfère-t-il?   *Quelles* pâtisseries aime-t-il?

The interrogative adjective **quel** and its forms mean _____. The

form of the word **quel** is followed by a _____. Look at the
nouns. Determine their gender (masculine or feminine) and their number (singular or plural). How do you know which form of **quel** to use?

Use **quel** before _____,

quels before _____,

quelle before _____,

quelles before _____.

Now compare these sentences:

> **Quel restaurant** *fréquente-t-il?*
> **Quel restaurant** *est-ce qu'il fréquente?*
>
> **Quelles pâtisseries** *aime-t-il?*
> **Quelles pâtisseries** *est-ce qu'il aime?*

When **quel**, **quelle**, **quels**, or **quelles** is followed by a noun that is the object of

the question, you can form the question by either _____ the

subject pronoun and the verb, or by using _____ before the subject and the verb.

ACTIVITÉS

E. Ask your friend which food he/she likes at the festival:

EXAMPLE:

Quels fruits aimes-tu?

1. _____

2. _____

3. _____

4. _____

5. _____

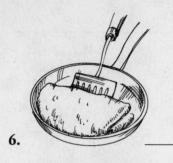

6. _____

7. _____

8. _____

9. _____

F. Complete the following questions with the correct forms of **quel**:

1. _____ restaurant fréquentez-vous?

2. _____ plats préparent-ils?

3. À _____ heure est-ce que la fête commence?

4. _____ salade choisit-elle?

5. _____ repas (singular) préférez-vous?

6. _____ tartes mange-t-il?

7. _____ fruits aimez-vous?

8. _____ crêpes prenez-vous?

Now look at these sentences:

Quel garçon **travaille à la fête?**
Quelle fille **prépare la salade?**

When **quel**, **quelle**, **quels**, or **quelles** is followed by a noun that is the subject of the question, neither inversion nor **est-ce que** is necessary.

___ ACTIVITÉ _____

G. There are many curious people at the food festival. Complete their questions with the correct form of **quel**:

1. _____ chef arrive à 9 heures?

2. _____ professeurs travaillent beaucoup?

3. _____ plat est délicieux?

4. _____ tartes sentent bon?

5. _____ soupe est excellente?

6. _____ filles préparent les desserts?

7. _____ garçons parlent aux enfants?

8. _____ femme goûte les crêpes?

 The adjective **quel** and its forms may be used before the verb **être** to ask questions. **Quel** must agree with the noun in the question:

Quel **est son plat préféré?** [masculine singular]
Quels **sont leurs desserts préférés?** [masculine plural]
Quelle **est la date de la fête?** [feminine singular]
Quelles **sont leurs adresses?** [feminine plural]

__ ACTIVITÉ _____

H. Complete with the correct form of **quel**:

1. _____ est son nom?

2. _____ est ta classe préférée?

3. _____ sont les dates importantes?

4. _____ sont les jours de la semaine?

5. _____ est ton numéro de téléphone?

6. _____ sont tes programmes préférés à la télévision?

7. _____ est sa nouvelle adresse?

8. _____ sont les chansons intéressantes?

Now look at these sentences:

> ***Quel dîner* délicieux!**
> ***Quels plats* intéressants!**

In exclamations, **quel** and its forms mean: _____.

__ ACTIVITÉ _____

I. Express that everything at the food festival is great:

EXAMPLE:

Quelles crêpes formidables!

1. _____

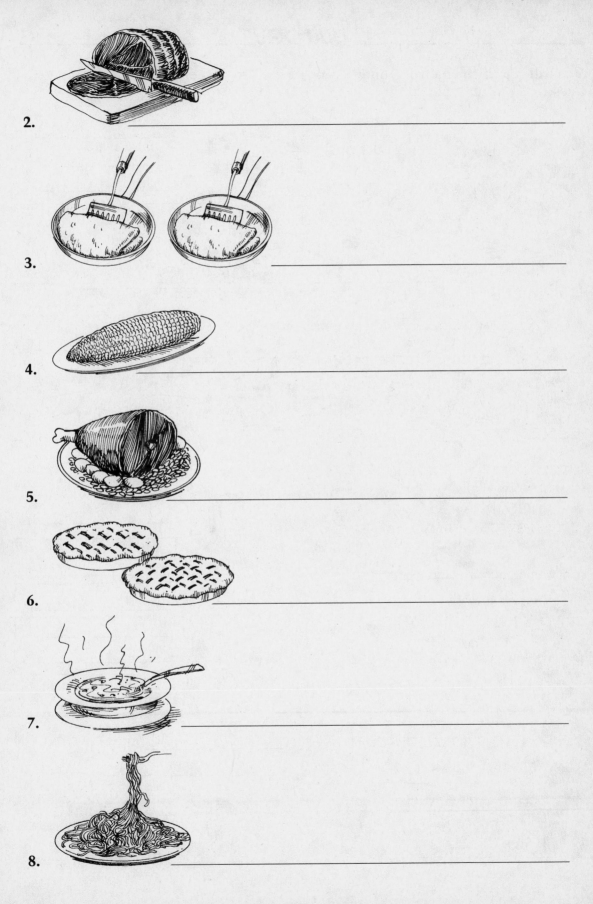

2. _____

3. _____

4. _____

5. _____

6. _____

7. _____

8. _____

DIALOGUE

Vous allez participer à la fête internationale de votre lycée. Votre professeur pose des questions et vous répondez:

_____ QUESTIONS PERSONNELLES _____

1. À quelle heure est-ce que votre mère/votre père sert le dîner?

_____

2. Quel plat sent bon?

_____

3. À quelle heure partez-vous pour l'école?

_____

4. Avec qui sortez-vous?

_____

5. Où dormez-vous?

_____

6. Quelle est votre adresse?

_____

_____ VOUS _____

You are in charge of the Foreign Food Festival for your school. Before preparing any dishes, you want to find out what the students like. Make up five questions that you could use for your food survey:

1. _____

2. _____

3. _____

4. _____

5. _____

COMPOSITION

You have just made a new friend in your class. Ask him/her for the following information:

1. Name _____

2. Address _____

3. Phone number _____

4. Favorite class _____

5. Favorite TV program _____

INTERVALLE CULTUREL

Plats typiques

Students from several French-speaking countries have prepared dishes for the school food festival. Which ones would you try?

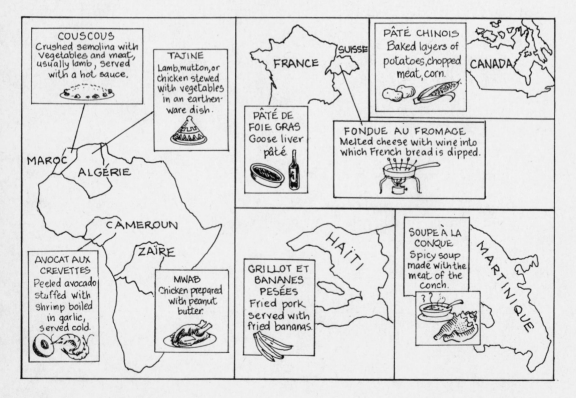

EXAMPLE: Je goûterais (*I would taste*) la fondue parce que j'aime le fromage.
            Je ne goûterais pas . . . parce que . . .

2 _Chez le bijoutier_

The Verb **mettre**; Negative Expressions

1 **Vocabulaire**

LA BIJOUTERIE « LE DIAMANT »

GRANDE VENTE DE BIJOUX

les pendants d'oreilles (m.)

l'anneau en or (m.)

les boucles d'oreilles (f.)

la broche d'émeraude

la montre (-bracelet)

la chaîne

le bracelet en argent

le collier de perles

la bague de diamants

__ ACTIVITÉS _____

A. Marie-Hélène has a job in a jewelry store. The manager has told her to place labels on all the articles in the showcase for the big sale. Can you help her?

bracelet en or $300   **anneau en argent $50**
bague de diamants $750   **broche d'émeraude $600**
collier de perles $500   **montre en or $125**

B. You are in the jewelry department of a store buying holiday presents. What should you buy for these people on your list:

EXAMPLE: votre père: J'achète une montre pour mon père.

1. votre ami Jean: _____

2. votre amie Annette: _____

3. votre mère: _____

4. votre sœur Jacqueline (16 ans): _____

5. votre frère Michel (18 ans): _____

☐2 What jewelry do you put on every day? Read the dialog and see if you can find all the forms of the verb **mettre** (*to put, to put on*):

Can you now fill in the correct forms of the verb **mettre**?

je _____   nous _____

tu _____   vous _____

il _____   ils _____

elle _____   elles _____

Other verbs conjugated like **mettre** are:

> **permettre** (*to allow, to permit*)
> **promettre** (*to promise*)
> **remettre** (*to postpone, to put back*)

____ ACTIVITÉS _____

C. Express what jewelry these people are putting on for their family reunion:

EXAMPLE: Paulette met une bague.

1. Nous _____ .

2. Régine _____ .

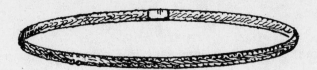

3. Je _____ .

4. Paul et Georgette _____ .

5. Tu _____ .

6. Vous _____ .

D. Complete with the correct form of the verb:

1. (mettre)   Tu _____ le bracelet.

2. (permettre)   Anne _____ cette surprise-partie.

3. (promettre)   Ils _____ d'être à l'heure.

4. (remettre)   Nous _____ l'examen à demain.

5. (mettre)   Je _____ mes gants.

6. (permettre)   Les filles _____ à Georges de partir.

7. (promettre)   Vous _____ un cadeau à l'enfant.

8. (remettre)   Il _____ la composition à lundi.

③ La magie

la magie *magic*

You already know that to make a sentence negative in French you simply put

_____ before the conjugated verb and _____ after the conjugated verb. There are, however, other important negative expressions in French. Read the following story and pay careful attention to the new negatives:

Un homme est assis sur une chaise devant un groupe de personnes. Ses yeux sont couverts. L'homme **ne** peut **plus** voir les spectateurs. Il **ne** voit **personne**. Il **ne** voit **rien**.

assis *seated*
couverts *covered*
ne ... plus *no longer*
  ne ... personne *no one*
ne ... rien *nothing*

Un assistant prend quelque chose d'un spectateur et dit: «Maître, mon très grand maître, j'ai quelque chose dans la main. Qu'est-ce que c'est? Donnez-moi la réponse.»

L'homme pense un moment et dit: «**Ne** dites **plus rien**. Je vois une chose qui **n'**est **ni** grande **ni** petite. Ce **n'**est **pas** un bracelet. C'est ... C'est ... C'est ... une montre!»

ne ... plus rien *nothing more*
ne ... ni ... ni *neither nor*

«Formidable, sensationnel!», crie l'assistant. «Le maître **ne** fait **jamais** d'erreurs. Il a toujours raison. Il **ne** dit **que** la vérité. Applaudissons!»

ne ... jamais *never*
ne ... que *only*
  la vérité *truth*

Mais, qu'est-ce qui se passe ici? Est-ce vraiment de la magie? Cet homme est-il un magicien ou a-t-il un truc? Comment a-t-il trouvé la réponse correcte?*

qu'est-ce qui se passe?
  what's happening?
truc *trick*

___ ACTIVITÉ ___

E. Vrai ou faux? If the sentence is incorrect, change it to make it correct:

1. Le magicien est assis sur **un lit.**

_____

2. Le magicien voit **les spectateurs**.

_____

3. Il voit **tout**.

_____

* L'assistant a dit: «MON TRÈS grand maître.»

4. Son assistant prend quelque chose d'**un spectateur**.

_____

5. L'assistant dit qu'il a quelque chose dans **la poche**.

_____

6. La chose est **très grande**.

_____

7. C'est **un bracelet**.

_____

8. Le maître fait **toujours** des erreurs.

_____

9. Le maître **ne** dit **pas** la vérité.

_____

10. Cet homme **est** un magicien.

_____

 Look at the words in bold type in the story and then insert the French negatives in the table:

not any longer, no longer	_____ · · ·	_____
no one, nobody	_____ · · ·	_____
nothing	_____ · · ·	_____
nothing more	_____ · · ·	_____
neither . . . nor	_____ · · ·	_____
not	_____ · · ·	_____
never	_____ · · ·	_____
only	_____ · · ·	_____

 Now read these sentences:

Il *ne* peut *plus* voir les
   spectateurs.
Il *ne* voit *personne*.
Il *ne* voit *rien*.

Ne dites *plus rien*.
Elle *n'*est *ni* grande *ni* petite.
Il *ne* fait *jamais* d'erreurs.
Il *ne* dit *que* la vérité.

Which little French word is used in all the negative sentences? _____ Which

familiar French word is replaced by other negative words? _____ Where is **ne**?

_____

Where is the other negative word? _____

___ ACTIVITÉS _____

F. Nathalie and Nicole are twin sisters who like different things. Give Nicole's
negative answers to Nathalie's questions:

    EXAMPLE: J'écoute la radio. Et toi?
                Je n'écoute pas la radio.

1. Je mets cet anneau. Et toi?

_____

2. Je joue au tennis. Et toi?

_____

3. Je danse bien. Et toi?

_____

G. Your friend does something, but you say that you do the opposite:

    EXAMPLE: Je sens quelque chose. Et toi?
                Je ne sens rien.

1. Je mange quelque chose. Et toi?

_____

2. Je vois quelque chose. Et toi?

_____

3. J'entends quelque chose. Et toi?

_____

4. Je prends quelque chose. Et toi?

_____

5. Je trouve quelque chose. Et toi?

_____

H. You still do the opposite of what your friend does:

> EXAMPLE: Je vois quelqu'un (*somebody*). Et toi?
> Je ne vois personne.

1. J'entends quelqu'un. Et toi?

_____

2. J'aime quelqu'un. Et toi?

_____

3. Je regarde quelqu'un. Et toi?

_____

4. J'adore quelqu'un. Et toi?

_____

5. Je cherche quelqu'un. Et toi?

_____

I. Say that you don't do the following things anymore:

> EXAMPLE: manger du chocolat
> Je ne mange plus de chocolat.

1. danser

_____

2. travailler

_____

3. chanter

_____

4. regarder ce programme

_____

5. jouer au tennis

_____

J. You don't like to eat certain foods. What do you say to your mother?

> EXAMPLE: les fruits . . . les légumes
> Je n'aime ni les fruits ni les légumes.

1. les frites . . . le maïs

_____

2. les pommes . . . les oranges

_____

3. la viande . . . le poisson

_____

4. le bifteck . . . le rosbif

_____

5. le veau . . . l'agneau

_____

K. Say that you never put on the following jewelry to go to school:

EXAMPLE:

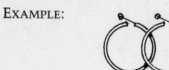

Je ne mets jamais de boucles d'oreilles.

1. _____

2. _____

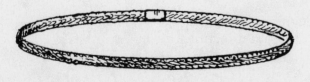

3. _____

4. _____

5. _____

L. What are the only things Anne eats?

EXAMPLE:

Elle ne mange que du rosbif.

1. _____

2. _____

3. _____

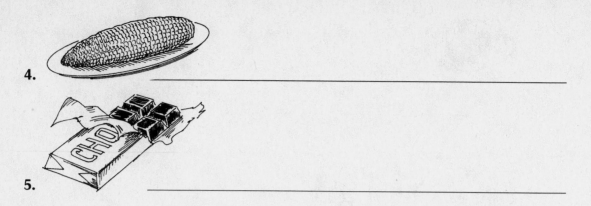

4. _____

5. _____

M. Change the sentences using the French equivalents of the expressions in parentheses:

1. (only) Il étudie le soir.

_____

2. (nobody) Nous voyons.

_____

3. (no longer) Je travaille au bureau.

_____

4. (never) Vous choisissez les fruits.

_____

5. (nothing) Mangez!

_____

6. (neither . . . nor) Marie aime les fruits et les légumes.

_____

 Note that **personne** and **rien** can be used as subjects:

> **Personne ne parle.**   _Nobody speaks._
> **Rien ne se passe.**   _Nothing is happening._

__ ACTIVITÉS _____

N. There's a test tomorrow. Say that no one is doing the following things tonight:

    EXAMPLE: écouter un disque
                Personne n'écoute de disque.

   1. regarder la télévision

   _____

   2. jouer au football

   _____

   3. faire une promenade

   _____

   4. parler au téléphone

   _____

   5. aller au cinéma

   _____

O. Today just isn't your day. Nothing is right. Express your negative feelings:

    EXAMPLE: important
                Rien n'est important.

   1. formidable _____

   2. intéressant _____

   3. superbe _____

   4. excellent _____

   5. parfait _____

_____ *VOUS* _____

Complete the following sentences to tell us something about yourself:

1. Je ne _____ personne.

2. Je n'aime ni _____ ni _____ .

3. Je ne _____ plus _____ .

4. Je ne _____ jamais _____ .

5. Je ne _____ que _____ .

6. Je ne _____ rien.

7. Je ne _____ pas _____ .

_____ QUESTIONS PERSONNELLES _____

1. Quels bijoux mettez-vous pour aller à l'école?

_____

2. Quels bijoux mettez-vous pour aller à une surprise-partie?

_____

3. Quels vêtements mettez-vous quand il fait froid?

_____

4. Quand mettez-vous une montre?

_____

5. Où mettez-vous vos livres?

_____

_____ COMPOSITION _____

Using different negative expressions, write a list of five things that you do not do:

EXAMPLE: Je ne mets jamais de pendants d'oreilles.

_____

_____

_____

_____

_____

DIALOGUE

Vous allez à une surprise-partie. Votre petit frère est très curieux. Que répondez-vous?

INTERVALLE CULTUREL

En avoir pour son argent

When you go shopping, especially in a foreign country, "do you get your money's worth?"

In the United States, the basic monetary unit is the dollar, which is also used in Canada, although it has a lesser value. What about the other French-speaking countries? What kind of money do you need if you want to go shopping in France? In Haiti? In Martinique? In Switzerland?

The basic monetary unit in France is the **franc**. The **franc** is also used in Belgium, Guadeloupe, Luxembourg, Martinique, Monaco, Switzerland, and in most French-speaking African countries (Cameroon, Chad, Djibouti, Gabon, Ivory Coast, Mali, Niger, Senegal, Togo), although not all the francs have the same value. Other countries have the following currencies:

Morocco — dirham   Haiti — gourde
Mauritania — ouguiya   Zaire — zaire

How many Swiss francs can you buy with a dollar? How many Belgian francs? Check the foreign-exchange table in your local newspaper for the latest exchange rates.

3 À la plage

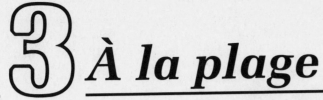

The Verb **ouvrir**;
Irregular Noun Plurals

1 Vocabulaire

le bateau

le maître-nageur

le requin

la vague

le parasol

la mer

le seau

le château
de sable

le panier

le trou

le sable

la pelle

les cailloux (m.)

le coquillage

— ACTIVITÉ

A. There's a phone booth near the beach. You decide to call your mother and tell her what you see:

EXAMPLES: Je vois la plage.
Je vois un trou.

1. _____

2. _____

3. _____

4. _____

5. _____

6. _____

7. _____

8. _____

9. _____

10. _____

11. _____

12. _____

2 You are at the beach with a group of friends. What do you all find as you open your picnic baskets? Read the dialog and try to discover all the forms of the verb **ouvrir** (*to open*):

Now fill in all the forms of the verb **ouvrir**:

j' _____   nous _____

tu _____   vous _____

il _____   ils _____

elle _____   elles _____

Other verbs conjugated like **ouvrir** are **couvrir** (*to cover*) and **découvrir** (*to discover*).

See if you can conjugate these verbs:

	couvrir	**découvrir**
je	_____	_____
tu	_____	_____
il	_____	_____
elle	_____	_____
nous	_____	_____
vous	_____	_____
ils	_____	_____
elles	_____	_____

___ ACTIVITÉS _____

B. Complétez les phrases avec les formes correctes des verbes entre parenthèses:

1. (ouvrir) Paulette _____ le parasol.

2. (couvrir) Vous _____ Jean de sable.

3. (découvrir) Je _____ des coquillages.

4. (ouvrir) Les garçons _____ leurs paniers.

5. (couvrir) Il _____ le trou.

6. (découvrir) Nous _____ le secret.

7. (ouvrir) _____ le panier, vous deux!

8. (couvrir) Tu _____ l'enfant.

9. (découvrir) Elles _____ le château de sable.

C. You are observing what's happening at the beach. Using suitable forms of **couvrir**, **découvrir**, or **ouvrir**, describe what these people do:

EXAMPLE:

Henri découvre un caillou.

1. Une petite fille _____.

2. Tous les enfants _____.

3. Un garçon _____.

4. Les filles _____ .

5. Le maître-nageur _____ .

6. M. et Mme Paul _____ .

③ Une aventure à la plage

Now let's read a story about an adventure at the beach:

Cet été, Jean-François passe ses vacances chez sa grand-mère, sur une petite île des Antilles. Chaque matin, de très bonne heure, il fait une promenade sur la plage avec son amie Nancy. Ce matin, tandis qu'ils marchent lentement, Jean-François aperçoit quelque chose qui brille dans le sable. C'est une bouteille avec une carte dedans. Jean-François et Nancy regardent la carte et commencent à rire. Voici ce qu'ils voient:

île *island*
de bonne heure *early*
tandis que *while*
lentement *slowly*
  aperçoit *notices*
brille *shines* **bouteille** *bottle*
rire *to laugh*
ce que *what*

«Quelle plaisanterie!» dit Jean-François.

plaisanterie *joke*

«C'est absolument ridicule!» répond Nancy.

Les deux jeunes gens continuent à marcher quand tout à coup ils arrivent au lieu indiqué sur la carte.

«Ce n'est pas possible!» s'exclame Jean-François.

s'exclame *shouts*

«Bah! Cherchons quand même ce trésor», dit Nancy. «Peut-être allons-nous trouver quelque chose?»

quand même *even so*
trésor *treasure*

Avec des cailloux et des coquillages ils cherchent dans le sable. À leur grande surprise, ils découvrent une boîte. Ils poussent un cri: à l'intérieur, ils voient des bijoux de toutes sortes — des colliers, des bracelets, des bagues — tous de grande valeur. Les voilà très agités.

boîte *box*
poussent un cri *shout*
valeur *value*

«Qu'est-ce que nous allons faire?» demande Nancy.

«Eh bien, mettons une annonce dans le journal. Si personne ne réclame ce trésor, alors . . . à nous la vie de château!»

annonce *announcement*
réclame *claims*
vie de château *life of ease*

___ ACTIVITÉ _____

D. Répondez par des phrases complètes:

1. Où Jean-François passe-t-il ses vacances?

_____

2. Que fait-il chaque matin?

_____

3. Que trouvent Jean-François et Nancy un matin?

_____

4. Qu'est-ce qu'il y a dedans?

_____

5. Pourquoi commencent-ils à rire?

_____

6. Où est-ce qu'ils arrivent?

_____

7. Que font-ils?

_____

8. Que découvrent-ils?

_____

9. Qu'est-ce qu'il y a dans la boîte?

_____

10. Que vont-ils faire maintenant?

_____

_____

 On their walk, Jean-François and Nancy see and find many things. When we speak about more than one person or thing, we must use the plural. Do you remember how to make most French nouns plural?

le trésor _____

la promenade _____

l'été _____

In French, to make most nouns plural, simply add _____ to the

_____ of the noun. Change the singular definite article **le**, **la**, **l'**

to the plural definite article _____.

Do you remember how to make the noun plural if it already ends in **s**?

le fils _____

If you wrote **les fils**, you are correct. Nouns that end in **s** do not change in the plural.

You also have learned some irregular plurals; for example:

le bureau	les bureaux
le chapeau	les chapeaux
l'hôpit*al*	les hôpit*aux*
le journ*al*	les journ*aux*

To form the plural of most nouns ending in **-eau**, add _____. To form the plural of most nouns ending in **-al**, change **-al** to _____.

__ ACTIVITÉ _____

E. Make the following nouns plural. Use the plural definite article:

1. le panier _____

2. le cheval _____

3. le bateau _____

4. l'autobus _____

5. le requin _____

6. le général _____

7. le bras _____

8. le couteau _____

 Now that your memory has been refreshed, it is time to learn about other irregular plural forms. Let's see if you can figure out the rules for each group of nouns. Look carefully:

le prix	les prix
la voix	les voix
la croix	les croix
le nez	les nez

How do you make a noun plural if it ends in **-x** or **-z**? _____

__ ACTIVITÉ _____

F. Make the following nouns plural. Use the plural definite article:

1. l'ami   _____

2. le repas   _____

3. le choix   _____

4. le prix   _____

5. le corps   _____

6. le gâteau   _____

7. la croix   _____

8. le nez   _____

| 6 | Look at this group of nouns with irregular plural: |

le feu   **les feux**
le lieu **les lieux**

Here's the simple rule: To make nouns ending in **-eu** plural, add _____ to the singular. Note this exception:

le pneu   **les pneus**

__ ACTIVITÉ _____

G. Make the following nouns plural. Use the plural definite article:

1. la fois   _____

2. le feu   _____

3. le palais   _____

4. la voix   _____

5. le jeu   _____

6. le pneu   _____

7. l'oiseau   _____

8. l'hôpital   _____

9. la robe   _____

10. le prix   _____

 Only seven nouns ending in **-ou** have an irregular plural that is formed by adding the letter **x** to the singular form:

le bijou	**les bijoux**
le caillou	**les cailloux**
le chou (*cabbage*)	**les choux**
le genou	**les genoux**
le hibou (*owl*)	**les hiboux**
le joujou (*toy*)	**les joujoux**
le pou (*louse*)	**les poux**

Except for these seven words, to form the plural of any nouns ending in **-ou**, simply add the letter **s** to the singular form:

le clou (*nail*)	**les clous**
le trou	**les trous**

ACTIVITÉS

H. Make the following nouns plural. Use the plural definite article:

1. le mois   _____

2. le bijou   _____

3. la pomme   _____

4. la voix   _____

5. le neveu   _____

6. le genou   _____

7. le gâteau   _____

8. le nez   _____

9. le hibou   _____

10. le lieu _____

11. l'eau _____

12. le trou _____

I. You and your friend are on a treasure hunt. Say what you are looking for:

EXAMPLE:

Nous cherchons des cailloux.

1. _____

2. _____

3. _____

4. _____

5. _____

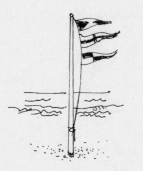

6. _____

7. _____

8. _____

8 Some nouns, most of which you already know, have irregular plurals:

le ciel	les *cieux*
l'œil	les *yeux*
madame	*mesdames*
mademoiselle	*mesdemoiselles*
monsieur	*messieurs*

The following nouns are normally used only in the plural in French:

les cheveux	*hair*
les ciseaux	*scissors*
les lunettes	*glasses*
les mathématiques	*mathematics*
les vacances	*vacation*

NOTE: Family names used in the plural do not end in **s**:

les Martin   *the Martins*

— ACTIVITÉS —————————————————————

J. You are playing with a group of children at the beach. Ask them to show you the following things:

EXAMPLE:

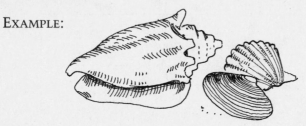

Montrez-moi vos coquillages.

1. _____

2. _____

3. _____

4. _____

5. _____

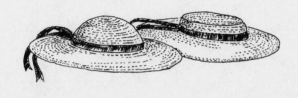

6. _____

7. _____

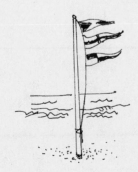

8. _____

K. Rewrite the sentences changing all the nouns to the singular. Make any other necessary changes:

> EXAMPLE: Ils vendent les bateaux.
> Il vend le bateau.

1. Les chevaux traversent (*cross*) la rue.

_____

2. Les gâteaux sont délicieux.

_____

3. Les drapeaux sont bleus, blancs et rouges.

_____

4. Mesdames, regardez ces films.

_____

5. Les palais sont magnifiques.

_____

6. Les hiboux sont dans les arbres.

_____

7. Ces jeux sont difficiles.

_____

8. Les repas sont bons.

_____

9. Les voix sont jolies.

_____

10. Ces messieurs sont élégants.

_____

_____ *VOUS* _____

You find a large chest at the beach. When you open it, what do you find? List five things:

1. _____   4. _____

2. _____   5. _____

3. _____

DIALOGUE

Pierre téléphone à Chantal. Que dit Chantal?

QUESTIONS PERSONNELLES

1. Combien de manteaux avez-vous?

   _____

2. De quelle couleur sont vos cheveux?

   _____

3. De quelle couleur sont vos yeux?

   _____

4. Quels journaux lisez-vous?

   _____

5. Portez-vous des lunettes?

   _____

6. Quels animaux aimez-vous?

   _____

7. En quelle saison allez-vous à la plage?

   _____

8. À quelle plage allez-vous?

   _____

   _____

COMPOSITION

Write a postcard to a friend in which you talk about your trip to the beaches of Southern France:

La Côte d'Azur
France

INTERVALLE CULTUREL

À la plage

Where would you like to go on vacation? If you like the beach and the opportunity to practice your French, the beautiful beaches along the Mediterranean on the Côte d'Azur in Southern France are a true tourist attraction, both to the French and to foreigners. In August, it is next to impossible to get a hotel room in Nice, Cannes, and St. Tropez on the Côte d'Azur (also called the Riviera).

If you prefer the beaches along the English Channel in Northern France, visit popular Deauville.

To enjoy a French-speaking atmosphere closer to home, the beaches on the Caribbean islands of Martinique, Guadeloupe, Haïti, and St. Martin are a must.

Would you like to spend your vacation at one of these beaches? What are you waiting for?

4 *Lettres au journal*

The Verbs **lire**, **écrire**, **dire**; Irregular Adjectives

1 Vocabulaire

LA POSTE

la boîte aux lettres

le code postal

le timbre (-poste)

l'enveloppe (f.)

la carte postale

le magazine/ la revue

LE JOURNAL

OE' DIGGER

LES NOUVELLES

LES BANDES DESSINÉES

UN ÉDITORIAL

UN ARTICLE

LE REPORTAGE SPORTIF

LES PETITES ANNONCES

___ ACTIVITÉS ___

A. List five activities required for writing and mailing a letter or a postcard:

EXAMPLE: J'achète (*I buy*) un timbre.

1. _____

2. _____

3. _____

4. _____

5. _____

B. Here are a couple of pages of a daily newspaper. Label the various sections in French:

You are certainly interested in other reading material besides newspapers and magazines:

le roman

le conte (de fées)

la pièce
(de théâtre)

le poème   l'histoire (f.)

___ ACTIVITÉ _____

C. Identify what Jeanne likes to read:

1. _____

2. _____

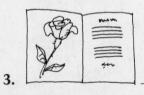

3. _____

4. _____

5. _____

3 Three common irregular French verbs, **lire** (*to read*), **écrire** (*to write*), and **dire** (*to say*), follow a similar pattern of conjugation. Read the dialog and see if you can spot all the forms of **lire**:

Now complete the table with the forms of **lire** used in our dialog:

je _____   nous _____

tu _____   vous _____

il _____	**ils** _____
elle _____	**elles** _____

___ ACTIVITÉ _____

D. Express in French what the following persons are reading:

EXAMPLE:    Je lis un conte.

1. Mon frère _____.

2. Nous _____.

3. Tu _____.

4. Mes parents _____.

5. Mme Robert _____ .

6. Vous _____ .

4 Here's another dialog. Try to find all the forms of the verb **écrire**:

Complete the table with the forms of **écrire**:

j' _____   **nous** _____

tu _____   **vous** _____

il _____   **ils** _____

elle _____   **elles** _____

___ ACTIVITÉ _____

E. Express in French what the following persons are writing:

EXAMPLE:    J'écris une carte postale.

1. Ma sœur _____.

2. Mes correspondants _____.

3. Tu _____.

4. Nous _____.

5. M. Colbert _____.

6. Vous _____.

 Another verb that is familiar to you is **dire**. See if you can find its forms in this dialog:

Now complete the table with the forms of **dire**:

je _____	nous _____
tu _____	vous _____
il _____	ils _____
elle _____	elles _____

ACTIVITÉ

F. From the list provided, choose what to say in the given situations:

Comment vas-tu?	**Quelle heure est-il?**
À bientôt.	**Je le regrette.**
Quelle est la date?	**Tu es sincère.**
Tu es charmant(e).	**Salut!**

EXAMPLE: Your friend is sick:
Je dis: «Comment vas-tu?»

1. You meet a friend:

Je _____

2. You leave friends:

Nous _____

3. You tell a friend what to say when he/she first meets a date:

Tu _____

4. You tell your friends what your French teacher says when he/she enters the classroom:

Il/Elle _____

5. You tell a girlfriend what the other students in the class say about her:

Ils _____

Let's take another look at our three new verbs side by side:

	lire	écrire	dire
je (j')	lis	écris	dis
tu	lis	écris	dis
il	lit	écrit	dit
elle	lit	écrit	dit
nous	lisons	écrivons	disons
vous	lisez	écrivez	dites
ils	lisent	écrivent	disent
elles	lisent	écrivent	disent

How are the verbs **lire** and **écrire** similar in their conjugations? _____

_____

How is **dire** different? _____

___ ACTIVITÉ _____

G. Complete the sentences with the correct forms of the verbs in parentheses:

1. (dire) Les filles _____ un mensonge.

2. (lire) Nous _____ un conte.

3. (écrire) Elles _____ une carte postale.

4. (dire) Je _____ «au revoir».

5. (lire) Vous _____ des bandes dessinées.

6. (écrire) Les garçons _____ une lettre.

7. (dire) Vous _____ «bonjour».

8. (lire) Elle _____ une histoire.

9. (écrire) Nous _____ un article.

10. (dire) Tu _____ la vérité.

11. (lire) Je _____ ce roman.

12. (écrire) Vous _____ un poème.

13. (dire) Paul _____ «à tout à l'heure».

14. (lire) Ils _____ un magazine.

15. (écrire) J' _____ l'éditorial de notre journal.

 Problèmes sentimentaux

Let's read about a special section of a newspaper: **la rubrique sentimentale** (*advice to the lovelorn*):

Chaque jour des millions de personnes dans le monde lisent les journaux. Que lisent tous ces gens? Les nouvelles? Les petites annonces? Les articles? Bien sûr. Mais ils lisent aussi une rubrique importante: «la rubrique sentimentale». Voici celle d'aujourd'hui:

une rubrique *section*
celle *the one*

Chère Louise,

J'ai quatorze ans et je suis amoureux pour la première fois. Elle a treize ans et elle est dans ma classe d'histoire. Elle est intelligente, charmante, élégante et très belle. Moi, je suis sérieux, studieux, généreux, loyal et sympathique. Le jour du bal approche et je donnerais tout pour avoir un rendez-vous avec elle. Malheureusement, je ne suis pas très courageux et j'ai peur de lui demander de sortir avec moi. Qu'est-ce que je peux faire?

amoureux *in love*
première *first*

approche *draws near*
je donnerais *I would give*
malheureusement
   unfortunately
lui *her*

Désespéré

désespéré *desperate*

Cher Désespéré,

Vous êtes un garçon formidable! Il est nécessaire d'avoir confiance en vous-même. Vous n'êtes ni paresseux ni cruel. Les jeunes filles préfèrent un garçon comme vous — gentil, sérieux et sincère. Soyez fier de vous-même. Pourquoi ne pas lui téléphoner? Si elle dit non, ne soyez pas triste parce que vous pouvez toujours sortir avec ma fille Josette. Son numéro de téléphone est le 21.55.64.78.

confiance *confidence*
   vous-même *yourself*
paresseux *lazy*
soyez fier *be proud*

Louise

__ ACTIVITÉ _____

H. Répondez aux questions par des phrases complètes:

1. Qui lit le journal?

   _____

2. Comment s'appelle une des rubriques importantes du journal?

   _____

3. Qui est Désespéré?

   _____

4. Quel est le problème de Désespéré?

   _____

5. Comment est la jeune fille qu'il décrit?

   _____

6. Comment est Désespéré?

   _____

7. Quel conseil (*advice*) donne madame Louise?

   _____

8. Êtes-vous d'accord avec son conseil? Pourquoi?

   _____

 Our story contains several new adjectives, words that describe a person or a thing. You remember that French adjectives agree in gender (masculine or feminine) and number (singular or plural) with the noun they describe. To check your memory, fill in the blanks:

Il est charmant.	**Elle est** _____.
Il est brun.	**Elle est** _____.
Il est triste.	**Elle est** _____.
Il est moderne.	**Elle est** _____.
Il est surpris.	**Elle est** _____.

For most adjectives, add **e** to the masculine to form the feminine. If the masculine already ends in **e**, the feminine remains the same.

Do you remember how to make adjectives plural? Fill in the blanks:

Ils sont charmant _____. **Elles sont charmante** _____.

Ils sont brun _____. **Elles sont brune** _____.

Ils sont triste _____. **Elles sont triste** _____.

Ils sont moderne _____. **Elles sont moderne** _____.

Ils sont surpris _____. **Elles sont surprise** _____.

To make most adjectives plural, add **s** to the singular forms. If the adjective already ends in **s**, the masculine plural remains the same.

 Now that your memory has been refreshed, let's learn some adjectives with irregular feminine forms. See if you can figure out the rules for each group:

Il est	Elle est	Ils sont	Elles sont
amour*eux*	amour*euse*	amour*eux*	amour*euses*
courag*eux*	courag*euse*	courag*eux*	courag*euses*
curi*eux*	curi*euse*	curi*eux*	curi*euses*
furi*eux*	furi*euse*	furi*eux*	furi*euses*
génér*eux*	génér*euse*	génér*eux*	génér*euses*
heur*eux*	heur*euse*	heur*eux*	heur*euses*
paress*eux*	paress*euse*	paress*eux*	paress*euses*
séri*eux*	séri*euse*	séri*eux*	séri*euses*
studi*eux*	studi*euse*	studi*eux*	studi*euses*
jal*oux*	jal*ouse*	jal*oux*	jal*ouses*

If an adjective ends in **-eux** or **-oux**, what do you notice about the masculine singular and plural forms? _____

The feminine singular of an adjective ending in **-eux** changes **-eux** to _____ and **-oux** to _____. To form the feminine plural, simply add _____ to the feminine singular.

Let's learn a few more useful adjectives in **-eux**:

affreux	*awful*	**merveilleux**	*marvelous*
dangereux	*dangerous*	**mystérieux**	*mysterious*
ennuyeux	*boring*	**peureux**	*fearful*
joyeux	*cheerful*	**précieux**	*precious*
malheureux	*unhappy*		

___ ACTIVITÉS _____

I. Complete the sentences with the correct forms of the adjectives:

1. (paresseux) Marie et Anne sont _____.

2. (amoureux) Ils sont tous les deux (*both*) _____.

3. (curieux) Paul est très _____.

4. (heureux) Liliane est _____.

5. (jaloux) Ces jeunes filles sont _____.

6. (furieux) Le professeur est _____.

7. (généreux) Ma mère est _____.

8. (sérieux) Sylvie et Régine sont _____.

9. (ennuyeux) Cette histoire est _____.

10. (dangereux) Ces sports ne sont pas _____.

J. A new student has just joined your class. Describe some of your classmates to her:

EXAMPLE: Jeanne/studieux
Jeanne est studieuse.

1. Marguerite/curieux

_____

2. Agnès et Nicole/sérieux

_____

3. Jean-Louis/généreux

_____

4. Henri et Nicolas/jaloux

_____

5. Chantal et Marie/peureux

_____

6. Georges et Olivier/courageux

_____

7. Monique/amoureux

_____

8. Antoine/paresseux

_____

 Here's another group of adjectives with irregular endings:

Il est	**Ils sont**	**Elle est**	**Elles sont**
acti*f*	acti*fs*	acti*ve*	acti*ves*
attenti*f*	attenti*fs*	attenti*ve*	attenti*ves*
destructi*f*	destructi*fs*	destructi*ve*	destructi*ves*
neu*f* (*new*)	neu*fs*	neu*ve*	neu*ves*
vi*f* (*lively*)	vi*fs*	vi*ve*	vi*ves*

The feminine singular of an adjective ending in **-f** changes **-f** to _____. Plu-

rals are formed by adding _____ to the singular.

___ ACTIVITÉ _____

K. Complete the sentences with the correct French forms of the adjectives:

1. (lively) Ces jolies couleurs sont _____.

2. (destructive) Ces animaux sont _____.

3. (attentive) Marie est _____.

4. (active) Les enfants sont _____.

5. (new) La boîte aux lettres est _____.

11 Look carefully at these adjectives and then complete the table:

Il est	Ils sont	Elle est	Elles sont
amer (*bitter*)	amers	amère	amères
cher (*expensive*)	_____	_____	_____
dernier (*last*)	_____	_____	_____
entier (*entire*)	_____	_____	_____
étranger (*foreign*)	_____	_____	_____
fier (*proud*)	_____	_____	_____
léger (*light*)	_____	_____	_____
premier (*first*)	_____	_____	_____

Let's formulate the rule: The feminine singular of an adjective ending in **-er** changes **-er** to _____. Plurals are formed by adding _____ to the singular.

_ ACTIVITÉ _____

L. You hear several statements. Using the nouns in parentheses, give your opinion:

> EXAMPLE: Ces fruits ne sont pas amers. (ces oranges)
> Mais ces oranges sont amères.

1. Ce collier n'est pas cher. (cette montre)

   _____

2. La famille n'est pas fière. (le fils)

   _____

3. Ces vêtements ne sont pas chers. (ces robes)

   _____

4. Ces hommes ne sont pas étrangers. (ces femmes)

   _____

5. Le dictionnaire n'est pas léger. (la revue)

   _____

Still another group of irregular adjectives has a pattern you can easily see. Complete the table:

Il est	Ils sont	Elle est	Elles sont
ég*al*	ég*aux*	ég*ale*	ég*ales*
général	_____	_____	_____
légal	_____	_____	_____
loyal	_____	_____	_____
national	_____	_____	_____
principal	_____	_____	_____
royal	_____	_____	_____
social	_____	_____	_____
spécial	_____	_____	_____

The masculine plural of an adjective ending in **-al** changes **-al** to _____ .
Feminine forms are regular in both the singular and plural.

___ ACTIVITÉ _____

M. One of your classmates describes some people and objects to you. You give your opinion about others:

> EXAMPLE: Les dimensions sont égales. (les prix)
> Les prix sont égaux aussi.

1. Cet article est général. (cette histoire)

   _____

2. Ces revues sont légales. (ces journaux)

   _____

3. Mes amis sont loyaux. (mes sœurs)

   _____

4. Le match est national. (l'équipe)

   _____

5. Les anniversaires sont spéciaux. (les fêtes)

_____

6. Le château est royal. (les jardins)

_____

 Now look carefully at the following table to determine how the adjectives are irregular. Then fill in the rest of the forms:

Il est	Ils sont	Elle est	Elles sont
ancien (old, ancient, former)	anciens	ancienne	anciennes
bon	bons	bonne	bonnes
bas (low)	bas	basse	basses
cruel	cruels	cruelle	cruelles
épais (thick)	_____	_____	_____
européen	_____	_____	_____
gentil (kind)	_____	_____	_____
gros	_____	_____	_____
haïtien	_____	_____	_____
italien	_____	_____	_____
parisien	_____	_____	_____

All of the adjectives above end in which letters in the masculine singular?

_____ or _____ or _____. For these adjectives, the final consonant is

_____ in the feminine form.

___ ACTIVITÉ _____

N. Give the correct form of the French adjective:

1. (kind) une femme _____

2. (cruel) des filles _____

3. (low) une voix _____

4. (thick) un cahier _____

5. (Parisian) ma tante _____

6. (European) des mères _____

7. (big) de _____ chiens

8. (good) un _____ film

 Some adjectives, like **beau**, **nouveau**, and **vieux**, usually come before the nouns they modify. Study the chart carefully and try to memorize their forms:

	MASCULINE before a consonant before a vowel	FEMININE before a consonant or vowel
SINGULAR PLURAL	**beau** ┆ **bel** **beaux**	**belle** **belles**
SINGULAR PLURAL	**nouveau** ┆ **nouvel** **nouveaux**	**nouvelle** **nouvelles**
SINGULAR PLURAL	**vieux** ┆ **vieil** **vieux**	**vieille** **vieilles**

Note the special masculine singular forms (**bel**, **nouvel**, **vieil**) used before vowel sounds only:

> un *bel* homme
> un *nouvel* étudiant
> un *vieil* artiste

But:

> **Cet homme est *beau*.**
> **Cet étudiant est *nouveau*.**
> **Cet artiste est *vieux*.**

Remember that, in the plural form, the partitive **de** is used before adjectives that precede the noun:

> **Ce sont *de* beaux garçons.**
> **Ce sont *de* nouvelles étudiantes.**

___ ACTIVITÉS _____

O. Complete with the correct form of the adjective:

1. Cet arbre est _____. (beau, bel, belle)

2. Ces livres sont _____. (vieil, vieux, vieilles)

3. Ce chapeau est _____. (nouveau, nouvel, nouvelle)

4. Cette université est _____. (beau, bel, belle)

5. Cet oncle est _____. (vieil, vieux, vieille)

6. Cette automobile est _____. (nouveau, nouvel, nouvelle)

P. Complete with the correct form of the adjective:

1. (beau) C'est une _____ histoire.

2. (nouveau) C'est un _____ ami.

3. (vieux) Ce sont de _____ chansons.

4. (beau) C'est un _____ appartement.

5. (nouveau) C'est une _____ amie.

6. (vieux) Ce sont de _____ hommes.

7. (beau) C'est un _____ cheval.

8. (nouveau) C'est un _____ disque.

9. (vieux) C'est un _____ avion.

10. (beau) Ce sont de _____ filles.

11. (nouveau) Ce sont de _____ robes.

12. (vieux) C'est une _____ personne.

13. (beau) Ce sont de _____ garçons.

14. (nouveau) Ce sont de _____ tableaux.

15. (vieux) C'est un _____ livre.

Q. You are helping your friend and her family move into a house they have just bought. Express what the previous owners left behind:

EXAMPLES:

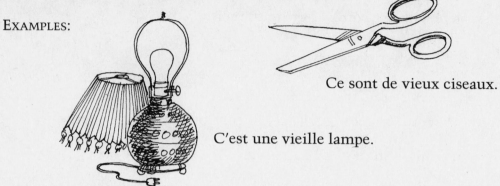

Ce sont de vieux ciseaux.

C'est une vieille lampe.

1. _____

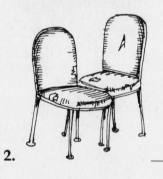

2. _____

3. _____

4. _____

5. _____

6. _____

7. _____

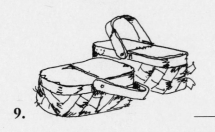

8. _____

9. _____

10. _____

R. Tell your friend how beautiful all the things in her house are:

EXAMPLE:

Quelle belle chaise!

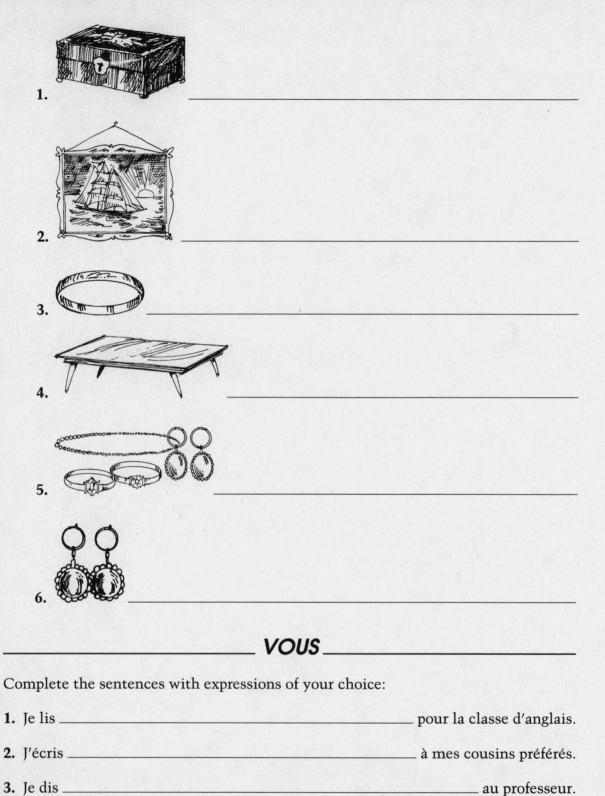

1. _____

2. _____

3. _____

4. _____

5. _____

6. _____

_____ VOUS _____

Complete the sentences with expressions of your choice:

1. Je lis _____ pour la classe d'anglais.

2. J'écris _____ à mes cousins préférés.

3. Je dis _____ au professeur.

4. Je lis _____ pour m'amuser.

5. J'écris _____ en classe.

DIALOGUE

Vous avez un problème personnel. La conseillère (*counselor*) de l'école veut vous aider. Que dites-vous?

COMPOSITION

You are writing to the "**Rubrique sentimentale**" of a newspaper. Tell them your name and age, describe yourself, and ask advice about a real or imaginary problem:

le _____ _____ 19_____

Cher (Chère) _____,

_____

_____

_____

_____

_____

_____

Cordialement,

_____

QUESTIONS PERSONNELLES

1. Quel est votre roman préféré?

_____

2. Quels magazines lisez-vous?

_____

3. À qui écrivez-vous des lettres?

_____

4. À qui dites-vous toujours la vérité?

_____

5. Quelles sont vos bonnes qualités?

_____

6. Quelles sont les bonnes qualités de votre meilleur(e) ami(e)?

_____

INTERVALLE CULTUREL

Les magazines et journaux français

Which of these French magazines would you choose to read?

FASHION	FILMS	HUMAN INTEREST STORIES
Elle	**Première**	**Paris Match**
Marie-Claire	**Cahiers du Cinéma**	**Confidences**

NEWS	COMICS	TEENAGERS
L'Express	**Tintin**	**Okay**
Le nouvel observateur	**Spirou**	**Salut les copains**

MUSIC

Best
Rock and Folk

Which of these French newspapers would you choose to read?

Le Monde   (the most literate and intellectual paper)

France-Soir
Le Figaro   (more popular papers)

L'Équipe   (a sports newspaper)

5 Les instruments de musique

The Verb **savoir**; Adverbs

1 Vocabulaire

les instruments à cordes

les instruments à vent

la clarinette

la flûte

le violon   la guitare

les cuivres

la trompette   le trombone

les instruments à percussion (m.)

le tambour

la batterie

le piano   l'accordéon

— ACTIVITÉ

A. Identify the instruments played by the members of this orchestra:

1. _____

2. _____

3. _____

4. _____

5. _____

6. _____

7. _____

8. _____

9. _____

10. _____

In French, the verb **jouer** means *to play:*

Les enfants aiment *jouer.*

When we speak about playing a musical instrument, **jouer** is followed by **de** plus the definite article (contracted if necessary):

Il *joue de la* guitare.
Nous *jouons du* piano.

When we speak about playing a sport, **jouer** is followed by **à** plus the definite article (contracted if necessary):

> **Je *joue au* tennis.**
> **Ils *jouent à la* balle.**

___ ACTIVITÉ ___

B. Express what the following people are doing:

EXAMPLES:

Hélène joue du tambour.   Vous jouez au tennis.

1. Éric et Simon _____ .

2. Lucie _____ .

3. Nous _____ .

4. François et Noëlle _____ .

5. Je _____ .

6. Vous _____ .

7. Tu _____ .

8. Nous _____ .

9. M. Dubois _____ .

10. Je _____ .

11. Vous _____ .

12. Nathalie _____ .

3 Let's take a closer look at the irregular verb **savoir** (*to know [a fact], to know how to [do something]*). See if you can find all the forms of **savoir** in the dialog:

Now complete the table with all the forms of **savoir**:

je _____   nous _____

tu _____   vous _____

il _____   ils _____

elle _____   elles _____

NOTE: **Savoir** + infinitive means *to know how to* (*do something*).

ACTIVITÉS

C. Fill in the correct form of the verb **savoir**:

1. Marie _____ parler français.

2. Nous _____ jouer du piano.

3. Je _____ ma leçon.

4. Les garçons _____ bien travailler.

5. Vous _____ danser.

6. Elles _____ lire.

7. Tu _____ faire du ski.

8. Il _____ bien nager.

D. Express which instruments the members of the school orchestra know how to play:

EXAMPLE: Paul sait jouer de la flûte.

1. Nous _____.

2. Raoul _____.

3. Je _____.

4. Renée et Justine _____.

5. Vous _____.

6. Tu _____.

4 Un succès musical

Here is a story about how to win a musical contest:

Guillaume est un garçon timide de quinze ans qui a
très peu d'amis. Il parle très doucement, très distinctement, très sérieusement et il est toujours
absorbé dans son travail scolaire. On le trouve souvent en train de lire ou d'écrire des compositions

peu *few*
   doucement *softly*
souvent *often*
en train de *in the middle of*

pour ses classes. Généralement, les autres élèves l'ignorent parce qu'ils ont très peu en commun avec ce garçon si studieux.

si *so*

Un jour, le directeur du lycée annonce une grande compétition musicale. Les étudiants sont invités à jouer de leurs instruments favoris pour gagner le titre de «Musicien par excellence du lycée Alexandre».

le titre *title*

Naturellement, tous les élèves populaires désirent participer pour impressionner leurs amis. Le jour venu, tout le monde est très enthousiaste de pouvoir écouter sa musique favorite à l'école.

le jour venu *when the day arrived*

Armand joue le premier. Malheureusement, il ne sait pas vraiment jouer de l'accordéon parce qu'il ne s'exerce jamais. Quand il termine, tout le monde a mal aux oreilles.

vraiment *really*
s'exerce *practices*

Ensuite, c'est le tour de Pierre, le garçon le plus populaire de l'école. Il joue assez bien de la guitare mais, franchement, cela n'a rien de très spécial.

ensuite *next* **le tour** *turn*
assez bien *rather well*
franchement *frankly*
  cela *it*

On écoute tous les autres. Une fille joue trop vite du violon, une autre trop lentement de la clarinette. Un garçon joue trop fort de la trompette et un autre joue trop doucement du trombone.

fort *loud*

Finalement, le tour de Guillaume arrive. Tout le monde commence à s'endormir et pense qu'il va certainement perdre la compétition. On pense également qu'il va probablement faire beaucoup d'erreurs. Guillaume se met au piano et joue de tout son cœur. Il joue facilement et tout le monde commence à écouter attentivement. Guillaume joue beaucoup mieux que tous les autres. On est absolument stupéfié par son talent. Il gagne la compétition et la réputation de musicien extraordinaire.

s'endormir *to fall asleep*
perdre *to loose*
également *as well*
se met *sits down*

mieux *better*
stupéfié *astounded*

Depuis, Guillaume est très populaire. Armand et Pierre sont ses amis. Il leur apprend à bien jouer de la musique et ils invitent Guillaume à leurs surprises-parties. Maintenant, les filles veulent sortir avec Guillaume. Il doit son succès à son talent

depuis *since then*
apprend à *teaches*

musical bien sûr, mais il peut également remercier **doit** *owes*
son père, le directeur du lycée Alexandre, d'avoir **remercier** *to thank*
organisé cette compétition!

___ ACTIVITÉ ___

E. Répondez par des phrases complètes:

1. Qui est Guillaume?

2. Pourquoi les autres élèves ignorent-ils Guillaume?

3. Qu'est-ce que le directeur annonce un jour?

4. Quel titre peut-on gagner?

5. Pourquoi les élèves désirent-ils participer à la compétition?

6. Pourquoi Armand ne joue-t-il pas bien?

7. Comment Pierre joue-t-il?

8. Qu'est-ce qu'on pense de Guillaume?

9. De quel instrument joue-t-il?

10. Comment joue-t-il?

11. Que fait Guillaume maintenant?

12. Pourquoi peut-il remercier son père?

5 | There are several new words in the story ending in **-ment**. Do you recall them? **Doucement, distinctement, sérieusement**, and others. These are called adverbs — expressions that describe a verb, an adjective, or another adverb. How are they formed? Very easily, **très facilement**. Look at the table to determine how adverbs are formed from adjectives:

ADJECTIVE		ADVERB	
autre	(*other*)	**autrement**	(*otherwise*)
poli	(*polite*)	**poliment**	(*politely*)
absolu	(*absolute*)	**absolument**	(*absolutely*)
vrai	(*real*)	**vraiment**	(*really*)

Look at the adjectives. What kind of letter do they end in? _____

Here's the simple rule: If the adjective ends in a vowel, simply add _____ to form the adverb (**-ment** is usually equivalent to English *-ly*).

Now see what happens if the adjective ends in a consonant in the masculine singular:

ADJECTIVE				ADVERB	
Masculine		Feminine			
parfait	(*perfect*)	**parfaite**		**parfaitement**	(*perfectly*)
naturel	(*natural*)	**naturelle**		**naturellement**	(*naturally*)
complet	(*complete*)	**complète**		**complètement**	(*completely*)
sérieux	(*serious*)	**sérieuse**		**sérieusement**	(*seriously*)
doux	(*sweet, soft*)	**douce**		**doucement**	(*sweetly, softly*)
franc	(*frank*)	**franche**		**franchement**	(*frankly*)

If the masculine singular adjective ends in a consonant, add **-ment** to the

_____ of the adjective to form the adverb.

ACTIVITÉS

F. Change the adjectives to adverbs:

1. facile _____

2. attentif _____

3. seul _____

4. triste _____

5. probable _____

6. heureux _____

7. certain _____

8. rapide _____

9. cruel _____

10. léger _____

G. Georges was chosen for the lead role in the school play. Tell why:

EXAMPLE: Il est doux.
          Et il parle doucement.

1. Il est sérieux.

_____

2. Il est naturel.

_____

3. Il est franc.

_____

4. Il est poli.

_____

5. Il est fier.

_____

H. You are asked to describe in French how some of your friends do certain things:

EXAMPLE: Victor participe _____activement_____ aux sports. (actively)

1. Rose parle _____ l'espagnol. (perfectly)

2. Fernand étudie _____ les mathématiques. (seriously)

3. Simone apprend _____ le français. (easily)

4. Jeanne est _____ intelligente. (really)

5. Michel écoute _____. (attentively)

6 There are other common adverbs that are not formed from adjectives. Here is a list of the most important ones:

assez *enough*	**moins** *less*
aujourd'hui *today*	**peu** *little*
beaucoup *much, a lot*	**plus** *more*
bien *well*	**près (de)** *near*
bientôt *soon*	**presque** *almost*
déjà *already*	**souvent** *often*
demain *tomorrow*	**surtout** *especially*
encore *still, yet*	**tard** *late*
ensemble *together*	**tôt** *early*
hier *yesterday*	**toujours** *always*
loin (de) *far (from)*	**très** *very*
longtemps *a long time*	**trop** *too much*
maintenant *now*	**vite** *quickly*
mal *badly*	

___ ACTIVITÉS _____

I. Jean-Paul always contradicts his older brother. Express what he says:

EXAMPLE: Janine danse bien.
Mais non, Janine danse mal.

1. Papa arrive tard.

_____

2. Raymond mange beaucoup de gâteau.

_____

3. Anne chante rarement.

_____

4. L'école est loin.

_____

5. Nicole écrit moins.

_____

6. Il va partir aujourd'hui.

_____

J. Tell your teacher when you are going to do the following:

1. Je vais faire mes devoirs de français _____. (tomorrow)

2. Je vais aller au cinéma _____. (today)

3. Je vais écrire une lettre _____. (soon)

4. _____ je vais sortir de la classe. (now)

5. Je vais lire le journal _____. (early)

7 Adverbs of quantity are followed by **de** (**d'** before a vowel sound):

> **assez de** *enough*
> **beaucoup de** *much, many, a lot of*
> **combien de** *how much, how many*
> **peu de** *little, few*
> **tant de** *so much, so many*
> **trop de** *too much, too many*

J'ai *beaucoup de* **disques.**   **Nous avons** *tant d'*amis.
Elle a *trop de* **devoirs.**   **Ils ont** *peu d'*argent.

— ACTIVITÉ

K. Tell your friend in French how much homework you have today:

EXAMPLE: (a lot) J'ai beaucoup de devoirs.

1. (little) _____

2. (so much) _____

3. (enough) _____

4. (too much) _____

Bien and **bon; mal** and **mauvais**

Remember that **bien** and **mal** are adverbs. They describe actions and do not change their form. **Bon** and **mauvais** are adjectives. They describe nouns and agree with them in gender and number:

Le repas est *bon*.   Le repas est *mauvais*.
La soupe est *bonne*.   La soupe est *mauvaise*.
Les légumes sont *bons*.   Les légumes sont *mauvais*.
Les pommes sont *bonnes*.   Les pommes sont *mauvaises*.

But:

Marie écrit *bien*.   Marie écrit *mal*.
Marie et Pierre écrivent *bien*.   Marie et Pierre écrivent *mal*.

___ ACTIVITÉS _____

L. Complete with the correct word: **bien** or **bon** (**bonne, bons, bonnes**):

1. Ces films sont _____.

2. Robert est un _____ élève.

3. Ça va _____.

4. Tu chantes et danses _____.

5. Je joue _____ de la guitare.

6. Tu reçois de _____ nouvelles de ta famille.

7. Le bébé dort _____.

8. La mousse est _____.

M. Repeat Activité L, using **mal** or **mauvais** (**mauvaise, mauvaises**):

1. _____

2. _____

3. _____

4. _____

5. _____

6. _____

7. _____

8. _____

Look at these sentences to determine the position of French adverbs in a sentence:

Je chante *bien*.   Nous ne travaillons pas *rapidement*.
Il danse *souvent*.   Vous ne parlez pas *doucement*.
Elle étudie *sérieusement*.   Ils ne sont pas *vraiment* contents.

Adverbs usually _____ the verb and usually _____ the adjective they modify. When an adverb describes an entire sentence, it may be at the beginning:

Maintenant je vais téléphoner au journal.

─────────── QUESTIONS PERSONNELLES ───────────

1. De quel instrument de musique savez-vous jouer?

_____

2. De quel instrument voulez-vous apprendre à jouer?

_____

3. Quel est votre instrument préféré?

_____

4. Quel plat savez-vous préparer?

_____

5. Comment parlez-vous français?

_____

6. Comment dansez-vous?

_____

7. Comment chantez-vous?

_____

8. Comment travaillez-vous?

_____

DIALOGUE

Votre amie Janine étudie la musique dans une école spécialisée. Posez-lui des questions au sujet de la musique:

_____ *VOUS* _____

You are applying for a job as a musician in a rock group. Tell the manager what you know how to do and how well you do it:

1. _____

2. _____

3. _____

4. _____

5. _____

_____ *COMPOSITION* _____

You would like to play in the school orchestra or band. Send a note to the music teacher in which you state the following:

1. which instrument you play.

   _____

2. what type of music (classical, rock, etc.) you know how to play.

   _____

3. that you like to play very much.

   _____

4. how well you play.

   _____

5. who your favorite musicians are.

   _____

INTERVALLE CULTUREL

La musique française

French rock music follows the American and British models. Our hits and those of the British are often imitated or translated. Johnny Halliday is noted for singing the French versions of our golden oldies. Some years ago, Françoise Hardy was known as the **yé-yé** girl from Paris. Today's pop singers include groups like Niagara or Rita Mitsouko and singers like Étienne Daho, Francis Cabrel, or Jean-Luc Lattage. French youths prefer pop music to rock. Old-time favorite singers who occasionally give concerts in the United States are Charles Aznavour and Gilbert Bécaud. Their music is probably more popular with your parents' generation. What American music would you recommend to a French visitor of your age?

If you're interested in French classical music, you might want to listen to the music of Camille Saint-Saëns (**la Danse macabre**); Claude Debussy (**Prélude à l'après-midi d'un faune**); Maurice Ravel (**Boléro**); Georges Bizet (**Carmen**); Charles Gounod (**Roméo et Juliette**); Jules Massenet (**Manon**), or Jacques Offenbach (**les Contes d'Hoffmann, la Vie parisienne**).

Révision I (Leçons 1–5)

Leçon 1

a. Irregular present-tense forms of the verbs **servir** (*to serve*), **dormir** (*to sleep*), **partir** (*to leave*), **sentir** (*to feel, to smell*), and **sortir** (*to go out*):

je	sers	dors	pars	sens	sors
tu	sers	dors	pars	sens	sors
il	sert	dort	part	sent	sort
elle	sert	dort	part	sent	sort
nous	servons	dormons	partons	sentons	sortons
vous	servez	dormez	partez	sentez	sortez
ils	servent	dorment	partent	sentent	sortent
elles	servent	dorment	partent	sentent	sortent

b. The interrogative adjective **quel** (*which, what*) has four forms:

Quel is used before masculine singular nouns.
Quels is used before masculine plural nouns.
Quelle is used before feminine singular nouns.
Quelles is used before feminine plural nouns.

Review pages 12–16 in Lesson 1 for the various uses of **quel** and its forms.

Leçon 2

a. Present-tense forms of the verb **mettre** (*to put, to put on*):

je mets	nous mettons
tu mets	vous mettez
il met	ils mettent
elle met	elles mettent

The verbs **permettre** (*to allow*), **promettre** (*to promise*), and **remettre** (*to postpone, to put back*) are conjugated like **mettre**.

b. Negative expressions:

ne . . . pas	*not*
ne . . . plus	*no longer, not any longer*
ne . . . personne	*nobody, no one*
ne . . . rien	*nothing*

ne . . . plus rien	nothing more
ne . . . ni . . . ni	neither . . . nor
ne . . . jamais	never
ne . . . que	only

The negative expressions **personne ne** and **rien ne** may be used as subjects:

Personne ne répond.
Rien n'est certain.

Leçon 3

a. Present-tense forms of the verb **ouvrir** (*to open*):

j'ouvre	nous ouvrons
tu ouvres	vous ouvrez
il ouvre	ils ouvrent
elle ouvre	elles ouvrent

The verbs **couvrir** (*to cover*) and **découvrir** (*to discover*) are conjugated like **ouvrir**.

b. To make most French nouns plural, add **s** to the singular form. Nouns that end in -**s**, -**x**, or -**z** remain unchanged in the plural:

le fil*s*	les fil*s*
la voi*x*	les voi*x*
le ne*z*	les ne*z*

Nouns that end in -**al** change -**al** to -**aux** in the plural:

| l'anim*al* | les anim*aux* |

Most nouns that end in -**eau**, or -**eu** add **x** to form their plurals:

| le chât*eau* | les chât*eaux* |
| le j*eu* | les j*eux* |

Exception: le pn*eu*   les pn*eus*

Nouns that end in -**ou** add **s** to form their plural, except for:

le bij*ou*	les bij*oux*
le caill*ou*	les caill*oux*
le ch*ou*	les ch*oux*
le gen*ou*	les gen*oux*
le hib*ou*	les hib*oux*
le jouj*ou*	les jouj*oux*
le p*ou*	les p*oux*

Some nouns with irregular plurals must be memorized. Review the nouns in this category on pages 49–50.

Leçon 4

a. Present-tense forms of the verbs **lire** (*to read*), **écrire** (*to write*), and **dire** (*to say*):

je (j')	lis	écris	dis
tu	lis	écris	dis
il	lit	écrit	dit
elle	lit	écrit	dit
nous	lisons	écrivons	disons
vous	lisez	écrivez	dites
ils	lisent	écrivent	disent
elles	lisent	écrivent	disent

b. Adjectives agree in gender and number with the noun they describe:

	MASCULINE	FEMININE
SINGULAR	charmant	charmante
PLURAL	charmants	charmantes

Adjectives with irregular feminine and plural endings follow these patterns:

MASC. SING.	MASC. PL.	FEM. SING.	FEM. PL.
-eux	-eux	-euse	-euses
-oux	-oux	-ouse	-ouses
-if	-ifs	-ive	-ives
-er	-ers	-ère	-ères
-al	-aux	-ale	-ales

Other irregular adjective forms must be memorized. Review them on pages 73–74.

Leçon 5

a. The verb **jouer** means *to play*. Use **jouer de** when speaking about playing a musical instrument and **jouer à** when speaking about playing a sport.

b. Present-tense forms of the verb **savoir** (*to know*):

je sais	nous savons
tu sais	vous savez
il sait	ils savent
elle sait	elles savent

Savoir + infinitive means *to know how to* (*do something*)

c. Adverbs describe a verb, an adjective, or another adverb. Adverbs are formed from adjectives as follows:

(1) Add **-ment** (equivalent to English *-ly*) to the masculine singular adjective if it ends in a vowel:

$$\textbf{vrai} \qquad \textbf{vrai}\textit{ment}$$

(2) If the masculine singular adjective ends in a consonant, add **-ment** to its feminine singular form:

$$\textbf{parfait} \qquad \textbf{parfait}\textit{e} \qquad \textbf{parfait}\textit{ement}$$

(3) Common adverbs that are not formed from adjectives must be memorized. Review these adverbs on pages 93–94.

d. Adverbs of quantity are followed by **de (d')**:

$$\textit{assez de} \text{ temps}$$
$$\textit{beaucoup d'} \text{argent}$$

e. NOTE: **Bien** and **mal** are adverbs; **bon** and **mauvais** are adjectives.

___ ACTIVITÉS _____

A. Qui est Marcel le magicien? Read the following sentences and then decide which one of the five men they describe. Put an X in the correct circle:

Il ne porte jamais de chapeau.
Il ne porte pas de cravate.
Il n'a pas beaucoup de cheveux,
   mais il a une barbe.

Il porte une boucle d'oreille.
Il porte aussi un collier en or.
Il ne porte jamais de veston.
Il porte de grandes lunettes.

B. How many of these words do you remember? Fill in the French words, then read
down the boxed column. What is Mme Laforestrie writing?

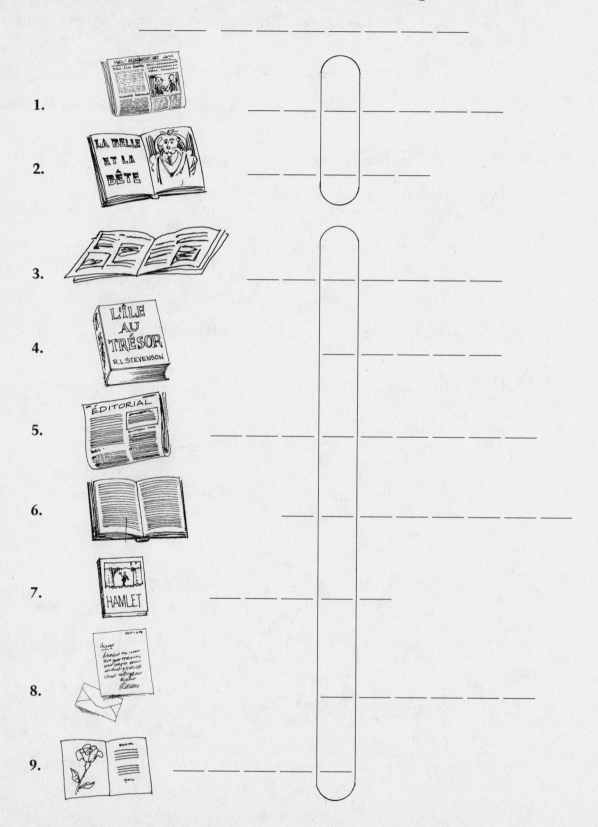

__ __ __ __ __ __ __ __ __

1. __ __ __ __ __ __ __ __

2. __ __ __ __ __

3. __ __ __ __ __ __

4. __ __ __ __ __

5. __ __ __ __ __ __ __ __ __

6. __ __ __ __ __ __ __ __ __

7. __ __ __ __ __ __ __

8. __ __ __ __ __ __

9. __ __ __ __ __ __

C. Here are eight pictures. Complete the description of each picture by using the correct form of one of these verbs:

aller	écrire	manger	ouvrir	répondre
choisir	faire	mettre	regarder	

1. Les enfants _____ jouer dans le jardin.

2. Michèle, _____ ces mots au tableau!

3. Vous _____ la télévision sur cette table.

4. J' _____ la fenêtre.

5. Nous ne _____ pas la télévision, nous _____ nos devoirs!

6. _____ vos épinards les enfants!

7. Les étudiantes _____ aux questions du professeur.

8. Marianne _____ la robe verte.

D. In the puzzle below, you will find hidden 15 things you might see at the beach. Circle the words from left to right, right to left, up or down, or diagonally:

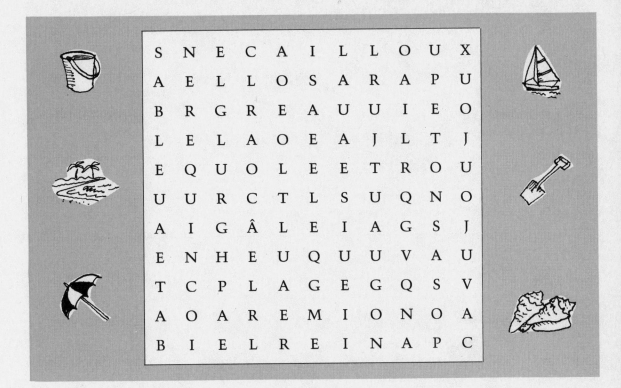

S N E C A I L L O U X
A E L L O S A R A P U
B R G R E A U U I E O
L E L A O E A J L T J
E Q U O L E E T R O U
U U R C T L S U Q N O
A I G Â L E I A G S J
E N H E U Q U U V A U
T C P L A G E G Q S V
A O A R E M I O N O A
B I E L R E I N A P C

E. Unscramble the words. Then unscramble the letters in the circles to find out the message:

G E B U A

R E M T O N

L E O C R I L

A M I T N A D

R E B C O H

Pour son anniversaire, Georgette reçoit un _____.

F. Make a comment about the pictures you see:

EXAMPLE:

Quel bon repas!

1. _____

2. _____

3. _____

4. _____

5. _____

G. Jacques and Hélène are in a restaurant looking at the menu. Something seems wrong! Whoever wrote the menu forgot to include the names of the dishes. Help Jacques and Hélène by filling in the names of the foods on the menu:

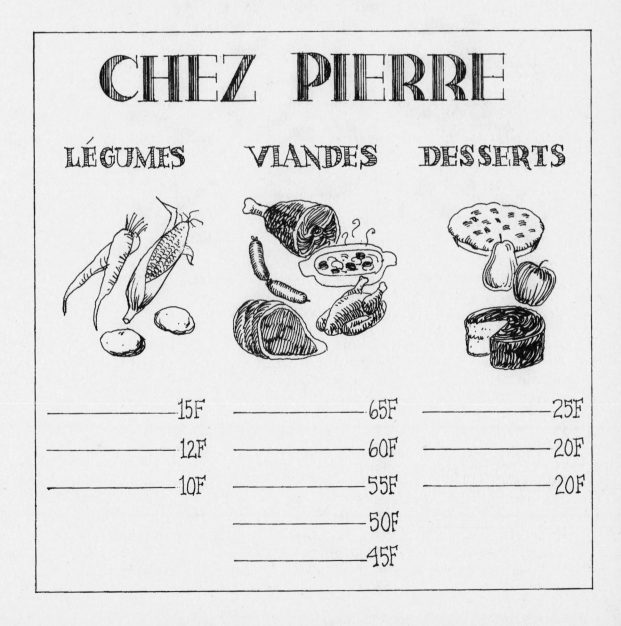

H. Mots croisés:

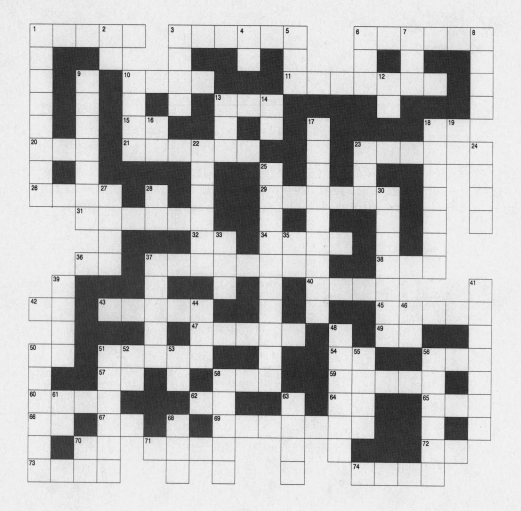

HORIZONTALEMENT

1. (écrire) il _____
3. (savoir) elles _____
6. (lire) ils _____
10. (sortir) Marie _____
11. (sortir) nous _____
13. my
15. he
18. some
20. (avoir) ils _____
21. to know
23. (dire) nous _____
26. (sentir) tu _____
29. (remettre) je _____
31. to go out
32. he

34. (mettre) tu _____
36. (avoir) tu _____
37. (écrire) ils _____
38. early
40. she
42. his/her
43. (écrire) tu _____
45. our
47. they
49. you
50. (être) tu _____
51. (dire) vous _____
54. (avoir) tu _____
56. (mettre) elle _____
57. he

58. (lire) il _____
59. your
60. (dormir) je _____
62. (avoir) j' _____
64. one
65. your
66. one
67. and
69. (servir) ils _____
70. year
71. to say
72. (être) tu _____
73. (savoir) elle _____
74. (avoir) vous _____

VERTICALEMENT

1. (écrire) nous ____
2. he
3. (servir) il ____
4. in
5. your
6. (lire) il ____
7. his/her
8. very
9. (mettre) nous ____
10. (savoir) tu ____
12. one
13. me
14. his/her
16. the
17. (permettre) vous ____

18. (dormir) elles ____
19. one
22. to open
23. (dire) il ____
24. (servir) je ____
25. (promettre) elles ____
27. (sortir) je ____
28. and
30. (sortir) les filles ____
33. (lire) je ____
35. in
37. (écrire) il ____
39. (partir) je ____
41. (sentir) ils ____

44. his/her
46. or
48. (savoir) nous ____
50. (endormir) tu ____
51. (dire) elles ____
52. he
53. in
55. (être) ils ____
56. (mettre) vous ____
58. (lire) vous ____
61. one
63. with
68. (dire) tu ____
70. (avoir) j' ____

I. Which instrument is Yvette playing? To find out, identify the objects in the pictures and write the letters in the spaces below:

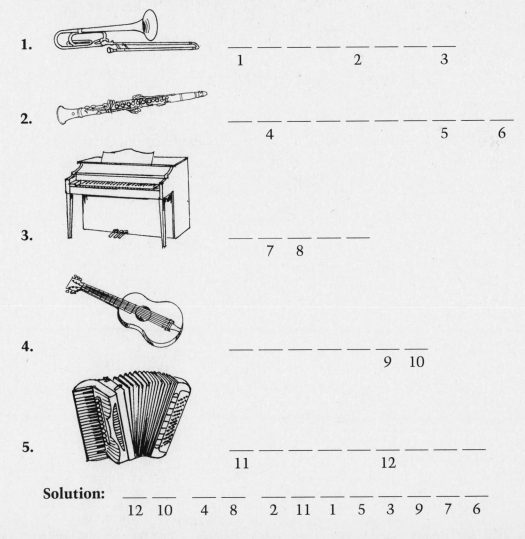

1. ___ ___ ___ ___ ___ ___
    1   2   3

2. ___ ___ ___ ___ ___ ___ ___ ___
    4   5   6

3. ___ ___ ___ ___ ___
    7 8

4. ___ ___ ___ ___ ___ ___
              9 10

5. ___ ___ ___ ___ ___ ___
    11   12

Solution: ___ ___ ___ ___ ___ ___ ___ ___ ___ ___ ___ ___
          12 10   4   8   2 11   1   5   3   9   7   6

J.   Picture story. Can you read this story? Much of it is in picture form. Whenever you come to a picture, read it as if it were a French word:

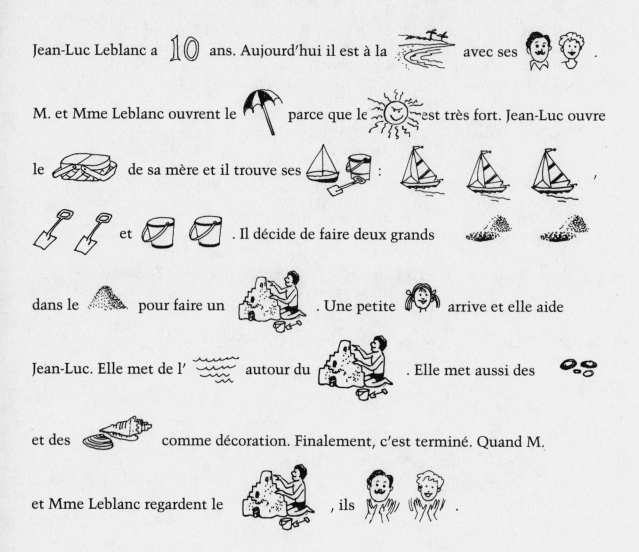

Deuxième Partie

6 *Le matin/le soir*

Reflexive Verbs

 Vocabulaire

The new words that follow are all verbs. They belong to a special family of verbs called REFLEXIVE VERBS. See if you can guess their meanings:

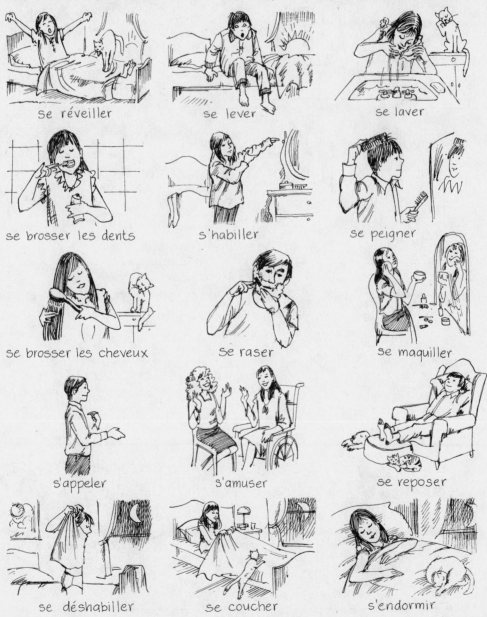

se réveiller

se lever

se laver

se brosser les dents

s'habiller

se peigner

se brosser les cheveux

se raser

se maquiller

s'appeler

s'amuser

se reposer

se déshabiller

se coucher

s'endormir

ACTIVITÉ

A. Match the descriptions with the pictures:

Il se peigne.   Vous vous brossez les dents.
Elles s'habillent.   Il se lève.
Tu te réveilles.   Marie se couche.
Nous nous reposons.   Je me lave.

1. _____

2. _____

3. _____

4. _____

5. _____

6. _____

7. _____

8. _____

2 A verb is reflexive when the subject does something to itself. To use a verb "reflexively," we add a special pronoun, called a reflexive pronoun, to indicate that the subject and object of the verb refer to the same person or thing. It's really not very difficult once you get the hang of it. You probably noticed, however, that some English verbs do not seem to be reflexive while their French equivalents are.

For example, **se lever** means *to get up*. The verb **lever** by itself, without the reflexive pronoun, means simply *to raise* or *to lift*:

> **Il *lève* la main.**   *He lifts his hand.*

> But:

> **Il *se lève*.**   *He gets up* (literally, *he lifts himself up*).

Let's look at some more reflexive verbs in French that are not reflexive in English. Just remember that the reflexive pronoun in French reflects the action expressed by the verb on the subject:

La grand-mère *amuse* les enfants.	*The grandmother amuses the children.*
La grand-mère *s'amuse*.	*The grandmother has fun* (*amuses herself*).
Le père *couche* le bébé.	*The father puts the baby to bed.*
Le père *se couche*.	*The father goes to bed* (*puts himself to bed*).
J'*appelle* Louis.	*I'm calling Louis.*
Je *m'appelle* Louis.	*My name is Louis* (*I call myself Louis*).

Most of the reflexive verbs in Sections 1 and 2 are **-er** verbs. Among these, **se lever** and **s'appeler** have special spelling changes that will be explained later. For now, put an **accent grave (`)** on the first **e** for all forms of **lever** except **nous**, **vous**, and the infinitive; double the **l** of **appeler** for all forms except **nous**, **vous**, and the infinitive. The irregular verb **s'endormir** is conjugated like **dormir** (see **Leçon 1**).

___ ACTIVITÉ _____

B. In each group, underline the sentence with the reflexive verb:

1. Elle se lave avec de l'eau froide.
   Elle lave l'automobile avec de l'eau froide.
2. La petite fille regarde la télévision.
   La petite fille se regarde dans le miroir.

3. Ma mère habille le bébé.
   Ma mère s'habille.
4. Vous vous réveillez tôt.
   Vous réveillez votre mère tôt.
5. Jean brosse son chien.
   Jean se brosse les cheveux.

 ## Un vrai champion

Read this story about a very popular sport: bicycle racing. How many reflexive verbs can you identify?

En France le cyclisme est plus qu'un sport, c'est une passion. Le «Tour de France» dure vingt-quatre jours et le gagnant de cette course célèbre est un héros national qui reçoit beaucoup d'argent et beaucoup de cadeaux. Écoutons l'interview d'un jeune cycliste populaire, Victor Vitesse:

dure *lasts*
le gagnant *winner*
course *race*

LE REPORTER: Bonjour, Victor. Nous désirons savoir comment vit un champion. Peux-tu décrire une journée typique?

vit *lives*

VICTOR: Eh bien, en général, je me réveille très tôt, à cinq heures du matin. J'aime m'entraîner quand il ne fait pas chaud.

s'entraîner *to train*

LE REPORTER: Bien sûr. Que fais-tu pour commencer ta journée?

VICTOR: Je me lève, je me lave la figure et les mains, je me rase et je me brosse les dents.

LE REPORTER: Oui, oui, je comprends. Nous faisons tout cela, nous aussi. Mais que fais-tu de spécial pour avoir l'avantage sur les autres cyclistes et être le champion?

VICTOR: Je mange un petit déjeuner léger. Je m'habille, je mets mes chaussures, je me brosse les cheveux et je sors m'entraîner deux ou trois heures. De retour chez moi, je prends une douche. Je déjeune vers midi et puis je me repose un peu.

de retour *back home*
douche *shower*
vers *around*

LE REPORTER: Et que fais-tu l'après-midi?

VICTOR: Plus ou moins la même chose. Je fais des exercices et je roule à bicyclette pendant quelques heures. Je me mets à table à sept heures et demie et je me couche avant dix heures. J'ai be-

même chose *same thing*
roule à bicyclette *ride a bicycle*

soin de beaucoup de repos et je n'ai pas le temps
de m'amuser.

LE REPORTER: Oui, c'est très intéressant tout cela. Je
vois qu'en fait tu ne fais rien de spécial. Tous les
jeunes gens ont autant de chances que toi de
devenir un grand champion. Tu n'as aucun avantage sur les autres. À propos, tu as une très belle
bicyclette. Combien coûte-t-elle?

VICTOR: Six mille dollars!

repos *rest*

en fait *in fact*
autant de *as many*
devenir *to become*
à propos *by the way*

___ **ACTIVITÉ** _____

C. Répondez par des phrases complètes:

1. Comment s'appelle la célèbre course cycliste française?

   _____

2. Que reçoit le gagnant en général?

   _____

3. Que veut savoir le reporter sur Victor Vitesse?

   _____

4. À quelle heure Victor se lève-t-il?

   _____

5. Qu'est-ce qu'il fait pour commencer la journée?

   _____

6. Quelle sorte de petit déjeuner Victor prend-il?

   _____

7. Que fait Victor après le déjeuner?

   _____

8. À quelle heure Victor se couche-t-il?

   _____

9. Selon le reporter, quelles chances ont les autres jeunes gens de devenir champion?

   _____

10. Combien coûte la bicyclette de Victor?

    _____

Now you can answer the following questions. In the sentence **Je me lave**, whom am I washing? _____ Is the action being performed on the subject or on someone else? _____ Do the subject (**je**) and the reflexive pronoun (**me**) refer to the same person or to two different people? _____ What do we mean by a reflexive verb?

_____

What is the position of the reflexive pronoun with respect to the subject? _____ What is the position of the reflexive pronoun with respect to the verb? _____

5 Different subjects require different reflexive pronouns:

je me lave	*I wash myself, I am washing myself*
tu te laves	*you wash yourself, you are washing yourself*
il se lave	*he washes himself, he is washing himself*
elle se lave	*she washes herself, she is washing herself*
nous nous lavons	*we wash ourselves, we are washing ourselves*
vous vous lavez	*you wash yourself/yourselves, you are washing yourself/yourselves*
ils se lavent	*they wash themselves, they are washing themselves*
elles se lavent	*they wash themselves, they are washing themselves*

___ ACTIVITÉS _____

D. What do you do in the morning?

EXAMPLE:

Je me réveille.

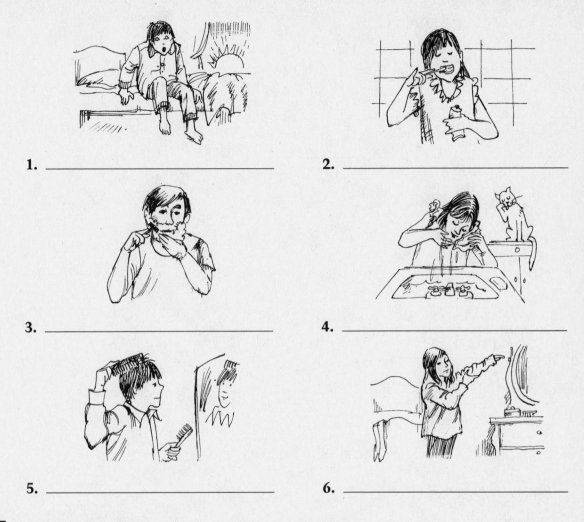

1. _____   2. _____

3. _____   4. _____

5. _____   6. _____

E. What is Gérard's routine? Look at the pictures and state what Gérard does at the time indicated:

EXAMPLE:

Gérard se réveille à six heures et demie.

1. _____

2. _____

3. _____

4. _____

5. _____

F. Complete each sentence with the correct reflexive pronoun:

1. Je _____ réveille à sept heures.

2. Elles _____ lèvent toujours tard.

3. Vous _____ couchez quand vous êtes fatigués.

4. Nous _____ habillons avant de sortir.

5. Il _____ amuse très bien.

6. Tu _____ endors tout de suite.

7. Chantal _____ maquille tous les jours.

8. Nous _____ brossons les cheveux chaque soir.

G. What are all these people doing? Complete the sentences with the correct form of the verb in parentheses:

1. (se coucher) Je _____ _____ tôt.

2. (se laver) Elle _____ _____ avec de l'eau froide.

3. (se maquiller) Tu _____ _____ avant d'aller à la fête.

4. (se coucher) Les enfants _____ _____ très tard.

5. (se brosser) Vous _____ _____ les cheveux souvent.

6. (s'habiller) Nous _____ _____ vite.

7. (se raser) Mes frères _____ _____ deux fois par jour.

8. (se reposer) Ma mère _____ _____ après le déjeuner.

9. (s'endormir) Je _____ _____ au cinéma.

10. (s'appeler) Est-ce que vous _____ _____ Paul?

 In French reflexive constructions, we do not use a possessive adjective with parts of the body, since the reflexive pronoun obviously refers to the subject. The definite article is used instead:

Je *me lave les* cheveux.	*I wash my hair.*
Tu *te brosses les* dents.	*You brush your teeth.*
Il *se rase la* figure.	*He shaves his face.*

__ ACTIVITÉ _____

H. Your mother wants to know what takes you so long in the morning. Tell her that

1. you're washing your face.

_____

2. you're brushing your teeth.

_____

3. you're brushing your hair.

_____

4. you're getting dressed.

_____

 In all the sentences up to this point, the reflexive pronoun came directly before the conjugated verb. In a negative sentence, the reflexive pronoun is not separated from the verb. Look at these examples:

> **Je _ne me lave pas_ avec de l'eau froide.**   _I don't wash myself with cold water._
> **Tu _ne te couches pas_ avant dix heures.**   _You don't go to bed before ten o'clock._

Where do we put **ne**? _____

Where do we put **pas**? _____

The reflexive pronoun remains _____ the verb in a negative sentence.

__ ACTIVITÉ _____

I. Combine one element from each column to tell what activities these people are NOT doing:

Charles	se coucher	à six heures du matin
je	se réveiller	à onze heures du soir
mes parents	se peigner	à minuit
tu	se déshabiller	à trois heures du matin
nous	s'endormir	à quatre heures de l'après-midi
vous	se lever	à deux heures de l'après-midi
ma mère	se brosser les dents	à midi

EXAMPLE: Tu ne te peignes pas à minuit.

1. _____

2. _____

3. _____

4. _____

5. _____

6. _____

7. _____

⦿ 8 What happens when the reflexive verb is used as an infinitive? Look at the following examples:

Je vais _me laver_ tout de suite.   _I'm going to wash myself right away._
Le bébé ne veut pas _se coucher._   _The baby doesn't want to go to bed._
Tu ne peux pas _t'endormir_ en classe.   _You can't fall asleep in class._

Where is the reflexive pronoun? _____

With what does the reflexive pronoun agree? _____

Let's summarize: When there are two verbs in the sentence and one of these verbs is a reflexive infinitive, the reflexive pronoun comes before the infinitive and agrees with the subject of the conjugated verb. The negative **ne** and **pas** are around the conjugated verb.

___ ACTIVITÉ _____

J. Complete the following sentences using the correct French form of the verb in parentheses:

1. (to wash) Il ne veut pas _____ les mains avec ce savon.

2. (to have fun) Philippe et moi, nous allons _____ à la fête.

3. (to go to bed) Va _____ tout de suite!

4. (to fall asleep) Le bébé ne peut pas _____ .

5. (to rest) Je n'ai pas le temps de _____ aujourd'hui.

6. (to get up) Vous allez _____ tôt demain matin.

7. (to put on makeup) Alice et Laure n'aiment pas _____ .

8. (to wake up) Je veux _____ tard.

9. (to comb your hair) Tu viens de _____.

10. (to rest) Vous pouvez _____ maintenant.

9 Look at these sentences showing how to form questions using inversion:

Tu te lèves.	*Te lèves-tu?*
Il se rase.	*Se rase-t-il?*
Nous nous lavons.	*Nous lavons-nous?*

Where does the reflexive pronoun remain? _____

Which pronoun is inverted with the verb? _____

How is the subject pronoun joined to the verb? _____

ACTIVITÉ

K. Change these statements to questions using inversion:

EXAMPLE: Tu te lèves tard.
          Te lèves-tu tard?

1. Il s'amuse beaucoup.

_____

2. Nous nous peignons.

_____

3. Ils s'endorment.

_____

4. Tu te brosses les dents.

_____

5. Vous vous reposez.

_____

6. Marie se couche à minuit.

_____

7. Jean se réveille à 8 heures.

_____

8. Les garçons s'habillent.

_____

10 Study these negative questions using inversion:

Ne te lèves-tu *pas?*
Ne se rase-t-il *pas?*
Ne nous lavons-nous *pas?*

Where is **ne**? _____

Where is **pas**? _____

___ ACTIVITÉ _____

L. Change the questions in Activité K to the negative:

   EXAMPLE: Ne te lèves-tu pas tard?

1. _____

2. _____

3. _____

4. _____

5. _____

6. _____

7. _____

8. _____

11 How are reflexive verbs used to give commands? Look at this short game of "Simon says" (the French say "**Jacques a dit**"):

Jacques a dit à tous les élèves:

Levez-vous!	Ne *vous levez* pas!
Lavez-vous!	Ne *vous lavez* pas!
Peignez-vous!	Ne *vous peignez* pas!

Jacques a dit à Jacqueline:

Lève-toi!	Ne *te lève* pas!
Lave-toi!	Ne *te lave* pas!
Peigne-toi!	Ne *te peigne* pas!

Jacques a dit:

Levons-nous!	**Ne** *nous levons* **pas!**
Lavons-nous!	**Ne** *nous lavons* **pas!**
Peignons-nous!	**Ne** *nous peignons* **pas!**

Which pronoun, the subject pronoun or the reflexive pronoun, is missing

from a command form? _____ .

Where is the reflexive pronoun in relationship to the verb? In the affirmative

command, the reflexive pronoun is _____ the verb and at-

tached to it by a _____ . The reflexive pronoun **te** becomes

_____ in an affirmative command.

In a negative command, the reflexive pronoun is _____ the

verb; **ne** is _____ the reflexive pronoun and **pas** _____
the verb.

___ ACTIVITÉS _____

M. Tell a friend in French to do the following:

1. wake up

_____

2. wash himself

_____

3. brush his teeth

_____

4. have fun

_____

5. go to bed

_____

6. get dressed

_____

N. Say to your friends in French: "Let's do (or not do)" the following:

    1. get up

    _____

    2. comb our hair

    _____

    3. have fun

    _____

    4. not fall asleep

    _____

    5. not put on makeup

    _____

    6. not go to bed

    _____

_____ **COMPOSITION** _____

You are away on vacation. Express in French that

    1. you wake up late every day.
    2. you do not get up before noon.
    3. you rest frequently.
    4. you go to bed after midnight.
    5. you are having a good time.

1. _____

2. _____

3. _____

4. _____

5. _____

DIALOGUE

Vous êtes un cycliste célèbre. Un journaliste veut écrire un article et vous pose des questions:

_____ QUESTIONS PERSONNELLES _____

1. À quelle heure vous levez-vous le matin?

_____

2. Comment vous appelez-vous?

_____

3. À quelle heure vous couchez-vous le samedi soir?

_____

4. Combien de fois par jour est-ce que vous vous brossez les dents?

_____

5. Quand est-ce que vous vous lavez?

_____

_____ VOUS _____

List five things you do in the morning before going to school:

1. _____

2. _____

3. _____

4. _____

5. _____

INTERVALLE CULTUREL

Les repas en France

Notice how French meals are different from ours:

Le petit déjeuner

Breakfast is very light.

Le déjeuner

Lunch is the main meal, served in courses starting with an appetizer (**hors-d'œuvre**). Salad is eaten after the main course and it is followed by cheese and then dessert.

Le dîner

Dinner is usually lighter than lunch and is also served in courses.

In smaller towns and villages, the tradition of the long lunch break from 12 noon to 2 p.m. continues. Stores close and workers return home for the main meal of the day. In Paris and in some other large cities, the number of fast-food restaurants is rapidly increasing to keep up with the faster pace of life. These self-service and fast-food restaurants serve not only the typical hamburger and fries but also French favorites like omelettes, ham or cheese sandwiches, pizza, and **croque-monsieur** (a ham-and-melted-swiss-cheese sandwich on toasted white bread).

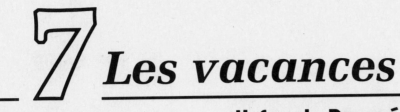

7 Les vacances

Il faut; Passé composé

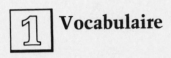

1 **Vocabulaire**

jouer au golf

faire du ski nautique

faire du ski alpin

prendre des photos

nager dans la mer

pêcher dans la rivière

faire de la planche à voile

faire une randonnée en montagne

faire une croisière

133

___ ACTIVITÉ _____

A. Here's a picture of a wonderful resort place. Describe some of the things the people are doing:

_____

_____

_____

_____

_____

_____

_____

_____

_____

_____

_____

_____

2 The students in M. Hervé's swimming class are discussing the class rules. Follow the dialog and learn about the verb **falloir** (*to be necessary, must*):

As you can see in the dialog, the verb **falloir** has only one form in the present tense:

_____. What does it mean? _____ What is the

form of the verb that follows **il faut**? _____

___ ACTIVITÉ ___

B. Your friend Gilbert wants to lose weight so that he will look his best at the beach. Tell him what he must do:

    EXAMPLE: manger moins
               Il faut manger moins.

1. faire attention aux calories

_____

2. aller à pied partout

_____

3. manger beaucoup de légumes

_____

4. éliminer les gâteaux

_____

5. faire du sport

_____

6. aller danser tous les soirs

_____

 Do you remember how to form the **passé composé** (*past tense*) of regular verbs? Since the **passé composé** expresses what "happened" or "has happened," you

must use a helping verb. Most French verbs use the helping verb _____

(*to have*) in the **passé composé**.

Refresh your memory and conjugate **avoir**:

          j' _____   **nous** _____

          tu _____   **vous** _____

          il _____   **ils** _____

        elle _____   **elles** _____

Now that you have the helping verb of the **passé composé**, you need the "happened" part, called the past participle:

parler   J'ai parlé.

To form the past participle of an **-er** verb, drop _____ from the infinitive and add _____.

finir   Elle a fini son sandwich.

To form the past participle of an **-ir** verb, drop _____ from the infinitive.

répondre   Vous avez répondu à la question.

To form the past participle of an **-re** verb, drop _____ from the infinitive and add _____.

Now let's combine the present tense of **avoir** and the past participle of some of the verbs you already know:

	parler	choisir	répondre
j'	_____	_____	_____
tu	_____	_____	_____
il	_____	_____	_____
elle	_____	_____	_____
nous	_____	_____	_____
vous	_____	_____	_____
ils	_____	_____	_____
elles	_____	_____	_____

___ ACTIVITÉ ___

C. You had a picnic in the park with your friends. Tell what each person did:

EXAMPLE: Rémi/acheter le pain
           Rémi a acheté le pain.

1. vous/chercher du bois

_____

2. Denis et moi, nous/allumer le barbecue

_____

3. Jules et Jim/préparer la salade

_____

4. tu/laver les fruits

_____

5. Agnès/choisir où faire le pique-nique

_____

6. je/servir les hamburgers

_____

7. Pierre et toi, vous/remplir les verres de soda

_____

8. nous/attendre tous nos amis

_____

9. les garçons/perdre la balle

_____

10. Luc/vendre de la glace

_____

 Now look at the negative and interrogative forms of verbs in the **passé composé**. Remember that negatives and questions are formed with the helping verb **avoir**:

> **Il n'a pas mangé.**
> **Avez-vous choisi cette robe?**
> **N'ont-elles pas répondu?**

In the negative sentence, where are **ne** and **pas**? _____

_____

In a question, where is the subject pronoun? _____

In a negative question, where are **ne** and **pas**? _____

_____

___ ACTIVITÉS _____

D. Tell what each student did on vacation:

> EXAMPLE: Alice/jouer au tennis
> Alice a joué au tennis.

1. Joseph/finir ses leçons de planche à voile

_____

2. Élise/nager dans la mer

_____

3. Raoul/vendre de la glace

_____

E. Change the sentences in Activité D to the negative:

> EXAMPLE: Alice n'a pas joué au tennis.

1. _____

2. _____

3. _____

F. Change the sentences in Activité D to questions using inversion:

> EXAMPLE: Alice a-t-elle joué au tennis?

1. _____

2. _____

3. _____

G. Change the questions in Activité F to the negative:

> EXAMPLE: Alice n'a-t-elle pas joué au tennis?

1. _____

2. _____

3. _____

H. Ask a classmate the following questions about his/her vacation:

> EXAMPLE: étudier pendant l'été
> As-tu étudié pendant l'été?

1. visiter la Maison Blanche

   _____

2. voyager en avion

   _____

3. vendre des souvenirs

   _____

4. pêcher dans la rivière

   _____

5. dormir très tard

   _____

6. jouer au tennis de temps en temps

   _____

I. Answer the questions in Activité H:

> EXAMPLES: (oui)   Oui, j'ai étudié pendant l'été.
> (non)   Non, je n'ai pas étudié pendant l'été.

1. (non) _____

2. (non) _____

3. (oui) _____

4. (non) _____

5. (oui) _____

6. (oui) _____

J. Your friends have just returned from Paris. You are very surprised that they did not do certain things while there. Ask them the following negative questions:

> EXAMPLE: visiter le Louvre
> N'avez-vous pas visité le Louvre?

1. marcher le long des Champs-Élysées

   _____

2. goûter les crêpes au chocolat

   _____

3. attendre le guide

   _____

4. manger à la terrasse d'un café

   _____

5. acheter des souvenirs

   _____

 ## Une petite lettre

Some French verbs have irregular past participles. Read the following story and see how many irregular past participles you can recognize:

le 23 avril

Chère Jeanne,

As-tu reçu mes lettres précédentes? J'ai écrit plusieurs fois, mais tu n'as pas encore répondu. Qu'est-
ce que tu as eu comme note en français? Moi, je n'ai
eu que C parce que je n'ai pas bien compris la leçon
sur le passé composé. Je n'ai pas su répondre à toutes
les questions. Et toi?

précédentes *preceding*

Maurice a été absent hier. Je n'ai pas pu savoir pourquoi parce qu'il n'a pas voulu répondre à mes questions. Mais Hervé a dit que Maurice a pris un jour de
vacances pour aller faire de la planche à voile. L'été
dernier il a fait de la planche à voile tous les jours.

Aujourd'hui j'ai bien appris ma leçon et j'ai lu une
histoire en français. Il faut que je travaille!

À bientôt,

Marie

__ ACTIVITÉ _____

K. Répondez par des phrases complètes:

1. Qui a écrit cette lettre?

   _____

2. Est-ce que Jeanne a répondu aux lettres de Marie?

   _____

3. Quelle note Marie a-t-elle eu en français?

   _____

4. A-t-elle bien compris la leçon?

   _____

5. Qu'est-ce qu'elle n'a pas su faire?

   _____

6. Qui a été absent hier?

   _____

7. Qu'est-ce que Marie a voulu savoir?

   _____

8. Qu'est-ce que Maurice a pris?

   _____

9. Qu'est-ce que Maurice a fait l'été dernier?

   _____

10. Qu'est-ce que Marie a fait aujourd'hui?

   _____

---

6 | Look again at Marie's letter. To form the **passé composé** of irregular verbs, which helping verb is used? _____ What must be done to the helping verb? _____

Does the past participle change if the subject changes? _____

Since there is no rule for the formation of the past participles of irregular verbs, you must memorize them. Below is a list of infinitives and some past participles. Fill in the missing past participles by referring back to the story:

INFINITIVE	PAST PARTICIPLE	INFINITIVE	PAST PARTICIPLE
avoir	_____	mettre	*mis*
lire	_____	prendre	_____
pouvoir	_____	apprendre	_____
recevoir	_____	comprendre	_____
savoir	_____	dormir	*dormi*
voir	*vu*	sentir	*senti*
		servir	*servi*
vouloir	_____	ouvrir	*ouvert*
dire	_____	être	_____
écrire	_____	faire	_____
décrire	*décrit*		

__ ACTIVITÉS _____

L. Express what happened to these persons on their cruise:

EXAMPLE: je/comprendre les ordres du capitaine
J'ai compris les ordres du capitaine.

1. je/voir un film

_____

2. Robert/recevoir des lettres

_____

3. nous/écrire des cartes postales

_____

4. elles/apprendre une chanson

_____

5. tu/lire un roman

_____

6. vous/ouvrir un paquet

_____

7. Anne/dormir tard

_____

8. Jacqueline et Hubert/être malades

_____

9. je/mettre un maillot de bain

_____

10. vous/dire «bonjour» à tout le monde

_____

M. Express that the following things happened yesterday:

    EXAMPLE: Tu manges de la glace au chocolat.
                  Tu as mangé de la glace au chocolat.

1. Vous pouvez aller au cinéma.

_____

2. Ils font de la planche à voile.

_____

3. Mon père met les provisions dans la cuisine.

_____

4. Les touristes voient des sites historiques.

_____

5. Nous faisons une longue promenade.

_____

6. Tu prends de très belles photos.

_____

7. Mon frère dort toute la journée.

_____

8. Je suis très malade.

_____

9. Vous avez une bonne note à l'examen.

_____

10. Marie et François écrivent un tas de cartes postales.

_____

DIALOGUE

Vous venez de rentrer d'un voyage en France. Répondez aux questions que votre petit frère vous pose:

VOUS

List five things you must do to succeed in school:

_____

_____

_____

_____

_____

COMPOSITION

Your family is spending a vacation at a fabulous summer resort. Write an entry in your travel diary expressing in which activities you participated that day:

QUESTIONS PERSONNELLES

1. Avez-vous fait du ski cet hiver?

   _____

2. Avez-vous nagé dans la mer l'été dernier?

   _____

3. Quel livre avez-vous lu récemment?

   _____

4. Pourquoi avez-vous reçu de bonnes notes en français?

   _____

5. Pour quelle classe est-ce qu'il faut faire beaucoup de devoirs?

   _____

6. Avec qui avez-vous fait une promenade?

   _____

La géographie de la France

Let's take a look at a map of France. France is a country of many contrasts in climate, landscape, and industry. Study the map below and see if you can answer the questions that follow.

1. Which other European countries border on France?
2. Which rivers are in France?
3. Which mountains separate France from other countries?
4. Which bodies of water border on France?

8 Un roman policier

The Verb **venir**; **Passé composé** of Verbs Conjugated with **être**

1 Vocabulaire

UN VOL À LA BANQUE

le complice

le témoin

la caissière

le pistolet

le voleur

___ ACTIVITÉ _____

A. Qu'est-ce qui se passe? Express in French what you see in the picture:

EXAMPLE: Je vois un vol à la banque.

1. _____

2. _____

3. _____

4. _____

5. _____

2 Here's some more new vocabulary:

LE TRIBUNAL

les empreintes digitales (f.)

le juge

l'avocat de la défense (m.)

l'accusé (m.)

la victime

le procureur

___ ACTIVITÉ _____

B. You are on jury duty. Express what's happening in the courtroom:

EXAMPLE: L'accusé a très peur.

1. L'agent montre les _____.

2. _____ veut savoir la vérité.

3. _____ parle très longtemps.

4. _____ perd patience.

5. _____ répond aux questions.

3 The verb **venir** (*to come*) is an important irregular verb. See if you can find all the present-tense forms of **venir** in the following dialog:

Fill in the correct forms of the verb **venir** from the dialog:

je _____   nous _____

tu _____   vous _____

il _____   ils _____

elle _____   elles _____

___ ACTIVITÉ ___

C. Express at what time the following people are coming to the school's end-of-term barbecue:

> EXAMPLE: Pierre/8:00
> Pierre vient à huit heures.

1. tu/7:45

_____

2. Bruno et Gaston/6:50

_____

3. nous/5:30

_____

4. je/5:15

_____

5. Delphine/6:35

_____

6. vous/7:20

_____

4 Here's a third group of words for you to learn:

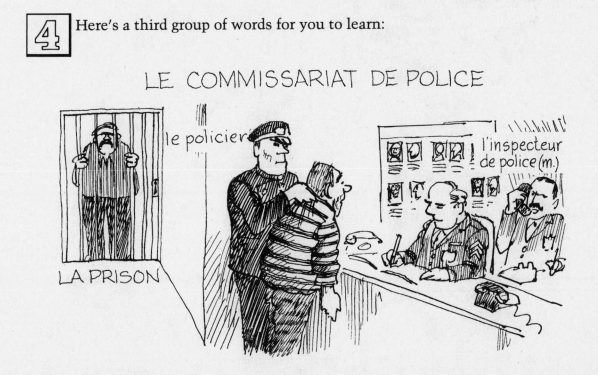

LE COMMISSARIAT DE POLICE

le policier

l'inspecteur de police (m.)

LA PRISON

___ ACTIVITÉ _____

D. Match the sentences with the pictures:

> L'inspecteur de police cherche des empreintes digitales.
> Le policier arrête le criminel.
> Le criminel va en prison.
> La victime va au commissariat de police.

1. _____

2. _____

3. _____

4. _____

 Other verbs conjugated like **venir** are:

devenir	_to become_
revenir	_to come back_
se souvenir de	_to remember_

ACTIVITÉ

E. Complete each sentence with the correct form of the verb:

1. (venir) Le témoin _____ au commissariat de police.

2. (devenir) La caissière _____ très nerveuse.

3. (revenir) Les criminels _____ en prison.

4. (se souvenir) La victime _____ du visage du voleur.

5. (venir) _____-tu aider la victime?

6. (devenir) Je _____ avocat cette semaine.

7. (revenir) Nous ne _____ pas à la banque.

8. (se souvenir) Les procureurs _____ de tous les détails.

9. (venir) Est-ce que vous _____ avec le juge?

10. (devenir) Le criminel _____ honnête.

Look carefully at these sentences showing a special use of the verb **venir** + **de**:

Je *viens de* manger.	*I have just eaten. I just ate.*
Ils *viennent de* finir.	*They have just finished. They just finished.*
Il *vient d'écrire* une lettre.	*He has just written a letter. He just wrote a letter.*

The verb **venir** plus **de** expresses an action just completed.

ACTIVITÉ

F. Tell what these people just did:

EXAMPLES: je/manger   Je viens de manger.
tu/se réveiller   Tu viens de te réveiller.

1. nous/jouer au tennis

   _____

2. elle/rencontrer le juge

   _____

3. je/écrire une lettre

   _____

4. il/acheter une voiture

   _____

5. ils/se raser

   _____

6. tu/se lever

   _____

7. elles/aller au commissariat

   _____

8. vous/se laver

   _____

Le crime ne paie pas

Now read this story about a burglary. Pay special attention to the verbs in bold type, all of which are in the **passé composé**:

L'inspecteur Maillot était en train de se reposer quand le téléphone a sonné. Madame Forêt, très agitée, a demandé à l'inspecteur de venir chez elle tout de suite. Vingt minutes plus tard, **l'inspecteur est arrivé** chez elle.

était *was*

MADAME FORÊT: Entrez, entrez, monsieur l'inspecteur. **Il s'est passé** quelque chose de terrible. **Je suis revenue** chez moi il y a une demi-heure. Quand **je suis arrivée** à la maison, j'ai trouvé la porte ouverte. J'ai entendu du bruit, **je suis entrée** et j'ai vu un homme dans le bureau de mon mari. Je n'ai pas pu voir son visage. Quand il m'a vue, **il est** tout de suite **sorti** par la porte qui donne sur le jardin. Je l'ai suivi, mais malheureusement **il est parti** très vite. **Je suis retournée** à la maison pour voir si quelque chose manquait. Dans le bureau j'ai trouvé le coffre-fort ouvert. Le voleur a pris tous mes bijoux, une fortune de plusieurs millions de francs. Heureusement, il y a deux mois, j'ai acheté une bonne assurance.

il y a *ago*

donne sur *faces*
suivi *followed*

manquait *was missing*
le coffre-fort *safe*

assurance *insurance*

L'INSPECTEUR: Y-a-t-il des suspects?

MADAME FORÊT: Oui, je pense que le voleur est Jean, le domestique que nous avons renvoyé la semaine passée. Il **est** souvent **allé** dans le bureau de mon mari. Et j'ai trouvé ce chapeau dans le jardin. C'est à Jean.

renvoyer *to fire*

être à *to belong to*

L'inspecteur a tout écouté très attentivement. Il a examiné le bureau. Tout était en désordre. Puis il **est allé** dans le jardin où il a vu les empreintes de pas d'un homme. Il a aussi vu des fleurs écrasées.

empreintes de pas *footsteps*
écrasées *crushed*

MADAME FORÊT: Monsieur l'inspecteur, voulez-vous d'autres renseignements sur Jean? Je veux tout faire pour vous aider à l'arrêter.

renseignements *information*

L'INSPECTEUR: Oui, madame. Je veux savoir la vérité et non pas ces mensonges que vous venez de me dire!

Comment l'inspecteur sait-il que madame Forêt a menti?

a menti *lied*

Solution: Elle dit qu'elle a suivi Jean dans le jardin mais l'inspecteur n'a trouvé que les empreintes de pas d'un homme. Madame Forêt a mis des souliers d'homme pour faire ces empreintes afin de recevoir une importante somme d'argent de la compagnie d'assurance.

afin de *in order to*

___ ACTIVITÉ _____

G. Répondez aux questions par des phrases complètes:

1. Pourquoi madame Forêt a-t-elle téléphoné à l'inspecteur Maillot?

_____

2. Qu'est-ce qui s'est passé?

_____

3. Quand est-elle revenue chez elle?

_____

4. Qu'est-ce qu'elle a trouvé?

_____

5. Qu'est-ce qu'elle a vu?

_____

6. Où a-t-elle suivi cet homme?

_____

7. Qu'est-ce que le voleur a pris?

_____

8. Qui est le suspect?

_____

9. Qu'est-ce que l'inspecteur a trouvé dans le jardin?

_____

10. Comment l'inspecteur sait-il que Mme Forêt a menti?

_____

8 There is still more to learn about the **passé composé**. Not all French verbs use **avoir** as the helping verb. Read the story again. Which other helping verb

occurred in the **passé composé**? _____ Do you remember how to conjugate this verb? Fill in the correct forms in the table:

je _____   nous _____

tu _____   vous _____

il _____   ils _____

elle _____   elles _____

You have already learned that the **passé composé** consists of a helping verb plus a past participle. Sixteen French verbs use **être** as the helping verb. Most of these verbs express coming and going. A good way to remember them is to think of a house, the house of **être**:

Except for the few verbs listed below, all past participles follow the rules for **-er**, **-ir**, and **-re** verbs. Fill in the missing past participles:

INFINITIVE   PAST PARTICIPLE

1. naître	*né*	9. retourner	_____
2. mourir	*mort*	10. rester	_____
3. arriver	_____	11. descendre	_____
4. entrer	_____	12. sortir	_____
5. rentrer	_____	13. partir	_____
6. tomber	_____	14. venir	*venu*
7. monter	_____	15. devenir	*devenu*
8. aller	_____	16. revenir	*revenu*

To help you remember the sixteen verbs that use **être** as a helping verb, here are DR. and MRS. VANDERTRAMP. DR. and MRS. VANDERTRAMP live in the house of **être**. Look at what happens when you write their name vertically:

Devenir
Revenir

Mourir
Rester
Sortir

Venir
Arriver
Naître
Descendre
Entrer
Retourner
Tomber
Rentrer
Aller
Monter
Partir

9 The **passé composé** formula is always the same:

helping verb conjugated + past participle
(**avoir** or **être**)

Now look carefully at the past participle in the examples below:

il est *arrivé*	elle est *arrivée*	ils sont *arrivés*	elles sont *arrivées*
il est *parti*	elle est *partie*	ils sont *partis*	elles sont *parties*
il est *venu*	elle est *venue*	ils sont *venus*	elles sont *venues*
il est *né*	elle est *née*	ils sont *nés*	elles sont *nées*

When **être** is the helping verb, what happens to the past participle?

_____

If the subject is feminine, you add _____ to the end of the past participle. If the subject is masculine plural, you add _____; if it is feminine plural, you add

_____ .

Look at this sentence:

Marie et Pierre sont *sortis*.

If the subject is both masculine and feminine, which form of the past participle do you use?_____

 Finally, look at these sentences:

Je suis *partie*.

Is the **je** of this sentence masculine or feminine?_____.

Nous sommes *arrivées*.

Is the **nous**, two boys, two girls, or a boy and a girl?_____.

Vous êtes *parti*.	**Vous êtes *partie*.**
Vous êtes *partis*.	**Vous êtes *parties*.**

When the subject is **vous**, why is it possible to have different endings?

_____

___ ACTIVITÉS _____

H. Complete the **passé composé** of the following verbs by applying the rules we have just formulated:

1. (partir)   Il est _____.

2. (entrer)   Elle est _____.

3. (retourner) Nous sommes _____.

4. (sortir)   Elles sont _____.

5. (rentrer)   Ils sont _____.

I. Who did it? Look carefully at the past participles and fill in the appropriate subject: **le garçon, la fille, les filles,** or **les garçons**:

EXAMPLE: Les garçons sont sortis.

1. _____ est arrivée au commissariat.

2. _____ sont venues à la banque.

3. _____ est né en France.

4. _____ sont tombés.

5. _____ sont restées à la maison.

6. _____ est entrée dans le tribunal.

7. _____ est retourné en prison.

8. _____ sont revenus au bureau.

J. Combine the following subjects with an appropriate verb chosen from the list:

est arrivé   est partie   sont rentrés   sont retournées

1. La mère _____.

2. Le garçon _____.

3. Les parents _____.

4. Les filles _____.

   5. Jacques et Monique _____ .

   6. Marie et Anne _____ .

   7. Yvonne _____ .

   8. Luc _____ .

   9. Robert et Gilles _____ .

   10. L'inspecteur _____ .

K.   Where is everybody? The weather is beautiful and today is a school holiday. Look at the pictures and tell where everyone went:

   EXAMPLE: je

   Je suis allé(e) à la piscine.

   1. Tu _____

   2. Elles _____

   3. Jacques _____ .

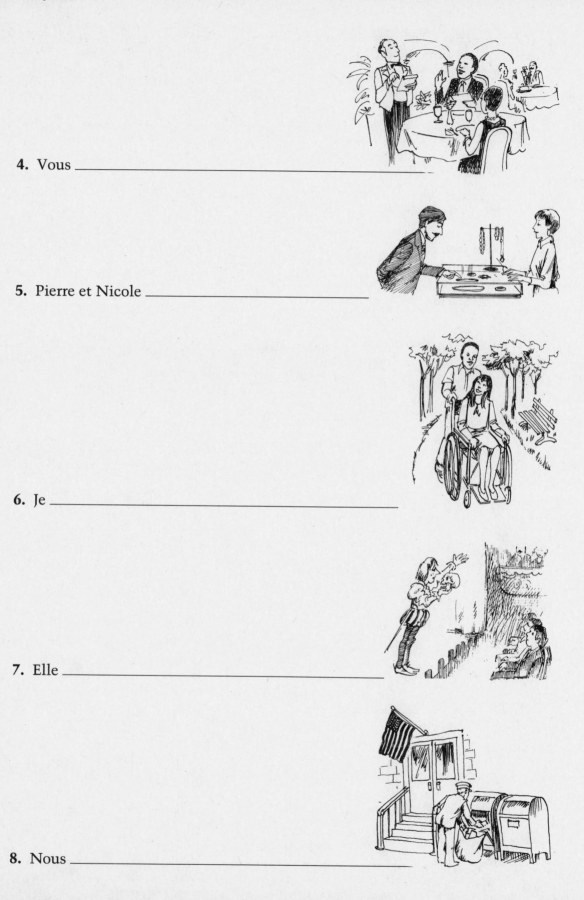

4. Vous _____

5. Pierre et Nicole _____

6. Je _____

7. Elle _____

8. Nous _____

L. On Tuesday morning, your teacher wants to know how you spent the four-day weekend. Complete the sentences with the correct form of the **passé composé**:

1. (arriver) Mercredi, mes cousins _____ de Montréal.

2. (venir) Ils _____ pour le mariage de ma sœur Jeannette.

3. (arriver) Pierre _____ en avion.

4. (venir) Ses parents _____ en voiture.

5. (aller) Nous _____ chercher Pierre à l'aéroport.

6. (rester) Ils _____ trois jours.

7. (sortir) Je _____ avec Pierre tous les soirs.

8. (aller, rentrer) Un soir nous _____ danser et nous _____ à la maison très tard.

9. (retourner) Pierre et ses parents _____ en voiture ensemble.

10. (rentrer) Ils _____ à Montréal très fatigués.

M. In your diary, you write down what you did when you visited your pen pal in Paris. You write everything as if it is happening in the present. Now you are telling your friends what you did in France:

EXAMPLE: J'arrive à l'aéroport Charles de Gaulle.
Je suis arrivé(e) à l'aéroport Charles de Gaulle.

1. Je descends de l'avion.

_____

2. J'arrive chez Jean.

_____

3. Je monte à la tour Eiffel.

_____

4. Je vais au Louvre.

_____

5. Je pars sur la Côte d'Azur.

_____

6. Je reste sur la plage.

_____

7. Je sors avec le cousin de Jean.

_____

8. Je reviens à Paris.

_____

9. Je vais à Versailles.

_____

10. Je reste à l'hôtel.

_____

11. Je monte dans l'avion.

_____

12. Je rentre à New York.

_____

13. Je sors de l'aéroport.

_____

14. Je retourne à l'école.

_____

N. You had an unusual experience in Paris. Now you are telling your friends about it. Complete the sentences in the **passé composé**, using **être** or **avoir**, as necessary:

1. Babette et moi, nous _____ en ville à dix heures du
                                (arriver)
matin.

2. Babette _____ voir sa cousine et moi, je
                (partir)

_____ à la banque.
     (aller)

3. Je _____ à dix heures dix.
      (arriver)

4. Deux hommes _____ derrière moi.
(entrer)

5. Tout à coup, ces deux types _____ la personne devant
(pousser)

moi violemment et elle _____ .
(tomber)

6. J' _____ si fort que les gens _____
(crier)   (avoir)

peur.

7. Les deux hommes _____ leurs pistolets et ils
(montrer)

_____ «Haut les mains!»
(crier)

8. Tout le monde _____ très nerveux, mais nous
(devenir)

_____ immobiles.
(rester)

9. Les voleurs _____ vers le guichet et ils
(aller)

_____ à la caissière de leur donner tout l'argent.
(dire)

10. La caissière _____ le temps de le faire.
(ne pas avoir)

11. Six policiers _____ si vite que les voleurs
(entrer)

_____ le temps de réagir (*react*).
(ne pas avoir)

12. La police _____ le vol et personne
(arrêter)

n'_____ .
(mourir)

13. Les voleurs _____ en prison.
(partir)

14. Les clients _____ très peur, mais ils
(avoir)

_____ de la banque sains et saufs.
(sortir)

15. La police _____ très rapide et très efficace (*efficient*).
(être)

To form the negative of verbs conjugated with **être**, use the same pattern as with **avoir**:

Je suis allé à la plage.   Je *ne suis pas allé* à la plage.
Nous sommes partis.   Nous *ne sommes pas partis.*

To form the interrogative, the **avoir** pattern also applies:

Vous êtes devenus riches.   *Êtes-vous devenus* riches?
Elles ne sont pas restées.   *Ne sont-elles pas restées?*

___ ACTIVITÉ ___

O. Make the following sentences negative:

1. Il est arrivé au tribunal.

_____

2. Sont-elles devenues nerveuses?

_____

3. Marianne est partie en retard.

_____

4. Es-tu entré avec l'avocat?

_____

5. Marc et Pierre sont nés en France.

_____

6. Le juge est-il sorti du tribunal?

_____

_____ *VOUS* _____

Make a list of five places you have gone to recently:

1. _____

2. _____

3. _____

4. _____

5. _____

DIALOGUE

Vous racontez (*tell*) à un ami un crime que vous avez vu. Répondez à ses questions:

QUESTIONS PERSONNELLES

1. Quand êtes-vous né(e)?

_____

2. Où êtes-vous allé(e) samedi soir?

_____

3. Avec qui êtes-vous sorti(e)?

_____

4. À quelle heure êtes-vous arrivé(e) à l'école aujourd'hui?

_____

5. À quelle heure êtes-vous rentré(e) chez vous hier soir?

_____

COMPOSITION

Write a note to a friend expressing what you did on your last day off from school:

_____

_____

_____

_____

_____

INTERVALLE CULTUREL

En cas d'urgence (*In case of emergency*)

In France, special phone numbers are assigned to emergency phone calls in order to provide fast responses from the appropriate services. For example, dialing 17 will connect you with **police secours**, which provides services equivalent to our 911. If you spot a fire, dialing 18 will reach a fire station. There are many other toll-free numbers (**numéros verts**) to assist people in any type of crisis or emergency. These numbers can be found in the yellow pages of any French phone book.

The **police judiciaire** takes care of investigating and solving crimes of all types. Also, each city has its own **police municipale**, which ensures the tranquility of the citizens. **La gendarmerie** is part of the army and deals with rescue operations and safety on the road.

Once arrested, a criminal must prove his innocence before being released from jail. There is no such thing as bail in France. Also, if suspected of an infraction, a person may be kept by the police in **garde à vue** (*custody*) for up to 48 hours.

Qu'est-ce qui se passe?

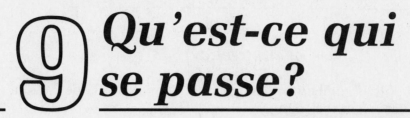

Passé composé of Reflexive Verbs

1 **Vocabulaire**

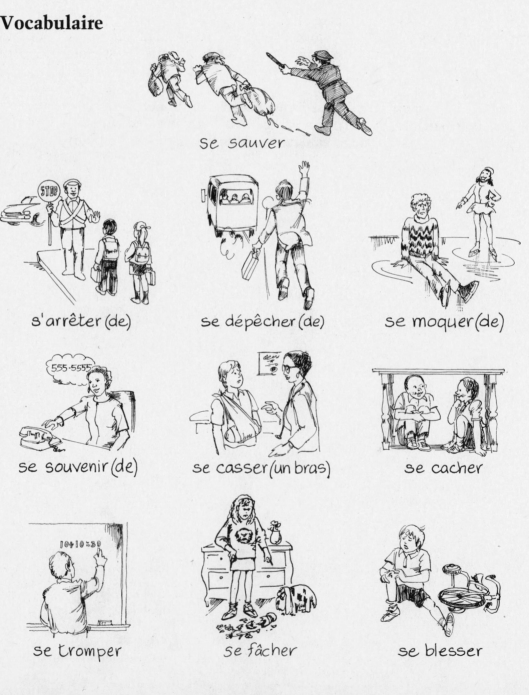

se sauver

s'arrêter (de)

se dépêcher (de)

se moquer (de)

se souvenir (de)

se casser (un bras)

se cacher

se tromper

se fâcher

se blesser

ACTIVITÉS

A. Match the descriptions with the related pictures:

Jean se moque de Marie.   Les enfants se cachent sous la table.
Le voleur se sauve.   L'élève se blesse.
Le professeur se fâche.   Elle se souvient du numéro.
M. Lambert se dépêche.   La voiture s'arrête devant le lycée.
Brigitte se trompe.   Georgette se casse le bras.

1. _____

2. _____

3. _____

4. _____

5. _____

6. _____

7. _____   8. _____

9. _____   10. _____

B. **Qu'est-ce qui se passe?** Form sentences using one element from each column:

Paul	se trompe	elle a perdu ses gants
l'homme	s'arrête	il n'écoute pas le professeur
Mme Guérin	se repose	ils sont en retard
les Dupont	se dépêchent	ils jouent aux voleurs
Jean et Paul	se sauvent	il voit un accident
l'enfant	se blesse	elle est fatiguée
Marie	se fâche	il ne fait pas attention

EXAMPLE: Paul se trompe parce qu'il n'écoute pas le professeur.

1. _____

2. _____

3. _____

4. _____

5. _____

6. _____

Une décision difficile

Now read this story about a job interview. Can you spot the **passé composé** of the reflexive verbs you have just learned?

Aujourd'hui, Alain Boucard avait une entrevue pour un poste de secrétaire. À deux heures de l'après-midi il s'est dépêché de partir parce qu'il avait peur d'être en retard.

avait *had*
une entrevue *interview*

Il s'est présenté dans le bureau de M. Restaud à trois heures. M. Restaud a posé beaucoup de questions et Alain ne s'est pas trompé dans ses réponses. Il s'est même souvenu de son numéro de sécurité sociale! L'entrevue s'est terminée et Alain est rentré chez lui très content. Il s'est arrêté dans une pâtisserie et a acheté un croissant au chocolat.

même *even*
sécurité sociale *social security*

À la maison, il s'est reposé et s'est fâché contre sa sœur qui s'est moquée de lui. Il n'a pas eu le temps de répondre car le téléphone a sonné.

M. Restaud lui a offert le poste d'ingénieur à la Compagnie Lamarche. Ingénieur? La Compagnie Lamarche? Alain ne comprend rien. Que s'est-il passé? Oh là là! Il s'est trompé d'étage et a été dans le mauvais bureau! Il n'est pas bon en maths et un ingénieur a toujours besoin de maths! Que faire? M. Restaud va se moquer de lui. Il peut dire qu'il s'est cassé la jambe ou qu'il s'est blessé et ne peut pas travailler . . .

ingénieur *engineer*

mauvais *wrong*

Il réfléchit pendant des heures. Finalement, il se décide: il va accepter le poste et apprendre les maths!

réfléchit *thinks about it*

___ ACTIVITÉ ___

C. Complete these sentences about the story:

1. Alain Boucard _____ de partir à deux heures.

2. Il avait peur _____ .

3. À trois heures il _____ dans le bureau de M. Restaud.

4. Alain ne _____ dans ses réponses.

5. Il _____ de son numéro de sécurité sociale.

6. Il _____ dans une pâtisserie.

7. Sa sœur _____ de lui, mais il n'a pas

_____ .

8. M. Restaud lui a offert un poste d' _____ .

9. Alain comprend qu'il _____ d'étage.

10. Il ne peut pas être ingénieur parce qu'il n'est pas _____
en maths.

11. Il peut dire qu'il _____ la jambe.

12. Il va _____ le poste et _____
les maths.

---

3 Let's look at some **passé composé** sentences from the story:

> **Il** *s'est dépêché* **de partir.**
> **Il** *s'est souvenu* **de son numéro.**
> **Il** *s'est fâché.*

The helping verb used with reflexive verbs in the **passé composé** is

_____ .

In the **passé composé**, the reflexive pronoun (**me, te, se, nous, vous**) comes

_____ .

Use this table to help you put sentences with reflexive verbs into the **passé composé**:

SUBJECT	REFLEXIVE PRONOUN	être (conjugated)	PAST PARTICIPLE
je	me	suis	arrêté(e)
tu	t'	es	fâché(e)
il	s'	est	dépêché
elle	s'	est	sauvée

nous	nous	sommes	blessé(e)s
vous	vous	êtes	caché(e)(s)
ils	se	sont	trompés
elles	se	sont	souvenues

NOTE: The reflexive pronoun is always before the conjugated form of **être**.

___ ACTIVITÉS _____

D. Who did it? Look carefully at the past participle and the reflexive pronoun of the following sentences and then complete them with the appropriate subject pronoun:

EXAMPLE: Elle s'est lavée.

1. _____ s'est moqué de Pierre.

2. _____ nous sommes blessés.

3. _____ t'es trompée.

4. _____ vous êtes sauvé.

5. _____ me suis fâché.

6. _____ se sont cachées.

7. _____ s'est souvenue de la date.

8. _____ se sont dépêchés.

E. **Qu'est-ce qui s'est passé?** Tell what happened:

EXAMPLE: un accident horrible/se passer
Un accident horrible s'est passé.

1. le criminel/se sauver

_____

2. la police/se tromper

_____

3. la voiture/s'arrêter

_____

4. il/se passer quelque chose de suspect

_____

5. elle/se blesser

_____

6. les garçons/se moquer des filles

_____

7. les filles/se fâcher

_____

8. elles/se décider à partir

_____

F. You had an accident the other day. Express what happened:

EXAMPLE: (s'amuser) avec mes amis
                   Je me suis amusé(e) avec mes amis.

1. (se moquer) de mon frère

_____

2. (se sauver) pour jouer

_____

3. (se trouver) dans le parc

_____

4. (s'arrêter) de courir

_____

5. (se cacher) derrière un arbre

_____

6. (se souvenir) de l'heure

_____

7. (se décider) à rentrer chez moi

_____

8. (se dépêcher)

_____

9. (se tromper) de chemin

_____

10. (tomber) et (se blesser) au genou

_____

4 Now look carefully at these groups of sentences:

I	II

Marie *s'est lavée*.
Marie washed herself.

Marie *s'est lavé* le visage.
Marie washed her face.

Les enfants *se sont peignés*.
The children combed themselves.

Les enfants *se sont peigné* les cheveux.
The children combed their hair.

Elles *se sont reposées*.
They rested (themselves).

Elles *se sont reposé* les pieds.
They rested their feet.

In Group I, what is the direct object of each sentence? _____
When the reflexive pronoun is the direct object of the verb, the past participle

of the reflexive verb _____ with the subject.

Now look at Group II, what is the direct object of each sentence?

_____ , _____ and

_____ .

When the reflexive pronoun is not the direct object of the verb, the past participle of the reflexive verb does not agree with the subject.

___ ACTIVITÉ _____

G. Tell what these people did to get ready for a party:

1. (s'acheter) Louise _____ une chemise.

2. (se raser) Les garçons _____ .

3. (se brosser) Jean et Anne _____ les dents.

4. (se reposer) Mme Dupont _____ .

5. (se peigner) Sylvie et Georgette _____ .

6. (se regarder) Alice _____ dans la glace.

7. (se brosser) Les filles _____ les cheveux.

8. (se laver) Marie _____ le visage.

Look back at the table on pages 176–177. Since the reflexive pronoun and the helping verb cannot be separated, where are **ne** and **pas** in a negative sentence? Observe:

> **Tu** *t'es* **trompé.**   **Tu** *ne t'es pas* **trompé.**
> **Nous** *nous sommes* **fâchés.**   **Nous** *ne nous sommes pas* **fâchés.**

To make a sentence negative, use **ne** _____ the reflexive pronoun and **pas** _____ the helping verb.

___ ACTIVITÉ _____

H. What didn't they do today?

> EXAMPLE: ils/se laver
> Ils ne se sont pas lavés.

1. vous/se peigner les cheveux

_____

2. ils/se brosser les dents

_____

3. tu/s'habiller

_____

4. nous/se reposer

_____

5. je/se réveiller à l'heure

_____

 Now look again at the table on pages 176–177. If you wanted to make a sentence into a question using inversion, what would you invert, the subject pronoun or the reflexive pronoun? _____

> **Tu** *t'es* **trompé.**   ***T'es-tu* trompé?**
> ***Ils se sont* amusés.**   ***Se sont-ils* amusés?**
> ***Elle s'est* fâchée.**   ***S'est-elle* fâchée?**

Can the reflexive pronoun be separated from the helping verb? _____
In an inverted question, what is between the helping verb and the subject pronoun? _____

__ ACTIVITÉS _____

I. Ask what the following people did:

> EXAMPLE: vous/s'amuser au cirque
> Vous êtes-vous amusé au cirque?

1. il/se raser ce matin

_____

2. tu/se tromper de classe

_____

3. elles/se moquer des garçons

_____

4. tu/se fâcher

_____

5. ils/se souvenir de l'adresse

_____

6. vous/se casser la jambe

_____

7. elle/s'arrêter de parler

_____

8. vous/se coucher tard

_____

J. Express whether or not you did the following things last weekend:

> EXAMPLES: se reposer
> Oui, je me suis reposé(e).
> Non, je ne me suis pas reposé(e).

1. se lever très tôt samedi et dimanche matin

(non) _____

2. se dépêcher de faire ses devoirs

(oui) _____

3. se reposer toute la journée

(oui) _____

4. s'endormir devant la télévision

(non) _____

5. se fâcher contre quelqu'un

(non) _____

6. se blesser

(non) _____

7. se coucher très tôt

(oui) _____

8. s'amuser avec des amis

(oui) _____

7 Finally, how would you ask a negative question when using a reflexive verb in the **passé composé**? Where are **ne** and **pas** in a negative question?

_____

Are the reflexive pronoun and the helping verb separated? _____

> Tu *ne t'es pas* amusé.   *Ne t'es-tu pas* amusé?
> Vous *ne vous êtes pas* reposé. *Ne vous êtes-vous pas* reposé?
> Ils *ne se sont pas* arrêtés.   *Ne se sont-ils pas* arrêtés?

In a negative question, where is the subject pronoun? _____

Where is the reflexive pronoun? _____

— ACTIVITÉS _____

K. Make these sentences negative:

    EXAMPLE: Vous êtes-vous endormi tard?
                 Ne vous êtes-vous pas endormi tard?

1. S'est-il levé tôt ce matin?

_____

2. Nous sommes-nous trompés d'adresse?

_____

3. Se sont-elles fâchées?

_____

4. T'es-tu moqué de lui?

_____

5. Vous êtes-vous blessé à la main?

_____

6. Se sont-ils arrêtés de chanter?

_____

7. T'es-tu souvenu de son anniversaire?

_____

8. S'est-elle couchée tard?

_____

L. Change these sentences to the **passé composé**:

1. Je ne me repose pas.

_____

2. Ne se dépêche-t-il pas?

_____

3. Personne ne se souvient de la date.

_____

4. Tu ne te sauves pas.

_____

5. Vous ne vous couchez pas de bonne heure.

_____

6. Ne se lavent-elles pas?

_____

7. Se trompe-t-il de numéro?

_____

8. Vous réveillez-vous à six heures?

_____

9. Te rases-tu?

_____

10. S'habillent-elles?

_____

_____ QUESTIONS PERSONNELLES _____

1. À quelle heure vous êtes-vous levé(e) ce matin?

_____

2. À quelle heure vous êtes-vous couché(e) hier soir?

_____

3. Vous êtes-vous amusé(e) hier à l'école?

_____

4. Vous êtes-vous fâché(e) hier?

_____

5. Qu'est-ce qui s'est passé en classe hier?

_____

_____ COMPOSITION _____

You had a good day yesterday. Express the following:

1. You had a lot of fun.

_____

2. You didn't get angry.

_____

3. You didn't rest a lot.

_____

4. You got up late.

_____

5. You didn't hurry up.

_____

DIALOGUE

Votre correspondant veut savoir en quelles occasions vous agissez (*act*) de cette manière:

VOUS

State five things that you have done or that have happened to you in the past. Use reflexive verbs:

1. _____

2. _____

3. _____

4. _____

5. _____

(INTERVALLE CULTUREL)

Le centre Georges Pompidou

As you walk around Paris, you will want to see the **Centre Pompidou** (also called **Beaubourg**), named after Georges Pompidou, the president of France from 1969 to 1974. This immense, modern, unusual-looking cultural center attracts not only the younger generation but all art lovers as well.

Approximately half of the area of the site is open and free, allowing for many unprogrammed outdoor events, such as games, meetings, and spontaneous public spectacles. In front of the **Centre** is a large plaza, where jugglers, artists, musicians, fire eaters, acrobats, and mimes attract large crowds.

Because of its network of pipes and tubes of all sizes and bold colors adorning the outside walls, the **Centre Pompidou** has sometimes been dubbed "the factory." Outside, glass-enclosed, tubular escalators afford a magnificent view of the city.

The **Centre** offers many activities and exhibits, all focused on contemporary art. Once inside, you will find a huge library, the center of industrial innovation, the museum of modern art, a movie library (**la cinémathèque**), and the institute for acoustic and musical research and coordination. And, best of all, it's free!

As many as 26,000 people visit the **Centre Pompidou** daily (35,000 on weekends) to meet friends, participate in the activities, or simply look around.

Would you like to visit the **Centre Pompidou**? Why?

10 *Le temps passe*

The Verb **connaître**;
Imperfect Tense

1 Vocabulaire

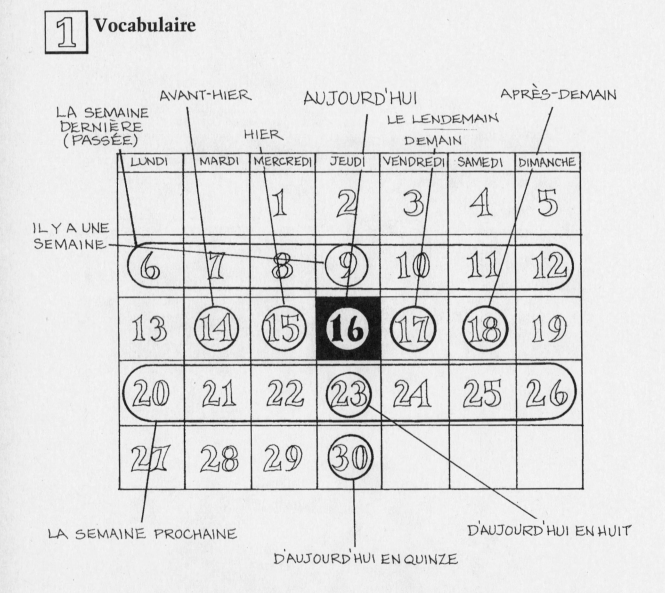

| LA SEMAINE DERNIÈRE (PASSÉE) | AVANT-HIER | HIER | AUJOURD'HUI | LE LENDEMAIN / DEMAIN | APRÈS-DEMAIN |

une minute = 60 secondes
une heure = 60 minutes
un jour = 24 heures
une semaine = 7 jours

un mois = 28/29/30/31 jours (4 semaines)
un an = 12 mois
un siècle = 100 ans
l'éternité

___ ACTIVITÉS ___

A. Si le 1ᵉʳ janvier est aujourd'hui, que sont ces dates?

EXAMPLE: le 1ᵉʳ février?   le mois prochain

1. le 31 décembre? _____

2. le 2 janvier? _____

3. le 30 décembre? _____

4. le 3 janvier? _____

5. le 8 janvier? _____

6. le 15 janvier? _____

B. Match the expressions in the left column with their definitions in the right column. Write the matching letter in the space provided:

1. 60 minutes _____
2. 60 secondes _____
3. 12 mois _____
4. dans deux semaines _____
5. deux jours avant aujourd'hui _____
6. le jour après aujourd'hui _____
7. cent ans _____
8. dans une semaine _____
9. deux jours après aujourd'hui _____
10. le temps infini _____
11. le mois à venir _____
12. les sept jours avant cette semaine _____

a. une minute
b. d'aujourd'hui en huit
c. d'aujourd'hui en quinze
d. une heure
e. après-demain
f. l'éternité
g. avant-hier
h. demain
i. un siècle
j. un an
k. la semaine dernière
l. le mois prochain

2 The verb **connaître** (*to know*) is an important irregular verb. See if you can find all the present-tense forms of **connaître** in the following dialog:

Fill in the correct forms of **connaître**:

je _____   nous _____

tu _____   vous _____

il _____   ils _____

elle _____   elles _____

Past participle: **connu**

ACTIVITÉS

C. Complétez avec la forme correcte du verbe **connaître**:

1. Tu _____ ce disque.

2. Nous _____ bien ce restaurant.

3. Ils _____ cette rue.

4. Il _____ Marie.

5. Elles _____ cette chanson.

6. Je _____ cette ville.

7. Vous _____ Paris.

8. Elle _____ Georges.

D. Complete the following conversation between Sylvie and Marise by filling in the appropriate form of **connaître**:

Sylvie: Marise, tu _____ très bien la France, n'est-ce pas?
　　　　　　　　　　　　　　　　1.

Marise: Oui, je _____ la France assez bien.
　　　　　　　　　　　　　2.

Sylvie: Alors, peux-tu me donner des renseignements sur le Midi (*south*)?

Marise: Pour le sud de la France, il faut demander à mes parents. Ils

_____ très bien le Sud parce qu'ils ont habité Nice
　　　　3.

pendant vingt ans. Mon frère Jean et moi, nous _____
　　　　　　　　　　　　　　　　　　　　　　　　　4.

beaucoup mieux le Nord: la Picardie et la Normandie. Tu sais, l'été dernier nous avons fait le tour du Nord en bicyclette.

Sylvie: Mais c'est formidable! Alors, non seulement vous _____
　　　　　　　　　　　　　　　　　　　　　　　　　　　5.

les grandes villes, mais aussi la campagne et les petits villages?

Marise: Oui, et mon frère _____ toutes les petites routes et les
　　　　　　　　　　　　　　　　6.

bons restaurants!

---

3 The verbs **connaître** and **savoir** both mean *to know*, but they are not used interchangeably. When do you use **connaître** and when do you use **savoir**? Let's look at some examples:

Je *connais* Michel, mais je ne *sais* pas où il habite.
I know (am acquainted with) Michel, but I don't know where he lives.

***Connaissez*-vous ce restaurant? Je *sais* qu'il est cher.**
Do you know (are you familiar with) this restaurant? I know it's expensive.

Can you see the difference? **Connaître** means *to know, to be acquainted with, to be familiar with* (*something or somebody*). **Savoir** means *to know facts, to have knowledge or information about something*. **Savoir** cannot be used with nouns that refer to people or places.

Remember: **savoir** + infinitive means *to know how to*:

Je *sais nager*.   *I know how to swim.*

___ ACTIVITÉ ___

E. Complete the following sentences with the correct form of **savoir** or **connaître**:

1. Je _____ danser.

2. Nous _____ que Janine parle italien.

3. Tu _____ monsieur Secret.

4. Ils _____ où se trouve le Louvre.

5. _____-vous la musique d'Édith Piaf?

6. _____-tu si la porte est fermée?

7. Elles _____ ce restaurant.

8. Je ne _____ pas comment s'appelle le professeur de biologie.

9. Nous _____ la France.

10. Nous _____ faire du ski.

11. Il _____ ma mère.

12. Tu _____ son adresse.

4 Chez madame Berthe

Since we are learning about time expressions, let's now read a story about a fortune teller (**une voyante**). Pay attention to the verbs in bold type. These verbs are in the imperfect, another past tense in French:

LISETTE: Georges, veux-tu venir avec moi consulter la vieille voyante Berthe mercredi prochain? On dit qu'elle peut voir le passé et prédire l'avenir.

GEORGES: Tu m'étonnes! Toi qui es une fille intelli-

prédire *to predict*
avenir *future*
étonner *to astonish*

gente et rationnelle, tu crois à ces choses-là? Enfin, si tu insistes, je t'accompagnes. Mais je ne vais pas payer pour entendre des bêtises.

bêtises *nonsense*

LISETTE: D'accord, je vais payer pour toi. À mercredi!

Le mercredi suivant, chez madame Berthe.

suivant *following*

BERTHE: Je vais commencer par discuter du passé de mademoiselle. Eh bien, mademoiselle, quand vous **étiez** jeune, vous **comptiez** sur les doigts des mains et des pieds. Vous n'avez appris à calculer que très récemment.

compter *to count*

LISETTE: Non, au contraire: j'**étais** très forte en maths.

BERTHE: Quand vous **aviez** treize ans, vous **étiez** si jalouse de votre meilleure amie que vous **disiez** toujours des mensonges sur elle.

meilleure *best*

LISETTE (qui rougit): Non, c'est faux!

rougir *to blush*

BERTHE: Enfin, vous **écriviez** toujours des billets doux anonymes à tous les beaux garçons de votre classe de français.

billets doux *love notes*

LISETTE: Mais tout ça est ridicule. Vous vous trompez!

BERTHE: Encore une chose: je ne vois pas de mariage dans votre avenir.

LISETTE (sur le point de pleurer): Tu **avais** raison, Georges. Comme je suis bête! Cette dame ne sait pas ce qu'elle dit. Allons-nous en!

être sur le point de *to be on the verge of*
pleurer *to cry*
Allons-nous en *let's go*

BERTHE: Attendez un moment. Je vois quelque chose de très intéressant vous concernant, monsieur.

GEORGES: Moi? Oh! Qu'est-ce que vous voyez?

BERTHE: Vous **étiez** un garçon très timide. À l'âge de dix ans, vous **suciez** encore votre pouce.

sucer *to suck*
encore *still*
pouce *thumb*

GEORGES: C'est embarrassant, mais vous avez raison.

BERTHE: Vous n'**aimiez** pas les œufs que votre mère vous **préparait** pour le petit déjeuner et vous les **jetiez** par la fenêtre.

jeter *to throw*

GEORGES: Mais oui, c'est vrai! Continuez, continuez, madame!

BERTHE: Quand vous **étiez** jeune, vous **écriviez** des messages méchants sur les murs de l'école.

méchants *naughty*
murs *walls*

GEORGES: Comment savez-vous ça?

BERTHE: Je sais tout. Je sais aussi que vous allez gagner un million de dollars à la loterie. Voilà, c'est tout pour aujourd'hui. Cinquante dollars, s'il vous plaît.

Georges paie et ils sortent dans la rue.

GEORGES: Je ne comprends pas comment elle **savait** toutes ces choses sur mon passé. Elle est fantastique!

LISETTE: Que tu es bête! Ta sœur a consulté Mme Berthe la semaine dernière. Et tu sais comme elle est bavarde, ta sœur . . .

bavarde *talkative*

___ ACTIVITÉ _____

F. Répondez aux questions par des phrases complètes:

1. Où est-ce que Lisette et Georges sont allés?

_____

2. Comment Lisette comptait-elle quand elle était jeune?

_____

3. Que disait-elle sur sa meilleure amie?

_____

4. Qu'est-ce qu'elle écrivait aux beaux garçons de sa classe?

_____

5. Que prédit Berthe pour son avenir?

_____

6. Pourquoi Lisette n'aime-t-elle pas Berthe?

_____

7. Où est-ce que Georges jetait les œufs que sa mère préparait?

_____

8. Qu'est-ce qu'il écrivait sur les murs de l'école?

_____

9. Qu'est-ce que Berthe prédit à Georges?

_____

10. Pourquoi Georges aime-t-il Berthe?

_____

11. Comment Berthe savait-elle tant de choses sur le passé de Georges?

_____

In French, we use two different past tenses to express actions in the past. You have already learned one of them, the **passé composé**. Now let's learn the other one, the imperfect (**l'imparfait**). Later on, we'll see the differences between the two. For now, let's concentrate on the forms of the imperfect. Look at the following examples:

	parler	**finir**	**vendre**
PRESENT	nous parl*ons*	nous finiss*ons*	nous vend*ons*
IMPERFECT	je parl*ais*	je finiss*ais*	je vend*ais*
	tu parl*ais*	tu finiss*ais*	tu vend*ais*
	il parl*ait*	il finiss*ait*	il vend*ait*
	elle parl*ait*	elle finiss*ait*	elle vend*ait*
	nous parl*ions*	nous finiss*ions*	nous vend*ions*
	vous parl*iez*	vous finiss*iez*	vous vend*iez*
	ils parl*aient*	ils finiss*aient*	ils vend*aient*
	elles parl*aient*	elles finiss*aient*	elles vend*aient*

Which present-tense form provides the stem for the **imparfait**? _____
If you answered the **nous** form, you are correct. To form the **imparfait**, add the following endings to the verb stem:

je	*-ais*	nous	*-ions*
tu	*-ais*	vous	*-iez*
il	*-ait*	ils	*-aient*
elle	*-ait*	elles	*-aient*

 So far you have learned the **imparfait** of verbs that are regular in the present. Notice what happens with verbs that are irregular in the present:

	faire	**avoir**
PRESENT	nous fais*ons*	nous av*ons*
IMPERFECT	je fais*ais*	j' av*ais*
	tu fais*ais*	tu av*ais*
	il fais*ait*	il av*ait*
	elle fais*ait*	elle av*ait*
	nous fais*ions*	nous av*ions*
	vous fais*iez*	vous av*iez*
	ils fais*aient*	ils av*aient*
	elles fais*aient*	elles av*aient*

For both regular and irregular verbs in the present, from which present-tense

form do we get the imperfect stem? _____

The only verb that does not derive its stem from the present-tense form **nous** is **être**. The imperfect stem for **être** is **ét-**:

j'*étais*	nous *étions*
tu *étais*	vous *étiez*
il *était*	ils *étaient*
elle *était*	elles *étaient*

Now let's formulate the rule for forming the **imparfait**. All verbs except **être** form the imperfect as follows:

nous form of the present minus **-ons** + imperfect endings

___ ACTIVITÉS _____

G. Complete the following table. You may want to review the present-tense forms of some irregular verbs:

INFINITIVE	**nous** FORM OF PRESENT	IMPERFECT
1. parler	_____	je _____
2. finir	_____	vous _____
3. répondre	_____	il _____
4. aller	_____	nous _____
5. avoir	_____	tu _____
6. connaître	_____	elles _____
7. croire	_____	vous _____
8. dire	_____	je _____
9. dormir	_____	ils _____
10. écrire	_____	nous _____
11. étudier	_____	tu _____
12. faire	_____	elle _____

13. lire _____ vous _____

14. mettre _____ elles _____

15. ouvrir _____ tu _____

16. partir _____ il _____

17. pouvoir _____ je _____

18. prendre _____ nous _____

19. recevoir _____ tu _____

20. savoir _____ elle _____

21. sentir _____ je _____

22. servir _____ vous _____

23. sortir _____ ils _____

24. venir _____ nous _____

25. voir _____ vous _____

26. vouloir _____ je _____

H. You are reminiscing with a friend about your childhood. Complete the sentences with the correct forms of the imperfect of the verbs in parentheses:

1. (passer) Ma famille _____ chaque été au bord de la mer.

2. (punir) Mes parents me _____ souvent.

3. (vendre) En été, je _____ de la limonade devant chez moi.

4. (être) Ma sœur _____ une petite fille sage.

5. (partir) Ma mère _____ de la maison très tôt.

6. (dire) Mes frères _____ toujours des mensonges.

7. (être) Mes parents _____ sévères.

8. (prendre) Tu _____ souvent ton petit déjeuner chez nous.

9. (venir) Mon frère et moi, nous _____ souvent te voir.

10. (vouloir) Je _____ devenir pompier.

11. (recevoir) Je _____ de beaux cadeaux pour mon anniversaire.

12. (se fâcher) Mes parents _____ souvent contre notre chien.

13. (aller) L'après-midi, nous _____ à la piscine.

14. (sortir) Ton frère et toi, vous _____ toujours avec moi.

15. (être) J'_____ un enfant heureux.

I. You are at a party where everyone is speaking about the past. Using the cues provided, make statements about the way it was:

EXAMPLE: je/jouer au base-ball dans le parc
Je jouais au base-ball dans le parc.

1. nous/aller chaque samedi chez notre grand-mère

   _____

2. il/dormir tard le week-end

   _____

3. elles/écrire des billets doux à Raymond

   _____

4. vous/lire des livres de science-fiction

   _____

5. tu/faire de longues promenades

   _____

6. je/prendre le train pour aller à l'école

   _____

7. Paul et Georgette/sortir tous les soirs

   _____

8. Douglas/jouer au golf

   _____

7 You have now learned two important tenses in French. Let's look at them side by side:

| imparfait | passé composé |

D'habitude il *arrivait* en retard,   **mais ce jour-là il *est arrivé* à l'heure.**
Il *jouait* toujours du piano,   **mais dimanche dernier il *n'a pas joué*.**
Luc *venait* tous les jours chez moi,   **mais avant-hier il n'*est pas venu*.**

In French, we use the imperfect to express what used to happen or happened over and over again — that is, repeated or habitual actions in the past. That's why the imperfect is often used with adverbial expressions like **d'habitude** (*usually*), **souvent** (*often*), **toujours** (*always*), **tous les jours** (*every day*). Most of these expressions relate to time.

The expressions **ce jour-là**, **dimanche dernier**, and **avant-hier** imply that the action happened at a specific time. In French, we use the **passé composé** to express specific events that are not habitual or that started and ended within a specific time frame. That's why the **passé composé** is often used with expressions that determine a specific time, like **hier soir** (*last night*), **ce matin** (*this morning*), **lundi dernier** (*last Monday*), and others.

___ ACTIVITÉS _____

J. Choose whether to use the **passé composé** or the **imparfait** in each sentence. Underline the correct choice:

1. Ils (sont allés, allaient) souvent au cinéma.

2. Qui (a préparé, préparait) les gâteaux hier soir?

3. Il (a étudié, étudiait) toujours très sérieusement pour ses examens.

4. Elle (est partie, partait) tôt ce matin.

5. Nous (avons pris, prenions) toujours le train en France.

6. Où est-ce que vous (avez rencontré, rencontriez) vos amis hier?

7. D'habitude (j'ai joué, je jouais) au football dans le parc.

8. Dimanche passé Jean (a visité, visitait) ses cousins.

9. Chaque vendredi ils (sont arrivés, arrivaient) tôt à la maison.

10. Vendredi dernier ils (sont rentrés, rentraient) tard.

K. You are at a party where everyone is talking about things they did. Complete the statements. Be careful, some verbs have to be used in the **passé composé** and some in the **imparfait**:

1. je/aller au cinéma samedi

   _____

2. nous/passer une semaine à New York

   _____

3. je/faire une promenade tous les soirs

   _____

4. Michel/lire deux romans l'été dernier

   _____

5. nous/jouer souvent au tennis ensemble

   _____

6. mes parents/partir en Europe chaque année

   _____

7. vous/aller au bord de la mer tous les étés

   _____

8. d'habitude ta sœur/travailler cinq heures par jour

   _____

9. mon oncle/revenir de France le mois dernier

   _____

10. tu/arriver toujours en retard à l'école

   _____

 There is still more to learn about the **imparfait** and the **passé composé**. Look carefully at these sentences:

> **J'*allais* à la cuisine quand le téléphone *a sonné*.**
> *I was going to the kitchen when the phone rang.*

> **Elle *regardait* la télé au moment où vous *êtes entré*.**
> *She was watching television when you came in.*

> **Il *étudiait* quand vous *êtes arrivé*.**
> *He was studying when you arrived.*

Paul *a téléphoné* pendant que nous *travaillions*.
Paul called while we were working.

How many actions occur in each sentence? _____ How many verb

tenses are used in each sentence? _____ Which tenses are they?

_____ and _____ .

Let's summarize: The **imparfait** describes an ongoing or continuous past action lasting an unspecified amount of time. In English, we usually say *was (were)* + . . . *ing*. The **passé composé** expresses a specific past action that happened at one point in time while the other action was in progress. Imagine two cameras — an instant and a video camera. Which one would represent the **imparfait**?

_____ the **passé composé?** _____

__ ACTIVITÉS _____

L. Answer the following questions using the correct form of the verb in parentheses:

EXAMPLE: Que faisiez-vous quand Jean a ouvert la porte? (danser)
Je dansais quand Jean a ouvert la porte.

1. Que faisiez-vous quand elles sont entrées? (lire)

_____

2. Que faisiez-vous quand Paul est venu? (travailler)

_____

3. Que faisiez-vous quand Hélène a téléphoné? (dormir)

_____

4. Que faisiez-vous quand le téléphone a sonné? (chanter)

_____

5. Que faisiez-vous quand les enfants sont arrivés? (partir)

_____

M. Complete the sentences with the correct form of the **passé composé** or **imparfait** of the verb in parentheses:

1. (rentrer) Tu _____ à quatre heures de l'après-midi.

2. (jouer) Samedi dernier, Dominique _____ au base-ball avec Jean.

3. (se coucher) D'habitude je _____ très tôt.

4. (écrire, être) Il _____ une lettre à Anne quand il

_____ en Corse.

5. (étudier, arriver) J'_____ quand tu _____ .

6. (faire, partir) _____-il ses devoirs quand tu _____ ?

7. (recevoir) Ils _____ toujours de belles cartes postales.

8. (naître, habiter) Quand mon frère _____, nous

_____ Avignon.

9. (dormir, entrer) Les enfants _____ quand je

_____ .

10. (lire, rentrer) Que _____-tu quand je _____ ?

 Read this short description of a holiday:

C'**était** le dix juin. Il **était** sept heures du matin. Le soleil **brillait** et il **faisait** un temps splendide. Nous **étions** dans un hôtel à côté de la plage et je **regardais** la mer par la fenêtre. Sur la plage il y **avait** un garçon. Il **était** grand et il **portait** un maillot de bain vert. Je **voulais** descendre à la plage, mais je **devais** attendre mes parents. J'**avais** seulement huit ans.

Which tense did the narrator use? _____ Right, he used the **imparfait** or the imperfect to describe circumstances and conditions in the past. The circumstances and conditions may refer to time, dates, weather, attitudes, states of mind, physical descriptions, age, or locations. All circumstances described in the **imparfait** happen over an unspecified amount of time.

What happens if the narrator wants to tell about an action that occurred at a specific point in time? Let's pick up the story from the last sentence:

J'**avais** seulement huit ans. Mes parents **dormaient** et je ne **voulais** pas attendre. J'**ai décidé** tout à coup de réveiller papa et maman. J'**ai ouvert** la porte de leur chambre et j'**ai crié** très fort: «Bonjour!»

Which tense is used to describe the narrator's actions that occurred at a specific moment? _____

___ ACTIVITÉS _____

N. You are writing a short paragraph describing your first years. Fill in the correct imperfect form of the verb in parentheses:

1. Quand j'_____ petit, ma famille _____ Paris,
   (être)   (habiter)
   dans un petit appartement.

2. Mon père _____ dans un garage.
   (travailler)

3. Quand il _____ tôt à la maison, papa et moi, nous
   (rentrer)
   _____ jouer au parc.
   (sortir)

4. En hiver, ma mère _____ du chocolat et j'_____
   (préparer)   (écouter)

   de la belle musique avec elle.

5. Nous _____ une famille heureuse et tranquille.
   (être)

O. Choose the **passé composé** or the **imparfait** to complete the story. Underline the correct form:

1. Nous (avons été, étions) au mois d'août et j'(ai été, étais) à Paris.

2. J'(ai eu, avais) une chambre d'hôtel au Quartier Latin.

3. Un jour je me (suis réveillé, réveillais) de bonne heure parce que (je suis allé, j'allais) visiter Versailles.

4. (J'ai voulu, Je voulais) voir ce palais magnifique.

5. Quand j'(ai ouvert, ouvrais) la fenêtre, le soleil (a brillé, brillait).

6. Comme nous (sommes allés, allions) faire la route dans un vieil autobus, je (me suis habillé, m'habillais) d'une façon confortable.

7. Le guide (a été, était) un jeune homme qui (a parlé, parlait) bien l'anglais.

8. Nous (sommes arrivés, arrivions) enfin au palais.

9. Pendant la visite, le guide (a raconté, racontait) beaucoup d'histoires intéressantes sur les anciens rois.

10. Versailles (a été, était) vraiment beau et je (me suis beaucoup amusé,
m'amusait beaucoup).

P. You are telling what happened on your way to school. Complete the paragraph
with the correct form of the **imparfait** or the **passé composé** of the verb in parentheses:

1. C'_____ le vingt juin, jour des examens finals.
   (être)

2. Il _____ déjà très chaud quand je _____.
   (faire)   (se réveiller)

3. Je _____ et je (j')_____ mon réveil.
   (se retourner)   (regarder)

4. Oh là là! Il _____ huit heures et quart.
   (être)

5. Je ne _____ pas arriver en retard pour mon examen de latin.
   (pouvoir)

6. Maître Corbeau _____ toujours la porte au moment où la
   (fermer)
   cloche (*bell*) _____.
   (sonner)

7. L'examen _____ commencer à huit heures quarante-cinq.
   (aller)

8. Je me _____ et je me _____
   (se lever)   (se depêcher)
   pour arriver à l'heure.

QUESTIONS PERSONNELLES

1. Quel temps faisait-il quand vous vous êtes réveillé(e) ce matin?

   _____

2. Où était votre mère quand vous êtes rentré(e) de l'école?

   _____

3. Que faisiez-vous hier soir à sept heures?

   _____

4. Qui était votre meilleur(e) ami(e) il y a deux ans?

   _____

5. Quel programme de télé était populaire il y a six mois?

   _____

DIALOGUE

Vous discutez de votre enfance avec un ami. Répondez à ses questions:

_____ *VOUS* _____

Complete this note to a friend telling how you were different when you were much younger:

Quand j'étais très jeune, _____

_____

_____

_____

_____

_____ *COMPOSITION* _____

Write a composition about how you used to spend your summer vacation when you were a child. Include the following information:

1. Where you used to go.

_____

2. What the weather was like.

_____

3. How you traveled there.

_____

4. What a typical day was like.

_____

5. Why you liked or disliked the vacation.

_____

Sites historiques

This map of France locates cities that have preserved remembrances of the past:

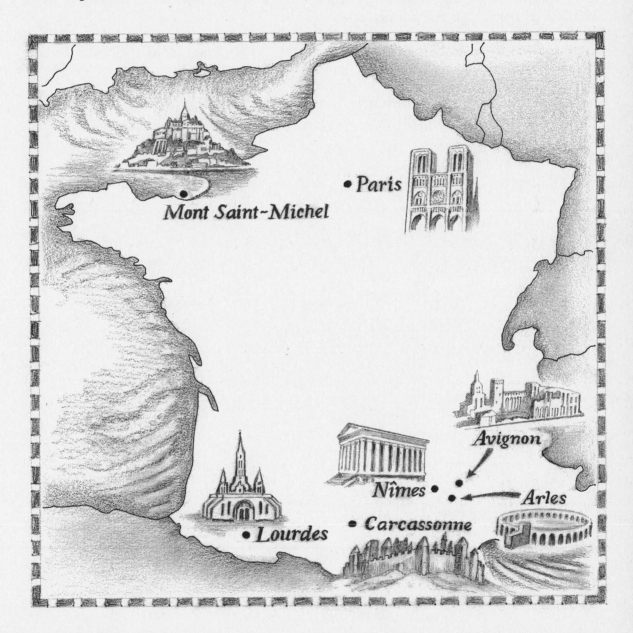

Carcassonne in southern France was named, according to the legend, for Dame Carcas, who helped save the besieged city during the Middle Ages. Famous for the walls and towers that surround it, Carcassonne is one of the finest examples of a medieval fortified city in Europe.

Mont-Saint-Michel is a rocky island off the coast of Normandy. Towering above the rock is a medieval abbey built in the 11th century. Surrounded by quicksand, the island can be reached only when the tide is low.

Every year, Catholics make a pilgrimage to **Lourdes**, a city at the foot of the **Pyrénées**, the mountains that separate France from Spain. It is believed that here, in 1858, the Virgin Mary appeared to the peasant girl Bernadette. For this reason, many people bathe in the sacred waters of the grotto where the vision took place, hoping to find a miracle that will restore their health.

Avignon, a city in Provence on the Rhône river, is famous for the Papal Palace that housed many popes during the 14th century.

Nîmes and **Arles**, also in Provence, contain some of the most beautiful and best-preserved Roman monuments, aqueducts, and arenas.

Révision II
(Leçons 6–10)

Leçon 6

a. Reflexive verbs have a special pronoun, called a reflexive pronoun, to indicate that the subject and object of the verb refer to the same person or thing:

se **laver**, *se* **coucher**, *s'***habiller**

b. Different subjects require different reflexive pronouns:

je me lave	*nous nous* lavons
tu te laves	*vous vous* lavez
il se lave	*ils se* lavent
elle se lave	*elles se* lavent

c. In French reflexive constructions, the definite article is used instead of the possessive adjective with parts of the body:

Tu te laves *le* **visage.**   *You wash your face.*

d. Some French reflexive verbs have nonreflexive English meanings:

se lever	*to get up*
s'amuser	*to have fun*
se coucher	*to go to bed*

e. The reflexive pronoun normally comes directly before the verb:

Je *me couche* tôt.
Tu ne *te dépêches* pas assez.
Comment *t'appelles*-tu?
Ne *se brosse*-t-il pas les dents?
Il ne veut pas *se reposer*.
Ne *vous endormez* pas!

In an affirmative command, the reflexive pronoun follows the verb and is attached to it by a hyphen. The reflexive pronoun **te** becomes **toi**:

Dépêche-*toi*!   **Dépêchez-*vous*!**   **Dépêchons-*nous*!**

Leçon 7

a. The verb **falloir** (*must, to be necessary*) is used only in the third person singular of the present tense. A verb that follows **il faut** is always in the infinitive:

*Il **faut** poser des questions.*

b. The **passé composé** of most French verbs consists of the present tense of the helping verb **avoir** and the past participle of the verb:

J'ai mangé.　　*Nous **avons étudié**.*

The past participle of regular verbs is formed as follows:

drop **-er** and add **-é** for **-er** verbs: **parl**er — **parl**é
drop **-r** for **-ir** verbs: **fini**r — **fini**
drop **-re** and add **-u** for **-re** verbs: **répond**re — **répond**u

c. Some French verbs have irregular past participles:

avoir	*eu*	mettre	*mis*
lire	*lu*	prendre	*pris*
pouvoir	*pu*	apprendre	*appris*
recevoir	*reçu*	comprendre	*compris*
savoir	*su*		
voir	*vu*	dormir	*dormi*
vouloir	*voulu*	sentir	*senti*
		servir	*servi*
dire	*dit*		
écrire	*écrit*	ouvrir	*ouvert*
décrire	*décrit*		
		être	*été*
		faire	*fait*

Leçon 8

a. Present-tense forms of the verb **venir** (*to come*):

je viens	nous venons
tu viens	vous venez
il vient	ils viennent
elle vient	elles viennent

The verbs **devenir** (*to become*), **revenir** (*to come back*), and **se souvenir** (*to remember*) are conjugated like **venir**.

b. **venir** + **de** + infinitive expresses an action just completed:

> **Je *viens de finir* mes devoirs.**   *I have just finished my homework.*

c. Not all French verbs use **avoir** as the helping verb in the **passé composé**. There are sixteen verbs that form the **passé composé** with the helping verb **être**. Most of these verbs express coming or going:

> **Devenir**
> **Revenir**
>
> **Mourir**
> **Rester**
> **Sortir**
>
> **Venir**
> **Arriver**
> **Naître**
> **Descendre**
> **Entrer**
> **Retourner**
> **Tomber**
> **Rentrer**
> **Aller**
> **Monter**
> **Partir**

The first letters of these verbs spell out DR. (and) MRS. VANDERTRAMP to help you remember them.

d. When the **passé composé** is formed with **être**, the past participle agrees in number and gender with the subject of the verb:

> **Elle est entr*ée*.**
> **René et Anne sont arriv*és*.**

Leçon 9

a. The **passé composé** of reflexive verbs is formed with the helping verb **être**:

> **Je *me suis peigné*.**
> **Ils *se sont amusés*.**

b. In the **passé composé**, the reflexive pronoun always comes before the helping verb **être**:

> **Je *me suis* promené.**
> **Nous ne *nous sommes* pas blessés.**
> ***S'est*-il arrêté?**
> **Ne *se sont*-elles pas fâchées?**

c. The past participle of reflexive verbs agree with the subject pronoun if the reflexive pronoun is the direct object:

Elle *s'est lavée.*
Ils *se sont peignés.*
Elles *se sont maquillées.*

But: Elle *s'est lavé* le visage.
Ils *se sont peigné* les cheveux.
Elles *se sont maquillé* les yeux.

Leçon 10

a. Present-tense forms of the verb **connaître** (*to know*):

je connais	nous connaissons
tu connais	vous connaissez
il connaît	ils connaissent
elle connaît	elles connaissent

Past participle: **connu**

Both **savoir** and **connaître** mean *to know* but they are not interchangeable. Review their use on pages 191–192.

b. The imperfect (**imparfait**) of all verbs except **être** is formed by taking the **nous** form of the present tense minus **-ons** and adding the imperfect endings:

je		*-ais*
tu		*-ais*
il	parl(-ons)	*-ait*
elle	finiss(-ons)	*-ait*
nous	vend(-ons)	*-ions*
vous		*-iez*
ils		*-aient*
elles		*-aient*

c. The only verb irregular in the imperfect is **être**:

j'étais	nous étions
tu étais	vous étiez
il était	ils étaient
elle était	elles étaient

d. Uses of the **imparfait** and the **passé composé**:

imparfait	passé composé
Describes repeated or habitual actions (equivalent to English *used to*):	Describes specific events that are not habitual:
J'*allais* au cinéma *tous les jours.*	Je *suis allé* au cinéma *hier.*

Describes an ongoing or continuous action (equivalent to English *was* [*were*] + *ing* . . .):

Michel *dormait* profondément pendant que son frère *regardait* la télé.

Describes circumstances and conditions (time, date, weather, attitude, age, physical description) that happened over an unspecified amount of time:

Il *était* sept heures et il *faisait* du soleil.
Un homme qui *portait* des lunettes *voulait* parler à ma mère.

Describes a particular action that happened while another action was in progress:

Paul *faisait* ses devoirs quand Georges *est arrivé* chez lui.

Describes an action that started and ended at a specific point in time:

Je me *suis levé* et je me *suis habillé*.

J'*ai appelé* ma mère et elle *est venue* ouvrir la porte.

___ ACTIVITÉS _____

A. Here are eight pictures showing what Pierre did yesterday morning. Following the clues given, complete the sentence under each picture and then number the sentences so that they follow the correct order of his activities:

Dans la salle de bains, il

et il _____.

_____ ,

il _____ ,

Il _____
immédiatement

Après le déjeuner il _____   il _____ ,

_____ .

Ensuite, il _____   Hier Pierre _____
et il est parti déjeuner.   à six heures.

B. Just look at your friends! Look at the following pictures and give your friends some advice:

Example:

Amuse-toi!

1. _____   2. _____

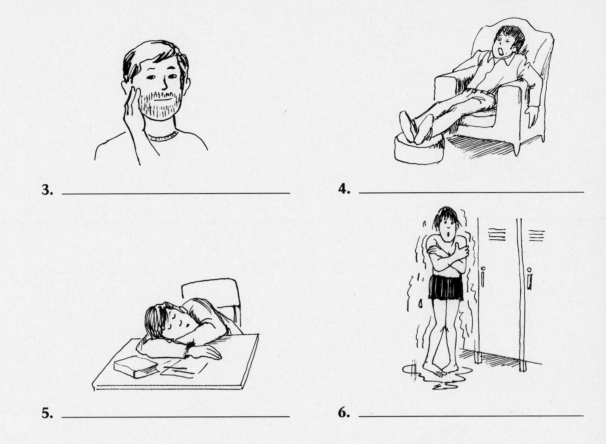

3. _____   4. _____

5. _____   6. _____

C. Time flies when you're having fun! Hidden in the puzzle below are 16 time-related French words. Circle the words from left to right, right to left, up, down, or diagonally. Note that hyphenated words are printed as one word in the puzzle:

A	V	A	N	T	H	I	E	R	É	O
U	P	E	S	E	S	D	M	O	T	I
J	A	R	I	M	R	E	E	E	E	L
O	R	S	È	P	U	R	T	É	R	E
U	I	L	C	S	I	D	U	N	N	N
R	N	A	L	I	D	N	N	I	D
D	E	P	E	O	E	E	I	A	T	E
H	V	T	A	M	M	V	M	C	É	M
U	A	H	L	S	A	O	I	A	T	A
I	D	N	U	L	S	N	N	O	I	I
X	E	R	U	E	H	É	U	H	U	N

D. **Qui est le criminel?** To find the answer, identify the objects and people in the pictures. Then write the letters indicated in the solution blanks below:

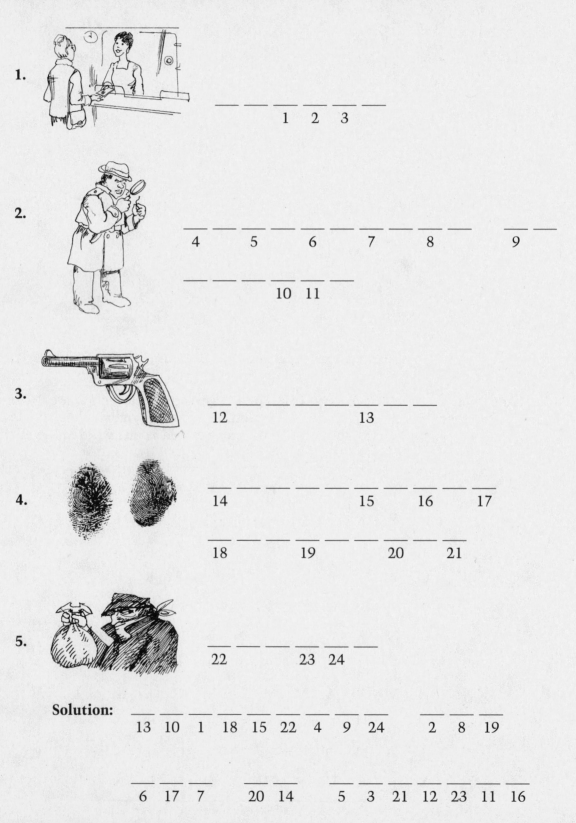

1.   __ __ __ __ __ __
        1 2 3

2.   __ __ __ __ __ __ __ __ __ __ __ __
     4   5   6   7   8   9

     __ __ __ __ __
        10 11

3.   __ __ __ __ __ __ __
     12   13

4.   __ __ __ __ __ __ __ __
     14   15 16 17

     __ __ __ __ __ __ __
     18   19   20 21

5.   __ __ __ __ __
     22   23 24

Solution: __ __ __ __ __ __ __ __ __   __ __ __
          13 10 1 18 15 22 4 9 24   2 8 19

          __ __ __   __ __   __ __ __ __ __ __ __
           6 17 7   20 14   5 3 21 12 23 11 16

E.   These people used to do different things during the summer. Complete the sentence under each picture, using the imperfect of the appropriate verb:

1. Rose _____.

2. Julie et Pauline _____.

3. Monsieur Gilbert _____.

4. Robert _____.

5. Vous _____.

6. Georges _____ .

7. Ils _____ .

8. Yvette _____ .

F. **Qu'est-ce qu'ils ont fait hier?** Complete the sentences with the correct forms of the verbs in the **passé composé**:

EXAMPLE:

Elle s'est cachée sous la table.

1. Je _____ dans le jardin.

2. Nous _____ de faire les courses (*shopping*).

3. Elle _____ contre sa petite sœur.

4. Vous _____ en classe.

5. Tu _____ légèrement au doigt.

G. Êtes-vous un bon témoin? You are walking down the street when a thief races out of a store and gets into a waiting car, which then speeds away. You have seen the whole incident and are asked to describe what you saw. Examine the following picture very carefully for one minute. Then cover the picture and try to answer the questions correctly:

1. Quelle heure était-il?

_____

2. De quelle couleur était la voiture?

_____

3. Quel était le numéro de la plaque (*plate*)?

_____

4. Le voleur avait-il le visage couvert?

_____

5. Avait-il une barbe ou une moustache?

_____

6. Portait-il un chapeau?

_____

7. A-t-il volé une banque ou une bijouterie?

_____

8. Combien de personnes y avait-il dans la voiture?

_____

9. Le voleur avait-il un pistolet?

_____

10. Combien de personnes y avait-il dans la rue?

_____

H. Madame Berthe, the fortune teller, has told you some things about your past and your future. The problem is that she didn't say when the things happened or will happen. Use the secret numbers to break the code and find out what she saw in her crystal ball. The numbers tell you which letters to put in the blanks. Then complete the sentences with expressions that make sense, following the clues given:

C L E F					
A₁	B₂	C₃	D₄	E₅	F₆
G₇	H₈	I₉	J₁₀	K₁₁	L₁₂
M₁₃	N₁₄	O₁₅	P₁₆	Q₁₇	R₁₈
S₁₉	T₂₀	U₂₁	V₂₂	W₂₃	X₂₄
Y₂₅	Z₂₆	É₂₇	È₂₈	Â₂₉	

1. ___ ___   ___ ___ ___ '___ ___ ___   ___ ___ ___ ___ ___   ___ ___
   20 21   20 5 19   3 1 19 19 27   12 5

___ ___ ___ ___   ___ '___ ___ ___ ___ ___
 2 18 1 19   12 1 14 14 27 5

___ ___ ___ ___ ___ ___ ___ ___ ___.

2. ___   ___ ___ ___   ___ ___ ___ ___ ___   ___ ___ ___ ___
     22 1 19   14 1 7 5 18   4 1 14 19

___ ___   ___ ___ ___   ___ ___ ___.
    3 5 20   27 20 27

3. ___ ___   ___ ___ ___   ___ ___ ___   ___ ___ ___ ___ ___ ___ ___
 20 1   22 9 5   3 8 1 14 7 5 18

___ ___ ___ ___.
 13 15 9 19

4. $\overline{}\ \overline{}\quad\overline{}\ \overline{}\quad\overline{}\ \overline{}\ \overline{}\ \overline{}\quad\overline{}\ \overline{}\quad\overline{}\ \overline{}\ \overline{}$
$\quad\ \ 20\ \ 21\qquad 1\ \ 19\qquad 6\ \ 1\ \ 9\ \ 20$

$\overline{}\ ,\overline{}\ \overline{}\ \overline{}\ \overline{}\ \overline{}\quad\overline{}\ \overline{}\ \overline{}\ \overline{}\ \overline{}.$
$12\ \ 8\ \ 9\ \ 22\ \ 5\ \ 18\qquad 16\ \ 1\ \ 19\ \ 19\ \ 27$

5. $\overline{}\ \overline{}\qquad\overline{}\ ,\overline{}\ \overline{}\quad\overline{}\ \overline{}\ \overline{}\ \overline{}\ \overline{}\ \overline{}\quad\overline{}\ \overline{}\ \overline{}\ \overline{}.$
$\qquad\qquad\qquad\qquad\qquad\ \ 2\ \ 12\ \ 5\ \ 19\ \ 19\ \ 27\qquad 8\ \ 9\ \ 5\ \ 18$

6. $\overline{}\ \overline{}\quad\overline{}\ \overline{}\ \overline{}\quad\overline{}\ \overline{}\quad\overline{}\ \overline{}\ \overline{}\ \overline{}\ \overline{}\ \overline{}$
$\quad\ \ 20\ \ 21\qquad 22\ \ 1\ \ 19\qquad\qquad 6\ \ 29\ \ 3\ \ 8\ \ 5\ \ 18$

$\overline{}\ \overline{}\quad\overline{}\ \overline{}\ \overline{}\ \overline{}$
$12\ \ 1$

$\overline{}\ \overline{}\ \overline{}\ \overline{}\ \overline{}\ \overline{}\ \overline{}\ \overline{}\ \overline{}.$
$16\ \ 18\ \ 15\ \ 3\ \ 8\ \ 1\ \ 9\ \ 14\ \ 5$

I. **Mots croisés:**

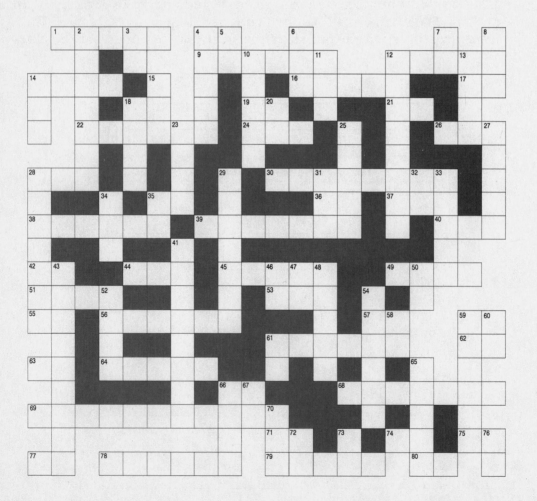

HORIZONTALEMENT

1. (écrire) j'ai _____
4. (your) _____ sœur
9. (ouvrir) tu _____
12. (vouloir) elle a _____
14. without
16. (sortir) il est _____
17. (avoir) j' _____
18. (pouvoir) ils ont _____
19. (not) Je _____ danse pas.
21. (avoir) j'ai _____
22. (arriver) tu es _____
24. (être) elle _____
26. (my) _____ lettres
28. (mettre) il a _____ une chemise.
30. (souvenir) Je me _____ de la date.
35. (some) Il a _____ pain.
36. (not) Je _____ chante pas.
37. (naître) Quand est-elle _____ ?
38. (which) _____ bague regardes-tu?
39. (appeler) Comment vous _____
    -vous?
40. nose
42. (être) tu _____

44. (être) il a _____
45. (se lever) tu te _____
49. (faire) elle a _____
51. names
53. one
55. you
56. (s'arrêter) il s' _____
57. (être) tu _____
59. (avoir) tu _____
61. (devenir) il est _____
62. the
63. (myself) Je _____ maquille.
64. (se fâcher) elle se _____
66. (my) _____ maison
68. (arriver) ils sont _____
69. (connaître) nous _____
71. one
74. one, people
75. (his) _____ bicyclette
77. (avoir) tu _____
78. (ouvrir) tu as _____
79. (rester) je suis _____
80. (savoir) nous avons _____

VERTICALEMENT

2. (connaître) je _____
3. he
4. (tomber) Le garçon est _____ .
5. (to the) _____ musée
6. (my) _____ amis
7. (lire) vous avez _____
8. who
10. (venir) vous _____
11. (her) _____ examen
12. (venir) elles _____
13. (se laver) je me _____
14. (his) _____ devoirs
15. him
18. (prendre) il a _____
20. (être) tu _____
23. (venir) vous êtes _____
25. (se lever) vous vous _____
27. (savoir) vous _____
28. (se moquer) ils se _____
29. (s'appeler) je m' _____
31. one
32. (naître) il est _____

33. (sentir) j'ai _____
34. they
35. of
41. (se dépêcher) tu te _____
43. (se souvenir) nous nous _____
46. (vois) tu as _____
47. in
48. (servir) il a _____
50. (to the) _____ lycée
52. except
54. (rentrer) il est _____
58. (savoir) vous avez _____
59. (aller) elles sont _____
60. (himself) il _____ lave
61. (some) _____ gâteau
65. (venir) tu _____
66. (mourir) il est _____
67. year
70. on
72. (not) Il _____ se repose pas.
73. and
76. (avoir) j' _____

J. Picture story. Can you read this story? Much of it is in picture form. Whenever you come to a picture, read it as if it were a French word:

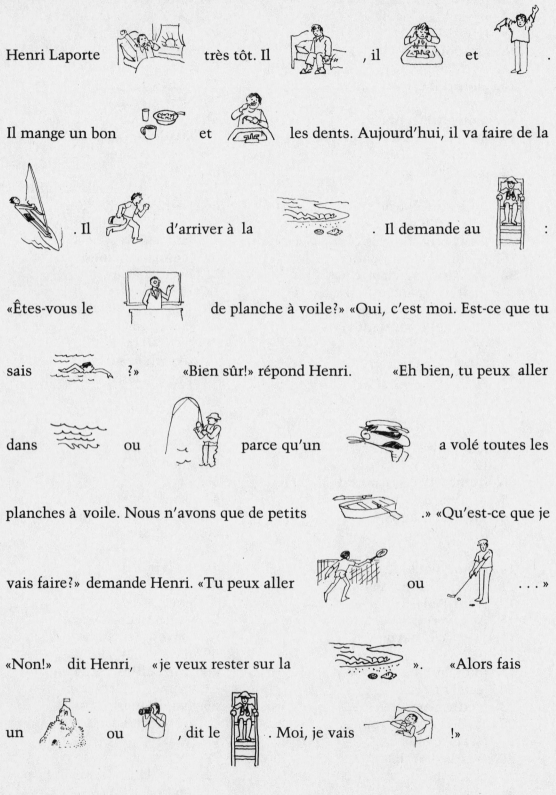

Henri Laporte [bed] très tôt. Il [sitting] , il [head] et [stretching] .

Il mange un bon [cereal/milk] et [brushing teeth] les dents. Aujourd'hui, il va faire de la

[windsurfing] . Il [running] d'arriver à la [beach] . Il demande au [lifeguard] :

«Êtes-vous le [man at window] de planche à voile?» «Oui, c'est moi. Est-ce que tu

sais [swimming] ?» «Bien sûr!» répond Henri. «Eh bien, tu peux aller

dans [water] ou [fishing] parce qu'un [thief] a volé toutes les

planches à voile. Nous n'avons que de petits [boat] .» «Qu'est-ce que je

vais faire?» demande Henri. «Tu peux aller [tennis] ou [golf] . . .»

«Non!» dit Henri, «je veux rester sur la [beach] ». «Alors fais

un [sandcastle] ou [camera] , dit le [lifeguard] . Moi, je vais [sleeping] !»

Troisième Partie

11 Au magasin de vêtements

The Verb **croire**; Direct Object Pronouns

1 Vocabulaire

le complet

le gilet

le sweat-shirt

le pyjama

l'imperméable

la robe de chambre

le blazer

le jean

le T-shirt

la chemise de nuit

les baskets

les bottes de cuir

les pantoufles

le short

l'écharpe

___ ACTIVITÉS ___

A. You need to buy some clothes and go shopping with your mother. What would you buy in this store?

1. _____   5. _____

2. _____   6. _____

3. _____   7. _____

4. _____   8. _____

B. You are writing a story and have four characters in mind. Here are their descriptions. What clothes would you have them wear? Use the new words and those you already know. Here are some more helpful expressions:

à manches courtes *short-sleeved*	**le tissu** *material, fabric*
à manches longues *long-sleeved*	**à rayures** *striped*
sans manches *sleeveless*	**à carreaux** *checkered, plaid*
le coton *cotton*	**le col** *collar*
la laine *wool*	**ultramoderne** *ultramodern*
large *wide*	**étroit(e)** *narrow*

Thomas: Un jeune homme de 20 ans. Il étudie à l'université. Il a des idées origi-
         nales et modernes. Il désire être acteur.

Michel: Un homme de 23 ans. Il travaille pour un avocat. Il est sérieux, intelli-
         gent et pratique. Il veut gagner beaucoup d'argent.

Denise: Une jeune fille de 21 ans. Elle est raffinée (*refined*) et élégante. Elle
         désire être mannequin (*model*). Elle aime bien la musique moderne.

Régine: Une jeune fille de 19 ans. Elle est secrétaire. Le soir, elle va à l'univer-
         sité. Elle veut devenir pharmacienne. Elle est studieuse, sympathique
         et agréable.

Thomas porte _____

_____

_____

Michel porte _____

_____

_____

Denise porte _____

_____

_____

Régine porte _____

_____

_____

After school, you and your friends discuss your French teacher. Read the following dialog and see if you can find all the forms of the verb **croire** (*to believe* [*something, someone*]; *to think*):

Fill in the correct form of **croire** from the dialog:

je _____   nous _____

tu _____   vous _____

il _____   ils _____

elle _____   elles _____

Past participle: **cru**

NOTE: **croire à** + object means *to believe in something*:

Il *croit au* père Noël.	*He believes in Santa Claus.*
Nous *croyons à* son histoire.	*We believe in his story.*

__ ACTIVITÉS _____

C. Combine one element from each column to express what the following people believe in:

nous	croient	aux revenants (*ghosts*)
il	croyons	aux extraterrestres
elles	croit	au père Noël
je	crois	aux voyants
tu	croyez	à la magie
vous		à son explication
Marie		aux contes de fées
les garçons		aux miracles

EXAMPLE: Il croit aux revenants.

1. _____

2. _____

3. _____

4. _____

5. _____

6. _____

7. _____

8. _____

D. Complete the following sentences with the correct forms of **croire**:

1. Nous _____ Jean.

2. Il ne _____ plus au père Noël.

3. Qu'est-ce que tu _____ ?

4. Hier, elle a _____ le voir dans la rue.

5. Ces garçons _____ tout savoir.

6. Les filles _____-elles aux excuses des garçons?

7. Je ne _____ jamais personne.

8. Vous _____ toujours vos parents.

③ Une robe particulière

Let's read a story about a special party dress and a girl's good luck. Pay special attention to the words in bold type:

Liliane vient de célébrer son dix-septième anniversaire. En cadeau, elle a reçu cent dollars de ses parents. Comment peut-elle **les** dépenser? Son amie Odette **l'**appelle: elle donne une fête ce week-end. Liliane décide donc de s'acheter une robe du soir magnifique. Elle va **la** porter à cette fête et sera la   **sera** *will be*
jeune fille la plus élégante. Elle veut une robe spéciale et elle sait exactement où **l'**acheter: chez Fifi, la boutique la plus chic de la ville. Quand Liliane entre dans la boutique, la vendeuse vient tout de suite **la** saluer.

VENDEUSE: Bonjour, mademoiselle. Est-ce que je peux vous aider?

LILIANE: Oui. Je veux une robe du soir. Taille 40, s'il   **taille** *size*
vous plaît.

VENDEUSE: Que pensez-vous de cette robe rouge en satin?

LILIANE: Non, je ne **l'**aime pas du tout. La couleur est trop vive.

VENDEUSE: Cette blouse blanche et cette mini-jupe noire forment un charmant ensemble. Voulez-   **ensemble** *outfit*
vous **les** essayer?   **essayer** *to try (on)*

LILIANE: Non. C'est un joli ensemble mais je **le** trouve trop simple. Je veux quelque chose de plus chic et de plus sophistiqué.

VENDEUSE: Je vois ce que vous voulez dire. Eh bien, voici une robe de soie bleue qui paraît faite pour   **soie** *silk*
vous. Je viens juste de **la** recevoir. Elle est unique.   **paraît** *seems*
C'est la seule que j'ai reçue. Décidez-vous vite   **la seule** *the only one*
avant que quelqu'un d'autre **l'**achète!

LILIANE: Oh, quelle belle robe! Où est-ce que je peux **l'**essayer?

VENDEUSE: Suivez-moi, mademoiselle.   **suivez** *follow*

Liliane **l'**essaie. Elle est enchantée.   **enchanté** *delighted*

LILIANE: Je l'adore. C'est décidé: je **la** prends. Combien coûte-t-elle?

VENDEUSE: Pour vous, deux cents dollars seulement.

LILIANE: Ah, mais je n'ai que cent dollars! Quel dommage! Tant pis. Je vais essayer le premier ensemble.

Liliane **l'**essaie. Elle **l'**aime beaucoup et son prix est raisonnable. Elle **le** prend.

Le soir de la fête arrive. Quand Liliane, habillée de son nouvel ensemble, entre dans le salon, elle pousse un cri de surprise. Ses trois amies, Julie, Claire et Murielle, paraissent fâchées et embarrassées. Elles sont toutes les trois habillées exactement pareil — d'une robe de soie bleue!

paraissent *seem*
pareil *the same*

LILIANE: Bonsoir tout le monde! Pourquoi portez-vous toutes les trois la même robe?

JULIE: Tu n'aimes pas cette robe qui paraît faite pour moi?

CLAIRE: Oui, elle est unique tu sais. C'est la seule du magasin.

MURIELLE: Vraiment, cette vendeuse de chez Fifi, j'ai envie de **l'**assassiner!

avoir envie de *to feel like*

___ ACTIVITÉ _____

E. Répondez aux questions par des phrases complètes:

1. Qu'est-ce que Liliane vient de célébrer?

_____

2. Qu'est-ce qu'elle a reçu en cadeau?

_____

3. Qu'est-ce qu'elle décide de s'acheter?

_____

4. Où va-t-elle?

_____

5. Qui vient la saluer?

_____

6. Pourquoi n'aime-t-elle pas la robe rouge?

_____

7. Quelle robe essaie-t-elle?

_____

8. Est-ce qu'elle l'achète? Pourquoi?

_____

9. Qu'est-ce qu'elle finit par acheter?

_____

10. Pourquoi est-elle contente le soir de la fête?

_____

_____

4 What do you think of these sentences in English?

I have a French book. I find my French book very useful. I read my French book, study my French book, and refer to my French book before taking a test.

Pretty repetitious! How about this version:

I have a French book. I find it very useful. I read it, study it, and refer to it before taking a test.

Much better, isn't it? What have we done? We have substituted an object pronoun (*it*) instead of repeating the same noun (*French book*). We can do the same thing in French. Look at these sentences:

I	II
Je veux _le complet_.	**Je _le_ veux.**
Tu prends _le gilet_.	**Tu _le_ prends.**
Il achète _le T-shirt_.	**Il _l'_achète.**

In Group I, which are the direct object nouns?_____,_____,

and _____. What is the gender of these nouns?_____

Are they singular or plural?_____

Now look at Group II. Which word has replaced the direct object nouns in the

first two examples?_____ What is the grammatical name for **le**?

_____

Where is **le** with respect to the verb? _____

If the verb starts with a vowel, what happens to **le**? _____

___ ACTIVITÉ _____

F. Replace the direct object noun with the direct object pronoun:

1. Je mets le T-shirt.

   _____

2. Il regarde le film.

   _____

3. Vous écoutez le disque.

   _____

4. Elles finissent le dessert.

   _____

5. Marie adore le professeur.

   _____

   _____

 Now look at these sentences:

I	II
Elle cherche *la robe de chambre*.	**Elle *la* cherche.**
Ils veulent *la chemise*.	**Ils *la* veulent.**
Vous aimez *la jeune fille*.	**Vous *l'*aimez.**

In Group I, what is the gender of the direct object nouns? _____

Are they singular or plural? _____

Look at Group II. What has replaced the direct object nouns in the first two

examples? _____ Where is the direct object pronoun **la** with respect to the verb?

_____

What happens to **la** if the verb starts with a vowel? _____

__ ACTIVITÉ __

G. Replace the direct object noun with the direct object pronoun:

1. Elles aiment la chemise de nuit.

_____

2. Nous mangeons la quiche.

_____

3. Vous voulez la robe de chambre.

_____

4. J'invite l'étudiante.

_____

5. Tu mets l'écharpe.

_____

 Finally, look at these sentences:

I	II
Je veux *les baskets.*	Je *les* veux.
Elles trouvent *les souliers.*	Elles *les* trouvent.
Nous aimons *les pantoufles.*	Nous *les* aimons.

In Group I, what are the genders of the direct object nouns?_____

_____ Are they singular or plural?_____

In Group II, what has replaced the direct object nouns?_____

Where is the direct object pronoun **les** with respect to the verb?_____

What happens to **les** if the verb starts with a vowel?_____

__ ACTIVITÉS __

H. Replace the direct object noun with the direct object pronoun:

1. J'adore les légumes.

_____

2. Nous voulons les bottes.

_____

3. Tu écris les exercices.

_____

4. Elles apprennent les chansons.

_____

5. Vous préparez les plats.

_____

6. Il achète les baskets.

_____

I. You are going on a trip and your mother wants to know what you are taking with you. Answer her questions:

EXAMPLE: Prends-tu la chemise bleue?
Oui, je la prends.

1. Prends-tu les pantalons noirs?

_____

5. Prends-tu le vieux gilet?

_____

2. Prends-tu l'écharpe verte?

_____

6. Prends-tu la robe de chambre?

_____

3. Prends-tu l'imperméable?

_____

7. Prends-tu les pantoufles?

_____

4. Prends-tu les bottes de cuir?

_____

8. Prends-tu les T-shirts?

_____

J. Carine has just met Roland at a party. They discover that they have a lot in common. Take the part of Roland and respond:

EXAMPLE: Carine: Je fais les devoirs le soir.
Roland: Moi aussi, je les fais le soir.

1. Carine: Je prends le bus pour aller à l'école.

Roland: _____

2. Carine: J'étudie les maths.

Roland: _____

3. Carine: J'aime beaucoup la cuisine marocaine.

Roland: _____

4. Carine: J'aime le base-ball.

Roland: _____

5. Carine: J'écoute souvent la radio.

Roland: _____

6. Carine: Je déteste la viande.

Roland: _____

7. Carine: J'étudie le français.

Roland: _____

8. Carine: J'adore les romans d'amour.

Roland: _____

 Now look at these sentences:

Je ne prends pas _la robe_.	**Je ne _la_ prends pas.**
Il n'aime pas _le pantalon_.	**Il ne _l'_aime pas.**
Nous ne voulons pas _les gants_.	**Nous ne _les_ voulons pas.**

In a negative sentence, the direct object pronoun comes _____ the verb.

___ ACTIVITÉ _____

K. You are giving a party and your best friend wants to know all the details. Answer his questions using direct object pronouns:

EXAMPLES: Est-ce que tu invites ton frère? (oui)
Oui, je l'invite.

Est-ce que tu invites Pierre? (non)
Non, je ne l'invite pas.

1. Est-ce que tu as les invitations? (non)

_____

2. Est-ce que tu invites Rose? (oui)

_____

3. Est-ce que tu mets ton complet? (non)

_____

4. Est-ce que Paulette amène ses amies? (oui)

_____

5. Est-ce que tu invites ton cousin? (non)

_____

6. Est-ce que tu sers les glaces au chocolat? (non)

_____

7. Fais-tu les sandwiches? (oui)

_____

8. Est-ce que ta mère prépare ton gâteau préféré? (oui)

_____

9. Est-ce que tu achètes le fromage que j'aime? (non)

_____

10. Est-ce que tu regardes la télévision? (non)

_____

 Where is the direct object pronoun when there are two verbs in a sentence? Let's look at the following examples:

> **Tu vas acheter _le pull-over_.**
> **Tu vas _l'acheter_.**
> **Tu ne vas pas _l'acheter_.**
>
> **Elle veut mettre _la robe_.**
> **Elle veut _la_ mettre.**
> **Elle ne veut pas _la_ mettre.**
>
> **Nous allons chercher _les enfants_.**
> **Nous allons _les_ chercher.**
> **Nous n'allons pas _les_ chercher.**

When there are two verbs in a sentence, the direct object pronoun comes

_____ the infinitive, whether the sentence is affirmative or negative.

Look at the following sentences:

Voilà *l'artiste.*	**Le** **voilà!**
Voilà *la robe.*	**La** **voilà!**
Voici *les clowns.*	**Les** **voici!**

Although **voici** and **voilà** are not verbs, where is the direct object pronoun

when used with those words? _____

 How do you form questions using direct object pronouns? Look at the following examples:

Cherches-tu *le disque?*
Le **cherches-tu?**
Ne *le* **cherches-tu pas?**

Voulez-vous *la robe?*
La **voulez-vous?**
Ne *la* **voulez-vous pas?**

Aime-t-il *les vacances?*
Les **aime-t-il?**
Ne *les* **aime-t-il pas?**

In a question, the direct object pronoun comes _____ the verb, whether the question is affirmative or negative.

___ ACTIVITÉ _____

L. Replace the direct object noun with the direct object pronoun:

1. Voici le livre.

_____

2. Aimez-vous la classe?

_____

3. Il ne peut pas trouver les stylos.

_____

4. N'apprend-il pas les leçons?

_____

5. Voilà l'écharpe.

_____

6. Elle va lire l'éditorial.

_____

7. Nous voulons écrire les lettres.

_____

8. Ne cherchez-vous pas les gants?

_____

_____

 Now look at these sentences:

Achète _le complet_!	**Achète-_le_!**	**Ne _l'_achète pas!**
Ouvrez _la fenêtre_!	**Ouvrez-_la_!**	**Ne _l'_ouvrez pas!**
Écrivons _les lettres_!	**Écrivons-_les_!**	**Ne _les_ écrivons pas!**

In an affirmative command, where is the direct object pronoun?_____

_____ How is it linked to the verb?_____

In a negative command, where is the pronoun with respect to the verb?

_____

NOTE: The direct object pronoun follows the verb and is linked to it by a
hyphen only in affirmative commands.

___ ACTIVITÉS _____

M. Repeat the following commands, replacing the direct object noun with a direct
object pronoun:

1. Apprends la leçon!

_____

2. Étudie les verbes!

_____

3. Ne caresse pas le chien!

_____

4. Achetons les revues!

_____

5. Ne réveille pas ta mère!

_____

6. Écoutez le professeur!

_____

7. Lis ces chapitres!

_____

8. N'ouvrez pas les fenêtres!

_____

N. Role-play with another student, who tells you to do certain things, and you answer that you are going to do them:

EXAMPLE: faire la vaisselle
           Ami(e): Fais-la!
           Toi: Je vais la faire.

1. écrire ces lettres

Ami(e): _____

Toi: _____
2. laver la voiture

Ami(e): _____

Toi: _____
3. lire l'article

Ami(e): _____

Toi: _____

4. manger les légumes

Ami (e): _____

Toi: _____

5. Ouvrir la fenêtre

Ami (e): _____

Toi: _____

O. Now role-play with a friend, who tells you not to do certain things, and you answer that you are not going to do them:

EXAMPLE: écrire les compositions maintenant
Ami(e): Ne les écrivez pas maintenant.
Vous: Nous n'allons pas les écrire maintenant.

1. manger les bonbons en classe

Ami(e): _____

Vous: _____

2. donner les réponses aux autres

Ami(e): _____

Vous: _____

3. regarder la télévision tard

Ami(e): _____

Vous: _____

4. consulter le dictionnaire

Ami(e): _____

Vous: _____

5. écouter la radio à l'école

Ami(e): _____

Vous: _____

Read this short dialog about an invitation to a party and find the other French direct object pronouns:

Here's a complete table of the French direct object pronouns:

me	*me*
te	*you* (familiar, singular)
le	*him, it* (masculine)
la	*her, it* (feminine)
nous	*us*
vous	*you* (formal singular, plural)
les	*them*

Remember: In affirmative commands, **me** and **te** become **moi** and **toi**:

Écoute-*moi*!   **Lave-*toi*!**

__ ACTIVITÉ _____

P. Complete the sentences with the correct direct object pronoun:

EXAMPLE: Je ____vous____ invite à la fête. (you, plural)

1. Nos amis _____ invitent souvent. (us)

2. Je _____ vois toujours avec elle. (you, familiar)

3. Tu _____ rencontres rarement. (them)

4. _____ écoutez-vous attentivement? (me)

5. Le professeur ne _____ punit pas souvent. (her)

6. Ils _____ admirent beaucoup. (you, formal)

7. Je ne _____ connais pas. (him)

 Now let's look at these sentences in the **passé composé**:

I	II
J'ai regardé *le garçon*.	**Je *l'*ai regardé.**
J'ai regardé *la fille*.	**Je *l'*ai regardée.**
J'ai regardé *les garçons*.	**Je *les* ai regardés.**
J'ai regardé *les filles*.	**Je *les* ai regardées.**

In these sentences, which helping verb is used? _____ Underline the direct object pronouns in Group II. Where is the pronoun with respect to the

helping verb?_____

Now look at the past participles. What happened to the past participles in

Group II?_____

With what do they agree?_____

Here is the simple rule: When a verb is conjugated with **avoir** in the **passé composé**, the past participle agrees with the direct object in gender and number if the direct object comes before the verb.

__ ACTIVITÉS _____

Q. Éric wants to go to the movies with his friends. When his father asks him about his chores, Éric says he has finished all of them:

> EXAMPLES: Tu as rangé ta chambre?
> Oui, je l'ai rangée.
>
> Tu as fait ton lit?
> Oui, je l'ai fait.

1. Tu as fait tes devoirs?

_____

2. Tu as lavé la vaisselle?

_____

3. Tu as fini ta composition?

_____

4. Tu as appelé ta sœur?

_____

5. Tu as mangé ton dîner?

_____

6. Tu as pris tes médicaments?

_____

7. Tu as réparé ta bicyclette?

_____

8. Tu as trouvé ton livre?

_____

R. Complete the following sentences in the **passé composé**, making the past participle agree whenever necessary:

> EXAMPLE: (voir) Tes chaussures? Je les ____ai vues____ dans ta chambre.

1. (finir) Tu _____ tes devoirs.

2. (voir) Je ne trouve pas mes cahiers. Est-ce que tu les _____?

3. (trouver) La robe? Elle l'_____ sous la chaise.

4. (acheter) Regardez cette voiture. Mon père l'_____ hier.

5. (punir) Le professeur nous _____ hier matin.

6. (croire) Elles _____ à mon explication.

7. (étudier) Les verbes? Je les _____ à l'école.

8. (oublier) J'_____ mes livres chez Lucien.

9. (choisir) Que penses-tu de ces bracelets? Mon mari les _____ pour moi.

10. (rencontrer) Isabelle et Sylvie? Je les _____ avant-hier en ville.

_____ QUESTIONS PERSONNELLES _____

1. Comment t'habilles-tu pour aller à une fête élégante?

   _____

2. Comment t'habilles-tu pour aller à l'école?

   _____

3. Quels vêtements as-tu reçus pour ton dernier anniversaire?

   _____

4. Qu'est-ce que tu as acheté la dernière fois (*time*) que tu as été au magasin?

   _____

5. À quels magasins vas-tu pour acheter tes vêtements?

   _____

_____ VOUS _____

Your parents just gave you $200 to buy clothes. How would you spend the money?
Make a list of at least five things you would buy, giving the material and colors:

1. _____

2. _____

3. _____

4. _____

5. _____

DIALOGUE

Vous allez au grand magasin pour acheter des cadeaux. Complétez le dialogue:

_____ *COMPOSITION* _____

Write a composition describing your favorite article of clothing. Include the following:

1. the article of clothing.
2. a description of the garment.
3. why you like it.
4. on what occasions you wear it.
5. your parents' opinion of it.

_____

_____

_____

_____

_____

La mode

Paris is renowned as one of the foremost fashion capitals of the world. Givenchy, Chanel, Yves Saint-Laurent, and Christian Dior are all famous French designers, whose fashions are popular worldwide and whose designs set the trend for the current year's styles. Although the French are, in general, very fashion-conscious, they do not all wear designer clothes or shop in the luxurious **maisons de couture** (*at the couturier's*). They frequent department stores, such as **la Samaritaine** or **Printemps**, and buy **prêt-à-porter** (*ready-to-wear clothes*). The **marchés aux puces** (*flea markets*) are also popular places where there are significant bargains.

French teenagers dress to fit the occasion. For casual wear, they prefer mostly jeans and sweatshirts or confortable clothes sporting the labels NAF-NAF, Ton-sur-Ton, or Lacoste, which are also popular in the United States. To learn about the latest styles in France, you can read French fashion magazines like **Elle** or **Marie-France**.

12 *En voiture!*

The Verb **devoir**;
Indirect Object Pronouns

1 Vocabulaire

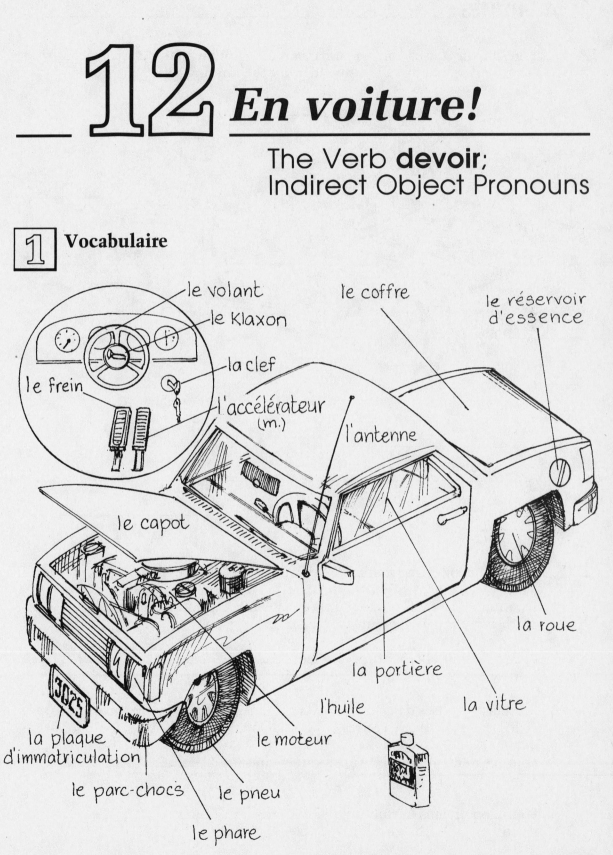

le volant

le Klaxon

le frein

la clef

l'accélérateur (m.)

le coffre

le réservoir d'essence

l'antenne

le capot

la roue

la portière

la vitre

l'huile

la plaque d'immatriculation

le moteur

le parc-chocs

le pneu

le phare

3025

— ACTIVITÉS —

A. You are buying a used car, a real bargain (**une bonne affaire**), but it needs some parts before you can drive it away. Identify the missing parts:

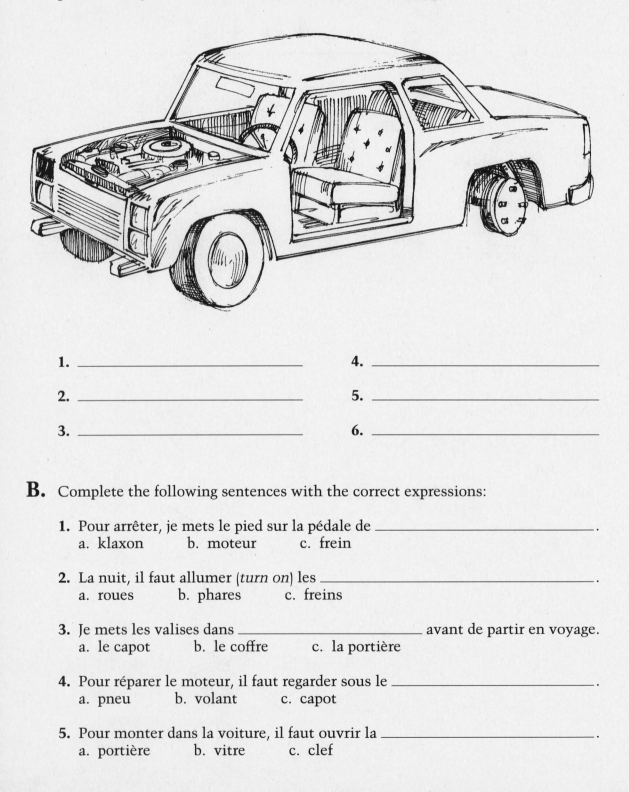

1. _____
2. _____
3. _____

4. _____
5. _____
6. _____

B. Complete the following sentences with the correct expressions:

1. Pour arrêter, je mets le pied sur la pédale de _____.
    a. klaxon   b. moteur   c. frein

2. La nuit, il faut allumer (*turn on*) les _____.
    a. roues   b. phares   c. freins

3. Je mets les valises dans _____ avant de partir en voyage.
    a. le capot   b. le coffre   c. la portière

4. Pour réparer le moteur, il faut regarder sous le _____.
    a. pneu   b. volant   c. capot

5. Pour monter dans la voiture, il faut ouvrir la _____.
    a. portière   b. vitre   c. clef

6. Le réservoir est presque vide, j'ai besoin _____.
   a. de pneus   b. de vitre   c. d'essence

7. Il faut toujours faire attention quand on est au _____.
   a. volant   b. roue   c. pare-chocs

2 Many things must be checked before taking a long car trip. Read the following dialog and see if you can find all the forms of the verb **devoir** (*to have to, must; to owe*):

Fill in the correct forms of the verb **devoir** from the dialog:

je _____   **nous** _____

tu _____   **vous** _____

il _____   **ils** _____

elle _____   **elles** _____

Past participle: **dû, due**

___ ACTIVITÉS _____

C. Express what the following people have to do:

EXAMPLE: Jean/chercher ses valises
Jean doit chercher ses valises.

1. je/visiter mes grands-parents

_____

2. Annette/aller au magasin

_____

3. tu/trouver ton livre

_____

4. M. et Mme Dufour/aller à la banque

_____

5. nous/faire les courses

_____

6. vous/écrire une lettre

_____

_____

D. Complete the following sentences with the correct forms of **devoir**:

1. Combien est-ce que je _____ à Paul?

2. Hier, elles ont _____ chanter en classe.

3. Nous _____ faire un voyage.

4. Il _____ aller au lycée.

5. Vous _____ le faire tout de suite.

6. _____ -elle partir?

7. Qu'est-ce que tu _____ faire aujourd'hui?

8. Ils _____ étudier.

Isabelle apprend à conduire

conduire *to drive*

You have already learned the direct object pronouns. Pay attention now to other pronouns you will find in this story:

Pour son anniversaire, les parents d'Isabelle vont **lui** donner une voiture de sport rouge. Avant de l'acheter, le père d'Isabelle a décidé de **lui** donner des leçons de conduite. C'est aujourd'hui sa première leçon et elle est très nerveuse parce que son père n'arrête pas de **lui** donner des conseils.

conduite *driving*

Il **lui** dit: «Tu vas conduire très lentement, s'il te plaît.» Il **lui** montre tout: «Voici le frein, l'accélérateur et le klaxon.» Il **lui** explique: «On met la clef ici pour faire démarrer la voiture.»

démarrer *to start*

Finalement, Isabelle se met au volant. Elle conduit assez bien. Pourtant son père n'arrête pas de **lui** crier: «Fais attention aux panneaux de signalisation! Conduis plus lentement! Ralentis, il y a un stop au coin! Regarde les autres voitures! Sois prudente! Fais attention aux piétons, surtout aux enfants!» Par la vitre de la voiture, il crie aux autres conducteurs: «Attention, ma fille apprend à conduire!»

pourtant *nevertheless*
panneaux de signalisation *road signs*
ralentir *to slow down*
 au coin *at the corner*
sois *be*
piétons *pedestrians*
conducteurs *drivers*

À la fin de la leçon, Isabelle est complètement épuisée et plus nerveuse qu'au début. Elle est très contente de reprendre sa place de passagère. Son père pousse un soupir de soulagement parce qu'Isabelle n'a pas eu d'accident. Il reprend le volant et **lui** dit: «Avant de **t'**acheter une voiture, je dois **te** donner beaucoup de leçons. Tu as encore beaucoup à apprendre.» Et il démarre.

épuisée *exhausted*
 début *beginning*
pousser un soupir de soulagement *to sigh with relief*

Tout d'un coup, ils entendent la sirène d'une voiture de police derrière eux. Ils s'arrêtent. L'agent s'approche et **leur** dit: «Monsieur, n'avez-vous pas vu le feu rouge? Je suis désolé, mais je dois **vous** donner une contravention. Je crois que vous avez besoin de quelques leçons de conduite. Qu'est-ce que vous en dites, mademoiselle?»

le feu rouge *traffic light*
 désolé *sorry*
une contravention *traffic ticket*

___ ACTIVITÉ _____

E. Répondez aux questions par des phrases complètes:

   1. Quel cadeau est-ce qu'Isabelle va recevoir?

   _____

   2. Qu'est-ce que son père a décidé de faire avant de l'acheter?

   _____

   3. Comment est Isabelle avant la leçon?

   _____

   4. Qu'est-ce que son père lui montre?

   _____

   5. Comment conduit Isabelle?

   _____

   6. À quoi Isabelle doit-elle faire attention?

   _____

   7. Qu'est-ce que le père d'Isabelle crie par la vitre de la voiture?

   _____

   8. Comment est Isabelle à la fin de la leçon?

   _____

   9. Pourquoi est-ce que la police arrête leur voiture?

   _____

  10. Qu'est-ce que l'agent de police fait?

   _____

 In this lesson, you will learn about indirect objects. First, let's look at some English sentences:

I	**II**
I write a letter TO MY FRIEND.	I write HIM a letter.
	I write a letter TO HIM.
He gives a present TO HIS MOTHER.	He gives HER a present.
	He gives a present TO HER.
You sell ice cream TO THE CHILDREN.	You sell THEM ice cream.
	You sell ice cream TO THEM.

In Group I, what are the subjects of the sentences? _____, _____, and

_____; the verbs? _____, _____, and _____; the

direct object nouns? _____, _____, and

_____. Which nouns are left? _____,

_____, and _____. What is the grammatical

name for these nouns? _____

Look at Group II. Which words have replaced the indirect object nouns?

_____, _____, and _____. What is the grammatical

name for the word that replaces the indirect object noun? _____

In French, too, the indirect object noun can be replaced by an indirect object
pronoun. Look at these sentences:

I	II
Catherine dit bonjour *à l'étudiant*.	**Elle *lui* dit bonjour.**
Nous vendons le livre *au garçon*.	**Nous *lui* vendons le livre.**
Elle donne de la glace *à Patrick*.	**Elle *lui* donne de la glace.**

What are the indirect object nouns in Group I? _____, _____,

and _____. What gender are they? _____ Are they sin-

gular or plural? _____ In Group II, which word has replaced

à l', **au**, **à** plus indirect object nouns? _____ What does **lui** mean? _____

Where is **lui** with respect to the verb? _____

___ ACTIVITÉ _____

F. Replace the indirect object nouns with indirect object pronouns:

1. Je parle à Robert.

_____

2. Vous donnez le livre au garçon.

_____

3. Elle parle au grand-père.

_____

4. Nous disons la vérité au professeur.

_____

5. Tu donnes le gâteau à l'enfant.

_____

 Now look at these sentences:

I   II

Il vend le disque _à la fille_.   **Il _lui_ vend le disque.**
Nous montrons les robes _à Josette_.   **Nous _lui_ montrons les robes.**
Vous dites au revoir _à l'étudiante_.   **Vous _lui_ dites au revoir.**

What are the indirect object nouns in Group I? _____ , _____ and

_____ . What is the gender of these nouns? _____

Are they singular or plural? _____ In Group II, which word has

replaced **à la**, **à**, **à l'** plus the indirect object nouns? _____ What does **lui**

mean here? _____ Where is the indirect object pronoun with respect

to the verb? _____

— ACTIVITÉ _____

G. Replace the indirect object nouns with indirect object pronouns:

1. Ils rendent les livres à Janine.

_____

2. Vous écrivez à votre grand-mère.

_____

3. Je parle à la jeune fille.

_____

4. Tu dis non à la femme.

_____

5. Elle donne le cadeau à Marie.

_____

6 Finally, look at these sentences:

<table>
<tr><td align="center">I</td><td align="center">II</td></tr>
<tr><td>

Il donne les gâteaux _à Luc et à Anne._
Elles montrent le disque _aux garçons._
Je rends les stylos _à Renée et à Lise._
</td><td>

Il _leur_ donne les gâteaux.
Elles _leur_ montrent le disque.
Je _leur_ rends les stylos.
</td></tr>
</table>

What are the indirect object nouns in Group I? _____,

_____, and _____ . What are the genders of these

nouns? _____ Are they singular or plural? _____

In Group II, which pronoun has replaced **à**, **aux** plus the indirect object noun?

_____ What does **leur** mean? _____ Where is **leur** with respect

to the verb? _____

NOTE: Indirect object pronouns (**lui/leur**) refer only to people.

ACTIVITÉS

H. Replace the indirect object nouns with indirect object pronouns:

1. Tu parles à Sylvie et à Hubert.

_____

2. J'écris aux enfants.

_____

3. Nous donnons l'argent aux hommes.

_____

4. Vous servez le repas aux étudiantes.

_____

5. Ils demandent la voiture à leurs parents.

_____

I.   Substitute an indirect object pronoun for the expression in bold type:

> EXAMPLE: Je dis au revoir **à mes amis**.
> Je **leur** dis au revoir.

1. Le père donne des leçons **à sa fille**.

_____

2. Le professeur explique la grammaire **aux étudiants**.

_____

3. Le policier donne une contravention **au conducteur**.

_____

4. Je dois vingt dollars **à mon amie Christine**.

_____

5. Il montre sa nouvelle voiture **à ses amis**.

_____

6. Les jeunes hommes portent des fleurs **aux jeunes filles**.

_____

7. Vous lisez le journal **à votre grand-père**.

_____

8. Les enfants disent toujours la vérité **à leurs parents**.

_____

9. Je donne le message **à mes sœurs**.

_____

10. Ils rendent (_return_) les clefs **à Janine**.

_____

7 Indirect object pronouns follow the same rules for position as direct object pronouns. Look at these examples:

> **Elle donne des bonbons *à Marie*.**
> **Elle *lui* donne des bonbons.**
> **Elle ne *lui* donne pas de bonbons.**
>
> **Tu vas parler *au garçon*.**
> **Tu vas *lui* parler.**
> **Tu ne vas pas *lui* parler.**
>
> **Écrivez-vous *à vos cousines*?**
> ***Leur* écrivez-vous?**
> **Ne *leur* écrivez-vous pas?**

When a sentence is negative, where does the indirect object pronoun remain?

_____

When there are two verbs in a sentence, before which verb does the indirect

object pronoun come? _____

In affirmative and negative questions, the indirect object pronoun comes

_____ the verb.

8 Look at these examples:

> **Donne l'argent *aux filles*!**
> **Donne-*leur* l'argent!**
> **Ne *leur* donne pas l'argent!**
>
> **Parlez *au professeur*!**
> **Parlez-*lui*!**
> **Ne *lui* parlez pas!**

Where does the indirect object pronoun come in an affirmative command?

_____ In a negative command? _____

The indirect object pronoun comes after the verb only in an _____.

The pronoun is joined to the verb by a _____.

⑨ Now look at the following sentences:

J'ai parlé *au garçon.*   Je *lui* ai parlé.
J'ai parlé *aux filles.*   Je *leur* ai parlé.

In the **passé composé**, where does the indirect object pronoun come?

_____

Is there agreement of the past participle with the preceding indirect object?

_____

If you said no, you are correct. In the **passé composé** using the verb **avoir**, only a preceding DIRECT object agrees with the past participle. Compare:

J'ai vu *Marianne.*   Je *l'*ai *vue.*
J'ai parlé *à Marianne.*   Je *lui* ai *parlé.*

___ ACTIVITÉS ___

J. You've had disagreements with some people and now you're not talking to them. Respond to the questions:

EXAMPLE: Parles-tu **à Paul**?
                 Non, je ne **lui** parle pas.

1. Parles-tu à tes frères?

_____

2. Parles-tu à ta sœur?

_____

3. Parles-tu à Luc et à Marie?

_____

4. Parles-tu à ton meilleur ami?

_____

5. Parles-tu à tes cousines?

_____

K. A friend asks you again about your disagreements. You respond:

EXAMPLE: Vas-tu parler **à Paul**?
                 Non, je ne vais pas **lui** parler.

1. Vas-tu parler à tes frères?

_____

2. Vas-tu parler à ta sœur?

_____

3. Vas-tu parler à Luc et à Marie?

_____

4. Vas-tu parler à ton meilleur ami?

_____

5. Vas-tu parler à tes cousines?

_____

L. Your friend persists. Tell what you're going to do:

EXAMPLE: Quand vas-tu parler **à Paul**?
Je vais **lui** parler demain.

1. Quand vas-tu parler à tes frères?

_____

2. Quand vas-tu parler à ta sœur?

_____

3. Quand vas-tu parler à Luc et à Marie?

_____

4. Quand vas-tu parler à ton meilleur ami?

_____

5. Quand vas-tu parler à tes cousines?

_____

M. One of your friends had the same problem. Ask her if she speaks to the following persons:

EXAMPLE: à son cousin
Lui parles-tu?

1. à sa tante

_____

2. à Lucie et à Annie

_____

3. à son frère

_____

4. aux jeunes gens

_____

5. à Pierre et à Corinne

_____

N. She hasn't apologized yet. Give her some advice:

EXAMPLE: à son cousin
Parle-lui face à face. Ne lui téléphone pas.

1. à sa tante

_____

2. à Lucie et à Annie

_____

3. à son frère

_____

4. aux jeunes gens

_____

5. à Pierre et à Corinne

_____

O. You've made up with everyone. Express the good news:

EXAMPLE: à Paul
Je lui ai parlé.

1. à tes frères

_____

2. à ta sœur

_____

3. à Luc et à Marie

_____

4. à ton meilleur ami

_____

5. à vos cousines

_____

P. Substitute an indirect object pronoun for the expression in bold type:

EXAMPLE: Jules doit dix dollars **à sa sœur**.
Jules **lui** doit dix dollars.

1. Tu vas donner le livre **à Jean**.

_____

2. Maman ne parle plus **aux Dupont**.

_____

3. Ne donne pas le magazine **à ton père**.

_____

4. Tu ne téléphones pas **à Claudine**.

_____

5. Je ne veux pas écrire **à mes cousines**.

_____

6. Écrivez-vous une lettre **à Marie**?

_____

7. Racontez l'histoire **à Anne et à Gérard**!

_____

8. Est-ce qu'elle a parlé **au garçon**?

_____

9. Je désire parler **au père de Marc**.

_____

10. Je ne peux pas demander le livre **au professeur**.

_____

11. Ne rendons pas les stylos **aux enfants**.

_____

12. N'avez-vous pas dit la vérité **à vos parents**?

_____

Look at these sentences:

Mes parents *me* donnent une voiture de sport.
My parents are giving me a sports car.

Qu'est-ce que ta mère *te* prépare pour le déjeuner?
What is your mother preparing for you for lunch?

Le professeur *nous* parle toujours en français.
The teacher always speaks to us in French.

Je *vous* achète le disque ce soir.
I am buying the record for you tonight.

What object pronouns do you recognize in these sentences? _____ ,

_____ , _____ , and _____ . In French, **me**, **te**, **nous**,
and **vous** are both direct and indirect object pronouns.

Here is a table of the indirect object pronouns:

me	*(to, for) me*
te	*(to, for) you*
lui	*(to, for) him, her*
nous	*(to, for) us*
vous	*(to, for) you*
leur	*(to, for) them*

___ ACTIVITÉ ___

Q. Identify the pronouns in bold type as direct or indirect object pronouns:

1. Il **me** voit. _____

2. Le garçon **te** sert le dîner. _____

3. Ils **nous** regardent. _____

4. Je **vous** donne le cadeau. _____

5. Tu **nous** trouves. _____

6. Vous **me** montrez le journal. _____

7. Je **t'**aime. _____

8. Il **vous** cherche. _____

The pronouns **me**, **te**, **nous**, and **vous** follow the same rules of position as **lui** and **leur**:

> Il ne *nous* a pas téléphoné.
> Nous *vous* avons dit la vérité.
> Est-ce que ta mère ne *te* comprend pas?
> Donnez-*moi* l'adresse!
> Ne *me* parle pas!
> Il va *t'*apprendre le russe.

___ ACTIVITÉ _____

R. Place the pronoun in parentheses in its proper position and make any necessary changes:

1. (me) Il veut parler.

   _____

2. (te) Il va expliquer la leçon.

   _____

3. (nous) Ne montrez pas la lettre.

   _____

4. (vous) Je veux dire la vérité.

   _____

5. (me) Donnez le livre.

   _____

6. (te) Je ne peux pas offrir cette voiture.

   _____

7. (nous) Ne va-t-il pas écrire?

   _____

8. (vous) Sert-il le repas?

   _____

_____ *QUESTIONS PERSONNELLES* _____

1. À qui expliquez-vous vos problèmes?

   _____

2. Lui parlez-vous souvent?

_____

3. Lui dites-vous vos secrets?

_____

4. Qui vous aime?

_____

5. À qui allez-vous téléphoner ce soir?

_____

6. Qui va vous donner un cadeau d'anniversaire?

_____

_____ VOUS _____

Refer back to the story and write five things you'd expect your driving instructor to say while you're learning to drive:

1. _____

2. _____

3. _____

4. _____

5. _____

_____ COMPOSITION _____

Your friend has expressed an interest in buying your car. Write him/her a note describing it:

_____

_____

_____

_____

_____

DIALOGUE

Vous apprenez à conduire à votre frère. Que lui dites-vous?

INTERVALLE CULTUREL

Les panneaux de signalisation

If you were to travel through a French-speaking country by car, you might see the following road signs. Can you guess their meanings?

1 2 3 4

5 6 7 8

13 *La fin de semaine*

The Verb **boire**; Pronouns **y** and **en**

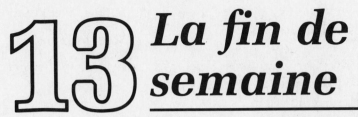

1 **Vocabulaire**

Que peut-on faire le week-end pour s'amuser?

faire des courses

voir une exposition

discuter entre amis

faire du patin à glace (patiner)

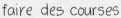

aller à la campagne

faire du cheval

faire une promenade en bateau

faire du patin

jouer au bowling

faire du vélo

aller écouter un concert

voir une pièce de théâtre

— ACTIVITÉ

A. Ask your friends if they want to do the following things this weekend:

EXAMPLE:

Voulez-vous voir une exposition?

1. _____

2. _____

3. _____

4. _____

5. _____

6. _____

2 If you are in France, you might go and have a cup of coffee with friends at a **café**. Coffee, however, is not everyone's preference. Read the dialog between the members of the Williams family and their French hosts, the Nalet family, sitting in an outdoor café, and see if you can find all the forms of the verb **boire** (_to drink_):

Fill in the correct forms of the verb **boire** from the dialog:

je _____   nous _____

tu _____   vous _____

il _____   ils _____

elle _____   elles _____

Past participle: **bu**

___ ACTIVITÉS _____

B. Everyday most of the students in the lunchroom come with their lunches and boxed drinks or cans from home. Express what they are drinking today:

EXAMPLE:

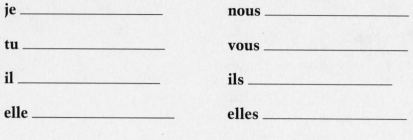

Paul boit du jus de raisin.

1. Vous _____.

2. Simone _____.

3. Je _____.

4. Marianne et Lisette _____ .

5. Nous _____ .

6. Tu _____ .

C. Complete the following sentences with the correct forms of **boire**:

1. Il _____ de l'eau.

2. Nous _____ du thé.

3. Je _____ du chocolat.

4. Elles ont _____ du jus de fruit.

5. Ils _____ du café.

6. Elle _____ du lait.

7. Vous _____ de l'orangeade.

8. Tu _____ du soda.

③ Un week-end mouvementé

mouvementé *eventful*

Let's read a story that will help you learn about the pronoun **y**. Try to figure out what **y** refers to whenever you meet it:

Après un long week-end, M. Vaillant, le professeur de français, demande à ses élèves: «Que vous est-il arrivé ce week-end?» Imaginez sa surprise quand Richard et son frère Georges lui racontent cette histoire:

arriver *to happen*

RICHARD: Nous avons passé un week-end mouvementé. Samedi, un voleur de bijoux est arrivé en ville.

GEORGES: Oui, et il **y** est arrivé avec son complice!

RICHARD: Ils voulaient aller à la bijouterie «Au quatorze carats».

GEORGES: Ils voulaient **y** aller tout de suite!

RICHARD: Ils sont vite arrivés devant la boutique.

GEORGES: Quand ils **y** sont arrivés, ils **y** sont entrés sans faire de bruit.

RICHARD: Ils sont allés derrière les rideaux.

rideaux *curtains*

GEORGES: Il **y** sont allés pour se cacher!

RICHARD: C'était en fin de journée et notre grand-mère, qui a soixante-cinq ans, était toute seule dans la boutique.

GEORGES: Oui, car le propriétaire n'**y** reste jamais l'après-midi.

RICHARD: Ma grand-mère est entrée dans le salon où les voleurs étaient cachés.

GEORGES: Quand elle **y** est entrée, les voleurs se sont précipités sur elle!

se précipiter *to jump*

RICHARD: Heureusement, ma grand-mère a suivi des cours de karaté au club de sport!

GEORGES: Elle **y** a beaucoup appris.

RICHARD: Elle a frappé les voleurs sur la tête et ils sont tombés par terre.

frapper *to hit*

GEORGES: Elle leur a ordonné: «Restez-**y**!»

ordonner *to order*

RICHARD: Quand les voleurs ont essayé d'aller vers la porte, elle leur a crié: «N'**y** allez pas ou je vous assomme!» Puis elle a appelé la police.

assommer *to knock out*

GEORGES: Quand la police est arrivée, elle a arrêté les voleurs.

RICHARD: Et maintenant notre grand-mère est une héroïne!

___ ACTIVITÉ _____

D. Répondez aux questions par des phrases complètes:

1. Qui est arrivé en ville?

_____

2. Avec qui est-il arrivé?

_____

3. Où voulaient-ils aller?

_____

4. Comment sont-ils entrés dans la boutique?

_____

5. Où se sont-ils cachés?

_____

6. Qui était dans la boutique?

_____

7. Qu'est-ce que la grand-mère a appris?

_____

8. Qu'a fait la grand-mère quand les voleurs se sont précipités sur elle?

_____

9. Qu'a-t-elle crié quand les voleurs ont voulu aller vers la porte?

_____

10. Qu'est-ce qui est arrivé aux voleurs?

_____

_____

 Let's look at some sentences:

Un voleur arrive *en ville*.	*A robber arrives in town.*
Il *y* arrive avec son complice.	*He arrives (there) with his accomplice.*
Ils arrivent *devant la boutique*.	*They arrive in front of the shop.*
Ils *y* arrivent.	*They arrive there.*
Je réponds *à la lettre*.	*I answer the letter.*
J'*y* réponds.	*I answer it.*

Which pronoun can take the place of phrases beginning with prepositions indicating location or phrases beginning with **à**? _____

What does **y** mean? _____ Where is the pronoun **y** in relation to the verb?

_____

Let's look at some other examples:

> **Elle *y* a beaucoup appris.**
> **Ils voulaient *y* aller tout de suite.**
> **Elle a crié: «Restez-*y*, n'*y* allez pas!»**

Where is **y** in the **passé composé**? _____

When there are two verbs? _____

In an affirmative command? _____

In a negative command? _____

Finally, you have learned that **-er** verbs drop **s** in affirmative familiar commands. Note what happens when **y** follows the verb:

***Va* en France!**	*Go to France!*
***Vas-y*!**	*Go (there)!*
***Reste* au lit!**	*Stay in bed!*
***Restes-y*!**	*Stay there!*

When **y** follows an affirmative familiar command, the letter _____ is retained. Can you tell why? _____

___ ACTIVITÉS _____

E. Your new friend wants to know more about you. Answer the questions:

EXAMPLE: Tu vas au cinéma?
          Oui, j'y vais.

1. Tu vas à Paris?

_____

2. Tu habites en ville?

_____

3. Tu travailles dans une pharmacie?

_____

F. Now answer the following questions in the negative:

    EXAMPLE: Tu vas au théâtre?
                 Non, je n'y vais pas.

1. Tu pars à la campagne?

_____

2. Tu restes chez Anne toute la journée?

_____

3. Tu joues au tennis cet après-midi?

_____

G. Ask your friend when he is doing the following things:

    EXAMPLE: Je vais en Bretagne.
                 Quand y vas-tu?

1. Je travaille dans un hôtel.

_____

2. Je dîne chez mes cousins.

_____

3. Je pars en Europe.

_____

H. You are very emphatic about how you will spend your four-day weekend:

    EXAMPLES: Veux-tu aller au Canada?
                  Oui, je veux y aller.

                  Ne veux-tu pas rester à la maison?
                  Non, je ne veux pas y rester.

1. Ne veux-tu pas travailler au restaurant?

_____

2. Penses-tu rester chez tes grands-parents?

_____

3. Vas-tu aller à la plage?

_____

4. Ne veux-tu pas aller au musée?

_____

5. Peux-tu passer le week-end chez ton ami?

_____

6. Ne veux-tu pas partir à Québec en train?

_____

I. You are spending the weekend at your friend's country house. You are trying to decide how to spend the day, but you and your friend can't seem to agree:

    EXAMPLE: Jouons aux cartes!
                Oui, jouons-y!
                Non, n'y jouons pas!

1. Allons au lac!

_____

_____

2. Restons à la maison!

_____

_____

3. Descendons au village!

_____

_____

J. Answer your teacher's questions affirmatively:

    EXAMPLE: Es-tu allé(e) à la bibliothèque?
                Oui, j'y suis allé(e).

1. Es-tu allé(e) au théâtre hier soir?

_____

2. As-tu dîné chez Pierre samedi dernier?

_____

3. As-tu joué au bowling ce week-end?

_____

5 | La préparation du pique-nique

The following story about a class picnic will help you learn about the pronoun **en**:

Tous les élèves de la classe reviennent de récréation. Quand ils **en** reviennent, ils discutent du pique-nique du lendemain. Ils **en** discutent pour vérifier leurs projets. Chaque élève doit apporter de la nourriture. Tout le monde doit **en** apporter. Le professeur, Mme Renan, demande à chacun ce qu'il va apporter. Ses élèves lui répondent: **récréation** *recess*

JEAN: J'aime les légumes, les carottes, les tomates, les radis. Je vais **en** apporter beaucoup.
PAUL: Moi, je vais apporter cinquante sandwiches.
LISE: Pourquoi **en** apporter autant? Nous ne sommes que vingt-cinq! **autant** *so many*
PAUL: Je vais **en** apporter cinquante parce que tout le monde va avoir très faim.
ANNE: J'aimerais manger de la salade. Marc, vas-tu **en** préparer? **J'aimerais** *I would like*
MARC: Bien sûr, je vais **en** préparer. René, ton père est boucher. Apporte des biftecks. S'il te plaît, apportes-**en** pour toute la classe, mais n'**en** apporte pas plus que nécessaire. **boucher** *butcher*
RENÉ: D'accord. Qui va acheter de l'orangeade?
LAURE: Personne. Je n'**en** bois jamais et c'est moi qui achète les boissons. Je vais apporter du soda parce que j'**en** bois toujours. Et vous, Mme Renan, qu'est-ce que vous allez faire?
MME RENAN: Du ragoût d'insectes.

Tous les élèves: Quoi? C'est une de vos spécialités françaises?

Mme Renan: Mais non! Je vais apporter de l'insecticide. Nous allons **en** avoir besoin contre les mouches, les moustiques et les abeilles. J'**en** ai tellement peur!

mouches *flies*
moustiques *mosquitoes*
abeilles *bees*
tellement *so*

___ ACTIVITÉ _____

K. Répondez aux questions par des phrases complètes:

1. D'où reviennent les élèves?

   _____

2. De quoi discutent-ils?

   _____

3. Qu'est-ce que chaque élève doit apporter?

   _____

4. Qu'est-ce que Mme Renan demande aux élèves?

   _____

5. Qu'est-ce que Jean aime?

   _____

6. Combien de sandwiches est-ce que Paul va apporter?

   _____

7. Pourquoi René va-t-il apporter du bifteck?

   _____

8. Pourquoi Laure ne va-t-elle pas apporter d'orangeade?

   _____

9. Qu'est-ce que Mme Renan va apporter?

   _____

10. De quoi Mme Renan a-t-elle peur?

   _____

In our story, you read many noun phrases beginning with **du**, **de la**, **de l'**, or

des. What meanings can these words have? _____ ,

_____ , and _____ .

Now let's look more closely at some examples:

Les élèves sortent *du lycée.*	*The students are coming out of the high school.*
Les élèves *en* **sortent.**	*The students are coming out (of it).*
Ils discutent *du pique-nique.*	*They are talking about the picnic.*
Ils *en* **discutent.**	*They are talking about it.*
Tout le monde doit apporter *de la nourriture.*	*Everyone must bring some food.*
Tout le monde doit *en* **apporter.**	*Everyone must bring some (of it).*

Which pronoun replaces phrases beginning with **du**, **de la**, **de l'**, or **des**? _____

What meanings can **en** have? _____

_____

 Now look at the following sentences:

J'apporte cinquante *sandwiches.*	*I'm bringing fifty sandwiches.*
J'*en* **apporte cinquante.**	*I'm bringing fifty (of them).*

What does **en** replace in this sentence? _____

When there is a number before the noun, **en** replaces only

_____ .

8 Finally, **en** follows the same rules of position as the other object pronouns you have learned so far:

J'*en* **apporte.**	**N'***en* **apporte pas.**
Je n'*en* **apporte pas.**	**Apportes-***en.*
J'*en* **ai apporté.**	*En* **apportes-tu?**
Je vais *en* **apporter.**	**Vas-tu** *en* **apporter?**

Where is **en** normally in relation to the verb? _____

In the **passé composé**? _____

When there are two verbs? _____

In a negative command? _____

In an affirmative command? _____

What letter is retained in an affirmative familiar command of **-er** verbs when

followed by **en**? _____

NOTE: **en** can be used only to replace **de** + an object or a place. The stress
pronouns **lui** (**eux**) or **elle** (**elles**) are used to replace the name of a person after **de**:

Je parle de *Luc*.	**Je parle de *lui*.**
Elle rêve de *ses amies*.	**Elle rêve d'*elles*.**

___ ACTIVITÉS _____

L. You are at a picnic with some friends. Respond negatively to the questions they
ask you:

> EXAMPLE: Bois-tu du jus d'orange?
> Non, je n'en bois pas.

1. Bois-tu du soda?

_____

2. Prends-tu des fruits?

_____

3. Manges-tu du fromage?

_____

4. Veux-tu de la salade?

_____

5. Achètes-tu de l'eau minérale?

_____

M. You are talking to your friend about his diet. Ask him if he does the following:

    EXAMPLE: acheter des bonbons
                  En achètes-tu?

1. manger du gâteau

    _____

2. choisir des légumes

    _____

3. faire de l'exercice

    _____

4. prendre des vitamines

    _____

5. boire de l'eau

    _____

N. Restate each sentence using **en**:

1. Je vais faire du vélo.

    _____

2. Ne préparez pas de légumes!

    _____

3. Achetez-vous du pain?

    _____

4. Elle ne fait pas de courses.

    _____

5. As-tu préparé des gâteaux?

    _____

6. Elles ne veulent pas manger de salade.

    _____

7. Mange du dessert!

    _____

8. Nous pouvons apporter de la soupe.

    _____

9. Ils discutent des différents plats.

_____

10. Vous sortez du restaurant.

_____

11. J'ai vu deux expositions.

_____

12. Il n'a jamais fait de promenade en bateau.

_____

9 Now that you have learned all the object pronouns, here is a summary table:

OBJECT
PRONOUN

le		le			possessive	
la	replace	la	ce	or	adjective	+ person/thing
l'		l'	or cet		(**mon**, **ma**,	
les		les	cette		**mes**, etc.)	

lui, leur   replace **à** (**au, à la, à l', aux**) + person

y   replaces preposition + place/thing
en   replaces **de** (**du, de la, de l', des**) + place/thing

___ ACTIVITÉ ___

O. Replace the words in bold type with an appropriate pronoun:

1. Il aime bien **cette fille**.

_____

2. Je bois **du thé**.

_____

3. Il ne va pas **au théâtre**.

_____

4. Je ne peux rien demander **aux garçons**.

_____

5. Regardez-vous **les tableaux**?

_____

6. N'apprenez-vous pas le français **en classe**?

_____

7. Nous sortons **du métro**.

_____

8. Téléphonez **à Marie**!

_____

9. Est-ce qu'elle cherche **la carte**?

_____

10. Il ne peut pas aller **en France**.

_____

11. N'écrivez pas de lettre **à Jean**.

_____

12. Elle a apporté **des stylos**.

_____

13. Je vois trois **voitures** derrière la maison.

_____

14. A-t-il trouvé **ses gants**?

_____

15. Je n'ai pas regardé **sous la chaise**.

_____

QUESTIONS PERSONNELLES

Répondez aux questions par des phrases complètes:

1. Je vais en France cet été. Y êtes-vous déjà allé?

_____

2. J'aime travailler à l'école. Aimez-vous y travailler aussi?

_____

3. J'aime rester à la maison. Aimez-vous y rester?

_____

4. J'adore voyager en Europe. Adorez-vous y voyager?

_____

5. Je fais mes devoirs à la bibliothèque. Y faites-vous vos devoirs aussi?

_____

6. Je suis allée à la Martinique. Votre famille y est-elle allée?

_____

7. J'ai une sœur. Combien en avez-vous?

_____

8. J'adore lire des romans d'amour. Adorez-vous en lire?

_____

9. Je suis sorti du lycée à trois heures. À quelle heure en êtes-vous sorti(e)?

_____

10. Je veux boire du soda. Voulez-vous en boire?

_____

11. J'écris des lettres à mes amis. En écrivez-vous à vos amis?

_____

12. J'ai envie d'aller au cinéma. En avez-vous envie aussi?

_____

VOUS

You lost your favorite record. Using the pronoun **y**, answer the questions:

EXAMPLE: As-tu cherché dans le tiroir?
           Oui, j'y ai cherché.

1. As-tu regardé sous le lit?

_____

2. Cherches-tu dans ta chambre?

_____

3. Vas-tu regarder derrière le stéréo?

_____

4. Est-il dans sa pochette (_sleeve_)?

_____

5. L'as-tu oublié chez ton ami?

_____

DIALOGUE

Vous expliquez à la diététicienne de l'école pourquoi vous n'aimez pas la nourriture.
Employez **y** et **en** dans vos réponses:

COMPOSITION

List five activities you and your friends can do over the weekend:

_____

_____

_____

_____

_____

(INTERVALLE CULTUREL)

Au café

The French café is a neighborhood spot where young and old go to socialize from early in the morning until late at night. The café is a place to meet friends, quietly read a newspaper, watch people, wait for a friend, have a drink or a sandwich, or just relax. Cafés serve croissants, sandwiches, and a wide variety of drinks. The most popular drinks at a café are beer, wine, cola, and mineral water.

14 À la pharmacie

Double Object Pronouns

1 Vocabulaire

le papier hygiénique

le savon

les aspirines

les mouchoirs en papier

les vitamines

le coton

les pansements

la brosse à dents

le rasoir

le peigne

le maquillage

la brosse

le dentifrice

le déodorant

__ ACTIVITÉS _____

A. Your mother has sent you to the drugstore. Express what she wants you to buy:

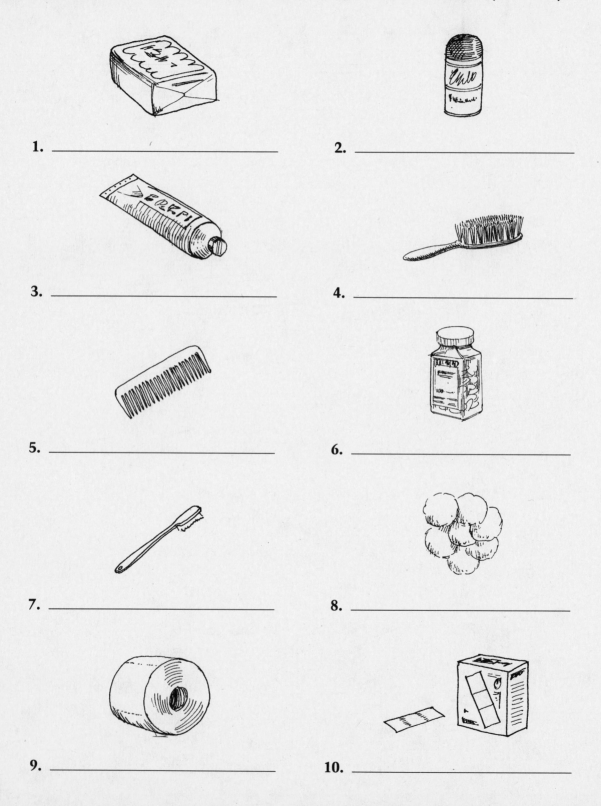

1. _____   2. _____

3. _____   4. _____

5. _____   6. _____

7. _____   8. _____

9. _____   10. _____

B. You are the pharmacist in the neighborhood drugstore. The people in the pictures below seem to be suffering from something. Express what they need (some people may need more than one item):

1. _____

2. _____

3. _____

4. _____

5. _____

6. _____

---

2 | Les annonces publicitaires

annonces publicitaires
advertisements

You have learned many different pronouns. So far, only one pronoun has been used in a sentence at a time. Two pronouns are often used together. Let's read the following story about advertisements and their promises. See if you can pick out the sentences where two pronouns are used together:

On ne peut pas échapper aux annonces publicitaires.   **échapper** *to escape*
On en trouve partout: dans les journaux, les maga-
zines, à la télévision, sur les panneaux des bus, du   **panneaux** *signs*

métro et dans les rues. Bien ou mal, elles influencent notre culture et notre vie quotidienne. Voici quelques annonces. Les connaissez-vous?

quotidienne *daily*

Soyez en forme pour l'été!

Sans exercice. Sans médicaments. Sans faim. Maigrissez de 21 livres en deux semaines seulement grâce à notre système unique. Laissez les machines faire tout le travail pendant que vous vous reposez. Vous désirez développer vos muscles? Notre programme spécial vous le permet en un temps record. Vous avez un problème particulier? Venez nous en parler. Nos machines peuvent tout faire! Résultats garantis! Nous vous le promettons.

soyez en forme *be in shape*

livres *pounds*
grâce à *thanks to*

garantis *guaranteed*

Vous avez perdu vos cheveux?

Ne souffrez plus parce que vous êtes chauve! Si vous croyez qu'il n'y a aucun remède à la calvitie, venez nous voir et nous en parler. Nous possédons la seule méthode d'implantation de cheveux qui donne une apparence naturelle. Et nous vous l'offrons à un prix incroyable! Nous sommes l'organisation la plus importante d'implantation de cheveux de tout le pays. Comparez nos services, nos installations et nos prix avec ceux des autres. Allez voir vos amis. Parlez-leur-en et venez vite prendre rendez-vous, nous vous le recommandons fortement.

souffrir *to suffer*
chauve *bald*
ne ... aucun *not any*
la calvitie *baldness*

ceux *those*

J'avais peur de sourire!

«J'avais peur d'ouvrir la bouche à cause de mes dents jaunies. J'avais une petite amie mais je ne voulais pas les lui montrer. J'avais honte de l'embrasser. Puis j'ai découvert le dentifrice Dentiblanc. Dentiblanc a une formule secrète à double action qui donne des dents blanches et une haleine fraîche.» Faites comme ce jeune homme, achetez-vous-en un tube et souriez à la vie. Vous n'êtes pas complètement satisfait? Apportez-le-nous et nous vous rendons votre argent. Nous vous le rendons sans poser de questions. Dentiblanc vous permet de sourire à nouveau avec confiance.

sourire *to smile*

jaunies *yellowed*
avoir honte *to be ashamed*

haleine *breath*

à nouveau *again*

___ ACTIVITÉ _____

C. Répondez aux questions par des phrases complètes:

1. Où voit-on les annonces publicitaires?

_____

2. Qu'est-ce que ces annonces influencent?

_____

3. Qu'est-ce que la première annonce vous propose?

_____

4. Qu'est-ce que le programme spécial vous permet de faire?

_____

5. Qui peut être intéressé par la deuxième annonce?

_____

6. Quelle sorte d'organisation est-ce?

_____

7. Quelle sorte de produit est Dentiblanc?

_____

8. Que donne Dentiblanc?

_____

9. Si vous n'êtes pas satisfait, que fait la compagnie?

_____

10. Qu'est-ce que Dentiblanc va vous permettre de faire?

_____

3 You have already learned the direct and indirect object pronouns. Sometimes you will have to use them together. Look at the following sentences:

Elle *me* donne *la brosse.*	*She gives me the brush.*
Elle *me la* donne.	*She gives it to me.*
Je *t'*apporte *le savon.*	*I bring you the soap.*
Je *te l'*apporte.	*I bring it to you.*
Notre mère *nous* achète *les peignes.*	*Our mother buys us the combs.*
Notre mère *nous les* achète.	*Our mother buys them for us.*

> **Votre frère *vous* rend *les mouchoirs***   *Your brother returns the tissues*
>   ***en papier.***   *to you.*
> **Votre frère *vous les* rend.**   *Your brother returns them to you.*

When you use two object pronouns together in French, where are they in relation to the verb? _____. Where are **me**, **te**, **nous**, and **vous** in relation to **le**, **la**, and **les**? _____

When these pronouns occur together, they follow this order:

$$
\left.\begin{array}{l}\textbf{me}\\\textbf{te}\\\textbf{nous}\\\textbf{vous}\end{array}\right\} \text{ before } \left\{\begin{array}{l}\textbf{le}\\\textbf{la}\\\textbf{les}\end{array}\right. \text{ before verb}
$$

__ ACTIVITÉS _____

D. You are sick and ask for help. Your friend tells you how she will help you, but you can't hear very well. Ask her questions using pronouns:

    EXAMPLE: Je te donne les aspirines.
                Tu me les donnes?

1. Je t'apporte les mouchoirs en papier.

    _____

2. Je t'achète le dentifrice.

    _____

3. Je te conseille la vitamine C.

    _____

4. Je t'offre ces revues françaises.

    _____

5. Je te montre le travail scolaire.

    _____

E. State your friend's answers using pronouns:

    EXAMPLE: Oui, je te les donne.

1. _____

2. _____

3. _____

4. _____

5. _____

F. Your friends are always asking questions and they often repeat them to make sure they have been understood. Restate their questions using pronouns:

EXAMPLE: Tu nous vends le livre?
Tu nous le vends?

1. Tu nous racontes l'histoire?

_____

2. Tu nous apportes le dictionnaire?

_____

3. Tu nous achètes ces cahiers?

_____

4. Tu nous montres la photo?

_____

5. Tu nous donnes les réponses correctes?

_____

G. State your answers to your friends' questions using pronouns:

EXAMPLE: Tu nous vends le livre?
Oui, je vous le vends.

1. _____

2. _____

3. _____

4. _____

5. _____

4   Now look at these sentences:

Marie *lui* donne *le peigne*.   *Marie gives him the comb.*
Marie *le lui* donne.   *Marie gives it to him.*

Nous *leur* disons *la vérité*.   *We tell them the truth.*
Nous *la leur* disons.   *We tell it to them.*

Je *leur* montre *les vitamines*.   *I show them the vitamins.*
Je *les leur* montre.   *I show them to them.*

Where are **le**, **la**, and **les** in relation to **lui** and **leur**? _____. When
these pronouns occur together, they are used in the following order:

$$\left.\begin{array}{l}\textbf{le}\\\textbf{la}\\\textbf{les}\end{array}\right\} \text{before} \left\{\begin{array}{l}\textbf{lui}\\\textbf{leur}\end{array}\right. \text{before verb}$$

Note that pronouns beginning with **l** are always used in alphabetical order.

___ ACTIVITÉ _____

H. You and your friend are describing what different people are doing. Confirm your
friend's statements:

EXAMPLE: Le docteur donne **les médicaments aux malades.**
          Oui, il **les leur** donne.

1. Le garçon sert le dîner aux clients.

   _____

2. Le boucher vend la viande à la femme.

   _____

3. La diététicienne conseille les vitamines aux sportifs.

   _____

4. Le garçon apporte le menu aux gens.

   _____

5. Le touriste envoie les cartes postales à ses amis.

   _____

6. Le professeur explique les exercices à l'étudiante.

   _____

7. Le conducteur ouvre la portière à la passagère.

_____

8. Le professeur enseigne (*teaches*) la biologie aux élèves.

_____

9. L'agent donne la contravention à mon frère.

_____

10. Le guide montre le monument au touriste.

_____

 The examples below will help you remember all the placements of the pronouns. Do not forget that in the **passé composé** the past participle agrees with a preceding direct object if **avoir** is the helping verb:

Il *me la* donne.	Il ne *me la* donne pas.
Est-ce qu'il *me la* donne?	Est-ce qu'il ne *me la* donne pas?
Me la donne-t-il?	Ne *me la* donne-t-il pas?
Donne-*la-moi!*	Ne *me la* donne pas!
Il va *me la* donner.	Il ne va pas *me la* donner.
Il *me l'*a donnée.	Il ne *me l'*a pas donnée.
Est-ce qu'il *me l'*a donnée?	Est-ce qu'il ne *me l'*a pas donnée?
*Me l'*a-t-il donnée?	Ne *me l'*a-t-il pas donnée?

___ ACTIVITÉS _____

I. Ask your teacher if he/she gave certain things to your classmates:

EXAMPLE: le cahier/à Rose
Le lui avez-vous donné?

1. le livre/à Michel

_____

2. les exercices/à Lucie

_____

3. l'examen/à Jean et à Luc

_____

4. les leçons/aux étudiants

_____

5. la règle/à Marianne

_____

6. les devoirs/aux filles

_____

J.   Your mother wants to know if you did certain things. Respond negatively:

EXAMPLE: As-tu donné **la nouvelle à ta sœur?**
Non, je ne **la lui** ai pas donnée.

1. As-tu acheté les brosses à dents à tes frères?

_____

2. As-tu expliqué ton problème au professeur?

_____

3. As-tu envoyé la carte postale à tes oncles?

_____

4. As-tu donné le message à Michelle?

_____

5. As-tu prêté tes disques à tes amis?

_____

6. As-tu servi le café à ton père?

_____

7. As-tu écrit la lettre au directeur?

_____

8. As-tu donné les vitamines à ta sœur?

_____

    Notice the order of **y** and **en** in the following sentences:

Ariane *lui* parle *de son voyage*.	*Ariane speaks to him about her trip.*
Ariane *lui en* parle.	*Ariane speaks to him about it.*
Il *m'achète des fleurs*.	*He buys me some flowers.*
Il *m'en* achète.	*He buys me some (of them).*
Je *les* invite *au restaurant*.	*I invite them to the restaurant.*
Je *les* y invite.	*I invite them there.*
Il *nous* amène *à la fête*.	*He brings us to the party.*
Il *nous* y amène.	*He brings us there.*

When **y** or **en** are used with another pronoun, where are they in relation to the

verb? _____ ; **y** and **en** remain closest to the verb whenever they are used with another object pronoun.

7 Finally, look at what happens when **y** and **en** are used together in a sentence:

Il y a *des mouchoirs en papier*.	*There are some tissues.*
Il y en a.	*There are some (of them).*
Est-ce qu'il y a *des aspirines*?	*Are there any aspirins?*
Est-ce qu'il y en a?	*Are there any (of them)?*

Where is **en** in relation to the verb when used together with **y**? _____

Here is a table summarizing all that we have learned so far about the order of object pronouns:

me te nous vous	before	le la les	before	lui leur	before	**y**	before	**en**	before	verb

_ ACTIVITÉS _____

K. Your friends are taking you out to dinner to celebrate your good grades. Describe the evening at the restaurant, substituting pronouns for the words in bold type:

EXAMPLES: Mes professeurs me donnent **des notes formidables.**
Mes professeurs m'**en** donnent.

Il m'accompagne **à la maison.**
Il m'**y** accompagne.

1. Mes amis m'amènent **en ville.**

_____

2. Ils m'invitent **au restaurant.**

_____

3. Quand nous arrivons, la serveuse nous accompagne **à notre table.**

_____

4. Le garçon nous apporte **des menus.**

_____

5. Jacques me commande **du vin excellent.**

_____

6. Le garçon nous recommande **des hors-d'œuvre.**

_____

7. Il nous sert **des spécialités de la maison.**

_____

8. Il nous montre **des desserts délicieux.**

_____

9. Nous lui parlons **du repas.**

_____

10. Nous lui faisons **des compliments.**

_____

L. Repeat the following sentences, replacing the nouns in bold type with the appropriate pronouns:

1. Nous n'avons pas rencontré **nos amis au cinéma.**

_____

2. N'a-t-il pas emmené **Marie au musée?**

_____

3. Vous parlez **de votre voyage à vos amis.**

_____

4. Je ne veux pas apporter **de sandwiches au pique-nique.**

_____

5. Le garçon offre **des fleurs à sa petite amie.**

_____

6. Ne mettez pas **les pieds sur la chaise!**

_____

7. Ne donnez pas **le chocolat à l'enfant.**

_____

8. A-t-il amené **l'enfant en Europe?**

_____

9. Tu as apporté **des livres en classe.**

_____

10. Il envoie (_send_) **des journaux à Paris.**

_____

M. Your friend is telling you what he/she usually does. Using pronouns, say that you do the same things:

>   EXAMPLES: Je lis des poèmes à ma grand-mère.
>   Moi aussi, je lui en lis.
>
>   J'accompagne mon frère à l'école.
>   Moi aussi, je l'y accompagne.

1. J'amène ma sœur au lycée.

_____

2. Je prête de l'argent à mon frère.

_____

3. Je mets mes vêtements sur la chaise.

_____

4. J'écris des lettres à mes cousins.

_____

5. J'invite mes amis au cinéma.

_____

6. J'amène souvent mon petit frère au parc.

_____

7. Je fais toujours des compliments à ma mère.

_____

8. Je demande rarement de l'argent à mes parents.

_____

 Do you remember where the single object pronoun is placed in sentences with

two verbs? _____
The same rule applies to double object pronouns:

Je vais donner _mon adresse à Lucie._	_I'm going to give my address to Lucie._
Je vais _la lui_ donner.	_I'm going to give it to her._
Il veut envoyer _des cartes postales à ses amis._	_He wants to send some postcards to his friends._
Il veut _leur en_ envoyer.	_He wants to send some (of them) to them._

__ ACTIVITÉ __

N. You make the same New Year's resolutions as your brother. Express what they are, using pronouns.

>EXAMPLES: Je vais acheter **des livres à ma cousine.**
>Je vais **lui en** acheter aussi.
>
>Je vais prêter **mes disques à ma sœur.**
>Je vais **les lui** prêter aussi.

1. Je vais lire des articles intéressants à mes parents.

    _____

2. Je vais apporter des bonbons à ma mère.

    _____

3. Je vais apprendre la musique à mon copain.

    _____

4. Je vais envoyer de l'argent aux pauvres.

    _____

5. Je vais présenter mes parents à mes professeurs.

    _____

6. Je vais faire des compliments à ma petite amie.

    _____

7. Je vais expliquer mes problèmes à mes parents.

    _____

8. Je vais prêter ma bicyclette à mon frère.

    _____

---

9   Do you remember where the single object pronoun is in affirmative commands?

_____ Here, too, the same rule applies to double object pronouns. Pronouns follow the verb and are attached to it and each other by hyphens:

Donnez *les cahiers aux filles.*   *Give the notebooks to the girls.*
Donnez-*les-leur.*   *Give them to them.*

Parlez *de votre voyage aux élèves.*   *Talk about your trip to the students.*
Parlez-*leur-en.*   *Talk to them about it.*

Emmène *les enfants au cirque.*   *Take the children to the circus.*

Emmène-*les-y.*   *Take them there.*

The order of pronouns is slightly different in affirmative commands:

$$
\text{Verb} + \begin{matrix} \text{le} \\ \text{la} \\ \text{les} \end{matrix} \ \text{before} \ \begin{matrix} \text{me} \\ \text{te} \\ \text{lui} \\ \text{nous} \\ \text{vous} \\ \text{leur} \end{matrix} \ \text{before} \ \textbf{y} \ \text{before} \ \textbf{en}
$$

NOTE: The pronoun **me** becomes **moi** except before **en**:

Donnez-*la-moi!*   *Give it to me!*

But:

Donnez-*m'en!*   *Give me some!*

__ ACTIVITÉS _____

O. You are in a very bossy mood today and repeat everything twice. Substituting pronouns for the words in bold type, express what you say to your brothers:

1. Apportez-moi **les livres!**

   _____

2. Lisez **l'histoire à Jacqueline!**

   _____

3. Mettez **le pain sur la table!**

   _____

4. Cherchez **les journaux sous la chaise!**

   _____

5. Donnez **le livre à Paul!**

   _____

6. Envoyez **cette carte à nos grands-parents!**

   _____

P. Change these commands to the affirmative:

1. Ne me la montre pas.

   _____

2. Ne lui en parlons pas.

   _____

3. Ne nous en achète pas.

   _____

4. Ne la lui lis pas.

   _____

5. Ne me l'envoyez pas.

   _____

6. Ne m'en parle pas.

   _____

7. Ne le leur donne pas.

   _____

8. Ne nous en écris pas.

   _____

Q. Your brother and sister are trying to help you. Of course, your brother does everything wrong. Your sister tries to tell him, but he won't listen. Emphasize what she says by replacing the words in bold type with pronouns:

1. N'apporte pas **les disques dans le salon.**

   _____

2. Ne donne pas **le sandwich au chien.**

   _____

3. N'amène pas **le chat dans la chambre.**

   _____

4. Ne montre pas **cette photo à Pierre.**

   _____

5. Ne sers pas **de fromage à papa.**

   _____

6. Ne mets pas **les papiers sur la table.**

   _____

7. Ne laisse pas **les magazines dans la chambre.**

_____

8. N'achète pas **de jouets au chien.**

_____

_____ QUESTIONS PERSONNELLES _____

Answer the questions using the object pronouns you have learned:

1. Offrez-vous des cadeaux à vos amis?

_____

2. Vous souvenez-vous de l'anniversaire de votre meilleur(e) ami(e)?

_____

3. Accompagnez-vous souvent votre frère (ou sœur) au cinéma?

_____

4. Racontez-vous votre journée à l'école à vos parents?

_____

5. Écrivez-vous des lettres à vos grands-parents?

_____

_____ VOUS _____

Write three sentences in French about things you do for other people. Then rewrite the sentences using object pronouns:

EXAMPLE: Je sers le café à ma mère.   Je le lui sers.

1. a. _____

   b. _____

2. a. _____

   b. _____

3. a. _____

   b. _____

DIALOGUE

On vous demande votre opinion sur un certain produit:

COMPOSITION

Write a note to your brother asking him to please go to the drugstore and explaining why:

_____

_____

_____

_____

_____

Pharmacies, drogueries et drugstores

In France there are **pharmacies**, **drogueries**, and **drugstores**.

A **pharmacie**, which is easily identified by its green cross above the door, sells over-the-counter and prescription drugs, items for personal hygiene, and some cosmetics.

At a **droguerie** you can buy chemical products, paints, household cleaners and accessories (brooms, buckets, etc.), some hygiene items, and cosmetics.

Finally, the **drugstore** is a huge place combining different functions and stores. There you will find a bar, a café-restaurant, varied shops (records, gifts, etc.), and sometimes even a movie theater.

15 *Les passe-temps*

Expressions of Time

1 Vocabulaire

collectionner les
bandes dessinées

faire de la photo

jouer aux jeux vidéo

faire de la poterie

cuisiner

collectionner les
pièces de monnaie

collectionner les
timbres

faire des modèles réduits

tricoter

lire

collectionner les
cartes de base-ball

dessiner

___ ACTIVITÉS _____

A. Express what the following people are doing in their spare time:

1. Jean-François _____.

2. Marc _____.

3. Vous _____.

4. André et Louise _____.

5. Les Ricard _____.

6. Janine _____.

7. Tu _____.

8. Mme Lafleur _____.

9. Sylvie et Lucie _____.

10. Le garçon _____.

11. Nous _____.

12. Laurent _____.

B. You are filling out a school questionnaire about hobbies. List five things that you like to do:

1. _____

2. _____

3. _____

4. _____

5. _____

 La chambre de Laure

In this lesson you will learn certain expressions of time. Read the following story about Laure and her hobbies and note how time is expressed:

Laure est une fille de quatorze ans qui s'intéresse à tout. Malheureusement, elle commence beaucoup de projets qu'elle n'arrive jamais à finir. Un jour, Marie, sa nouvelle camarade de classe, vient lui rendre visite. Quand Marie entre dans la chambre de Laure, elle ouvre de grands yeux. Quel désordre! Par terre il y a des bandes dessinées de toutes sortes, quelques vases en poterie, un album de timbres et un autre de photos. Sur le lit il y a un pull et sur le bureau elle voit plusieurs modèles réduits d'avions et de bateaux. Marie est étonnée de voir tous ces objets. Il y en a partout!

Comme elle est très curieuse, elle demande à son amie: «Depuis quand tricotes-tu ce pull bleu?»

depuis *since, for*

LAURE: Oh, pas depuis longtemps. Depuis quatre mois seulement. Le tricot est mon passe-temps préféré.

MARIE: Depuis quand fais-tu de la photo?

LAURE: Je prends toutes sortes de photos depuis mon enfance. Elles sont superbes, n'est-ce pas?

MARIE: Et ces bandes dessinées, depuis combien de temps les collectionnes-tu?

LAURE: Depuis huit jours. C'est mon passe-temps le plus récent. Comme tu vois, je préfère «L'homme aux nerfs d'acier».

nerfs *nerves*
acier *steel*

MARIE: Regarde tous ces vases! Depuis quand fais-tu de la poterie?

LAURE: Depuis l'année dernière. Mon prochain projet est de faire un autre vase.

MARIE: Combien de temps y a-t-il que tu fais des modèles réduits?

LAURE: Il y a six mois que j'en fais. Ils te plaisent?

MARIE: Oui, ils sont chouettes, mais il y a une chose que je veux absolument savoir. . .

chouettes *great*

LAURE: Quoi?

MARIE: Combien de temps passes-tu à nettoyer ta chambre le week-end?

passer *to spend*
nettoyer *to clean*

LAURE: Nettoyer? Tu rigoles ou quoi? J'ai promis à maman de tout nettoyer dès que mes projets seront terminés. Mais comme je découvre toujours un nouveau passe-temps avant d'en finir un. . . Je suis maligne, n'est-ce pas?

rigoler *to joke*
dès que *as soon as*
seront *will be*

maligne *clever*

___ ACTIVITÉ _____

C. Répondez aux questions par des phrases complètes:

1. Qui est Laure?

   _____

2. Que fait Marie quand elle entre dans la chambre de Laure?

   _____

3. Depuis quand est-ce que Laure tricote le pull bleu?

   _____

4. Depuis quand est-ce que Laure fait de la photo?

   _____

5. Depuis combien de temps est-ce que Laure collectionne les bandes dessinées?

   _____

6. Depuis quand est-ce que Laure fait de la poterie?

   _____

7. Depuis combien de temps est-ce que Laure fait des modèles réduits?

   _____

8. Quand Laure nettoie-t-elle sa chambre?

   _____

9. Qu'est-ce que Laure a promis à sa mère?

   _____

10. Pourquoi Laure commence-t-elle toujours un nouveau projet avant d'en finir
    un autre?

    _____

 Up to now you have learned how to express actions and events in three differ-

ent tenses. To express actions that are happening now, you use the _____

tense. To express actions that took place yesterday or last week, you use the

_____ tense. To express what was happening or what used to

happen yesterday or last week, you use the _____ .

Now you are going to learn how to express an action that began in the past and is still continuing at present. Look at the following sentences:

Depuis quand **tricotes-tu ce pull?**	*Since when have you been knitting this sweater?*
Je tricote ce pull *depuis* **4 mois.**	*I have been knitting this sweater for 4 months.*
Depuis quand **fais-tu de la photo?**	*Since when have you been taking pictures?*
Je fais de la photo *depuis* **mon enfance.**	*I have been taking pictures since my childhood.*
Depuis combien de temps **collectionnes-tu les bandes dessinées?**	*For how long have you been collecting comic books?*
Je collectionne les bandes dessinées *depuis* **8 jours.**	*I have been collecting comic books for 8 days.*
Depuis combien de temps **fais-tu des modèles réduits?**	*For how long have you been making models?*
Je fais des modèles réduits *depuis* **6 mois.**	*I have been making models for 6 months.*

In which tense are the verbs in the questions?_____

In which tense are the verbs in the statements?_____

Which word appears in all the questions?_____

Which word appears in all the statements?_____

What does **depuis** mean in the statements?_____

What does **depuis quand** mean?_____

What does **depuis combien de temps** mean?_____

In French, to express an action that began in the past and is still continuing at present, use:

PRESENT TENSE + **depuis** + TIME EXPRESSION

Je tricote   **depuis**   **quatre mois.**

___ ACTIVITÉS _____

D. The following people are talking about hobbies. Complete their dialogs by asking since when they have been engaged in the activity and by answering the question:

EXAMPLE:

/2 weeks
Pierre: Depuis quand cuisines-tu?
Robert: Je cuisine depuis deux semaines.

1. /3 months

Lucie: _____

Agnès: _____

2. /2 years

Éric: _____

Michel: _____

3. /6 months

Paul: _____

Georgette: _____

4. /10 years

Mme Lebois: _____

Mme Caron: _____

5. /8 days

Henri: _____

Anne: _____

6. /9 months

Jacques: _____

Thomas et Édith: _____

E. Ask a classmate how long he/she has been doing the following things. Provide the replies:

> EXAMPLE: étudier le français
> Vous: Depuis combien de temps étudies-tu le français?
> Camarade: J'étudie le français depuis un an.

1. habiter cette ville

Vous: _____

Camarade: _____

2. aller à cette école

Vous: _____

Camarade: _____

3. jouer à ton sport préféré

Vous: _____

Camarade: _____

4. dessiner

Vous: _____

Camarade: _____

5. jouer aux jeux vidéo

Vous: _____

Camarade: _____

6. connaître le professeur de français

Vous: _____

Camarade: _____

4 Here's another way of expressing how long an action has been going on:

***Combien de temps y a-t-il que* tu fais de la poterie?**	*How long have you been making pottery?*
***Il y a* une semaine *que* je fais de la poterie.**	*I have been making pottery for a week.*
***Combien de temps y a-t-il que* tu tricotes ce pull bleu?**	*How long have you been knitting this blue sweater?*
***Il y a* quatre mois *que* je le tricote.**	*I have been knitting it for four months.*
***Combien de temps y a-t-il que* tu dessines?**	*How long have you been drawing?*
***Il y a* cinq ans *que* je dessine.**	*I have been drawing for five years.*

In these questions, what phrase is used to express time in place of **depuis combien de temps?** _____

Note that the subject pronoun and the verb are not inverted after **combien de temps y a-t-il que.** Now look at the statements. In what tense is the verb?

_____ What replaces **depuis?**_____ To give an

answer to a question with **combien de temps y a-t-il que,** start with _____

+ a period of time + **que** + verb in the _____ tense.

__ ACTIVITÉ _____

F. Repeat the dialog of Activité D with **combien de temps y a-t-il que** and **il y a** + time + **que:**

EXAMPLE: Pierre: Combien de temps y a-t-il que tu cuisines?
Robert: Il y a deux semaines que je cuisine.

1. Lucie: _____

Agnès: _____

2. Éric: _____

Michel: _____

3. Paul: _____

Georgette: _____

4. Mme Lebois: _____

Mme Caron: _____

5. Anne: _____

Henri: _____

6. Jacques: _____

Thomas: _____

 One more point: To ask how long an action lasts in the present, use **combien de temps** + present tense. In a statement, use present tense + **pendant:**

Combien de temps travailles-tu chaque jour?   *How long do you work each day?*

Je travaille *pendant* **six heures.**   *I work for six hours.*

Note that **pendant,** like *for* in English, may be omitted:

Je travaille six heures.

To express how long an action completed in the immediate past lasted, use **combien de temps + passé composé** in a question and **passé composé + pendant** (which may be omitted) in a statement:

Combien de temps as-tu travaillé hier?	*How long did you work yesterday?*
J'ai travaillé (pendant) deux heures.	*I worked (for) two hours.*

___ ACTIVITÉS _____

G. You are interviewing people for an article you are writing for the school newspaper. Ask each person for how long he/she does the following activities:

EXAMPLE:

Combien de temps dessines-tu chaque jour?

1. _____

2. _____

3. _____

4. _____

5. _____

H. Write down the answers to your questions in Activité G, using the cues provided:

EXAMPLE: (1 hour)
Je dessine pendant une heure.

1. (3 hours)

   _____

2. (45 minutes)

   _____

3. (30 minutes)

   _____

4. (8 hours)

   _____

5. (2 hours)

   _____

I. You are going to interview a new French student who has just arrived in your class. Prepare some questions that you intend to ask, using appropriate expressions of time:

1. _____

2. _____

3. _____

4. _____

5. _____

_____ **VOUS** _____

Express for how long you engage in the following activities each day:

EXAMPLE: se brosser les dents
           Je me brosse les dents pendant cinq minutes.

1. jouer aux jeux vidéo

_____

2. manger

_____

3. dormir

_____

4. étudier le français

_____

5. écouter la radio

_____

6. regarder la télé

_____

7. parler au téléphone

_____

8. s'amuser

_____

9. se laver

_____

10. se reposer

_____

DIALOGUE

Votre amie s'intéresse beaucoup à votre passe-temps favori. Elle vous pose beaucoup de questions. Écrivez vos réponses:

QUESTIONS PERSONNELLES

1. Depuis quand étudiez-vous le français?

   _____

2. Combien de temps passez-vous à faire vos devoirs?

   _____

3. Quel est votre passe-temps favori?

   _____

4. Depuis quand avez-vous ce passe-temps?

   _____

5. Combien de temps lisez-vous par jour?

   _____

COMPOSITION

Write a composition in French in which you tell about your hobbies. Include the following information:

1. Your favorite hobby.

   _____

2. For how long you have been doing it.

   _____

3. Why you like it.

   _____

4. Where you do your hobby.

   _____

5. How much time you spend doing your hobby each day.

   _____

INTERVALLE CULTUREL

Les sorties (*Going out*)

Since French schools do not offer a wide range of extracurricular and sporting activities, most teenagers go out to movies, discos, or parties in groups. It is not unusual for as many as ten to twelve young adults to arrange to go places together or to plan get-togethers called "**boums.**" A **boum,** which may be organized in celebration of a special event, is just an informal gathering with music, dancing, and food. **Boums** are usually held on Saturday afternoons and last until early evening. Evening parties, held for older teenagers, are called **soirées.**

Dating, as we know it, does not start until much later, when a young man or woman is more inclined to make a commitment. Going out with just one person, rather than in a group, is seen as the beginning of a more serious relationship.

Révision III
(Leçons 11–15)

Leçon 11

a. Present-tense forms of the verb **croire** (*to think, to believe*):

je crois	**nous croyons**
tu crois	**vous croyez**
il croit	**ils croient**
elle croit	**elles croient**

Past participle: **cru**

NOTE: **croire à** + object means *to believe in something*:

Je *crois aux* extraterrestres.

b. Direct object pronouns:

me	*me*		**nous**	*us*	
te	*you*	(familiar)	**vous**	*you*	(plural; formal)
le	*him, it*	(masculine)	**les**	*them*	
la	*her, it*	(feminine)			

c. The direct object pronoun normally comes directly before the verb:

Je *le* vois tous les jours.	*I see him everyday.*
***Le* cherches-tu?**	*Are you looking for him?*
Nous ne *vous* invitons pas.	*We are not inviting you.*
Il *m'*a appelé hier.	*He called me yesterday.*

d. When used with an infinitive, the direct object pronoun precedes the infinitive:

Je veux *l'*acheter.	*I want to buy it.*
Je ne peux pas *te* présenter.	*I can't introduce you.*

e. In affirmative commands, the direct object pronoun follows the verb and is attached to it by a hyphen:

Ouvrez-*la*.	*Open it.*
Amenez-*nous* à la gare.	*Take us to the station.*

f. In negative commands, the direct object pronoun precedes the verb:

Ne *la* prends pas.   *Don't take it.*
Ne *nous* appelle pas.   *Don't call us.*

g. In the **passé composé** with the helping verb **avoir**, the past participle agrees in gender and number with the preceding direct object pronoun:

Je *les* ai *vus*.   *I saw them.*
Tu *l'*as *invitée*.   *You invited her.*

h. The direct object pronoun precedes **voici** and **voilà**:

***Les* voilà!**   *Here they are!*
***Le* voici.**   *Here it is.*

Leçon 12

a. Present-tense forms of the verb **devoir** (*to have to, must; to owe*):

je dois	**nous devons**
tu dois	**vous devez**
il doit	**ils doivent**
elle doit	**elles doivent**

Past participle: **dû, due**

b. Indirect object pronouns:

me (to, for) *me*	**nous** (to, for) *us*
te (to, for) *you*	**vous** (to, for) *you*
lui (to, for) *him, her*	**leur** (to, for) *them*

c. The indirect object pronoun follows the same rules for position as the direct object pronoun:

Je *t'*écris une lettre.	*I write a letter to you.*
***Me* donnez-vous ces bonbons?**	*Are you giving me these candies?*
Je vais *lui* parler.	*I am going to talk to him.*
Tu *leur* as acheté des fleurs.	*You bought flowers to them.*
Achète-*lui* un cadeau.	*Buy her (him) a present.*
Ne *leur* réponds pas.	*Don't answer them.*

Leçon 13

a. Present-tense forms of the verb **boire** (*to drink*):

je bois	nous buvons
tu bois	vous buvez
il boit	ils boivent
elle boit	elles boivent

Past participle: **bu**

b. The pronoun **y** always refers to things or places. It generally replaces **à** + noun but may also replace other prepositions of position + noun:

Allez-vous *à l'école?* — *Are you going to school?*
Oui, j'y vais. — *Yes, I am (going there).*

Est-ce que les lettres sont *sur le bureau?* — *Are the letters on the desk?*
Oui, elles y sont. — *Yes, they are (on it).*

c. The pronoun **en** replaces **de** + noun and generally refers to things. It usually is equivalent to English *some, any, of it* (*them*), *from there*:

J'ai acheté *des cerises.* — *I bought some cherries.*
***En* voulez-vous?** — *Do you want some?*

Vient-il *de la ville?* — *Does he come from the city?*
Oui, il *en* vient. — *Yes, he comes from there.*

en is also used to replace a noun that follows a number:

Hier, j'ai reçu deux *cartes postales.* — *Yesterday, I received two postcards.*
Aujourd'hui, j'*en* ai reçu trois. — *Today, I received three (of them).*

d. **y** and **en**, like other object pronouns, generally come before the conjugated verb, except with infinitives and affirmative commands:

Je vais y répondre. — *I'm going to answer it.*
Il veut en acheter. — *He wants to buy some.*
Allons-y! — *Let's go there!*
Prenez-en! — *Take some!*

NOTE: In affirmative familiar commands, when followed by **y** or **en**, **-er** verbs retain the letter **s**:

Amènes-y les enfants. — *Take the children there.*
Goûtes-en un peu. — *Taste a little (of it).*

Leçon 14

a. The order of direct and indirect object pronouns in French is as follows:

$$
\begin{matrix}
\text{me} \\
\text{te} \\
\text{nous} \\
\text{vous}
\end{matrix}
\quad \text{before} \quad
\begin{matrix}
\text{le} \\
\text{la} \\
\text{les}
\end{matrix}
\quad \text{before} \quad
\begin{matrix}
\text{lui} \\
\text{leur}
\end{matrix}
\quad \text{before } \mathbf{y} \text{ before } \mathbf{en} \text{ before verb}
$$

Examples:

Isabelle *me le* donne.	*Isabelle gives it to me.*
Nos parents *nous les* achètent.	*Our parents buy them for us.*
Il *la leur* montre.	*He shows it to them.*
Je vais *la lui* offrir.	*I am going to offer it to her.*
Le prof *nous y* invite.	*The teacher invites us there.*
Armand *lui en* a parlé.	*Armand spoke to him (her) about it.*
Il *y en* a beaucoup.	*There is (are) a lot (of it) (of them).*
Nous les offre-t-il?	*Is he offering them to us?*

b. Double object pronouns follow the verb in affirmative commands and are joined by hyphens. Note the order of the object pronouns in affirmative commands:

$$
\text{verb} \quad \text{before} \quad
\begin{matrix}
\text{le} \\
\text{la} \\
\text{les}
\end{matrix}
\quad \text{before} \quad
\begin{matrix}
\text{moi (m')} \\
\text{toi (t')} \\
\text{lui} \\
\text{nous} \\
\text{vous} \\
\text{leur}
\end{matrix}
\quad \text{before } \mathbf{y} \text{ before } \mathbf{en}
$$

Examples:

Donnez-*la-moi*!	*Give it to me!*
Prêtez-*les-nous*!	*Lend them to us!*
Apportez-*les-y*!	*Bring them there!*
Vendez-*m'en* trois!	*Sell me three of them!*

Leçon 15

a. The present tense is used with **depuis quand**, **depuis combien de temps**, **combien de temps y a-t-il que** in a question and with **depuis, il y a** + time + **que** in a statement to express an action that started in the past and is continuing in the present:

Depuis quand habitez-vous ici?	*Since when have you been living here?*
Nous habitons ici *depuis* 1980.	*We have been living here since 1980.*
Depuis combien de temps fais-tu du ski?	*For how long have you been skiing?*
Je fais du ski *depuis* douze ans.	*I have been skiing for twelve years.*

Combien de temps y a-t-il que tu étudies?

How long have you been studying?

Il y a une heure que j'étudie.

I have been studying for one hour.

b. To express how long an action lasts in the present, use the present tense with **combien de temps** in a question and **pendant** in a statement:

Combien de temps nages-tu chaque jour?

How long do you swim each day?

Je nage (pendant) une heure.

I swim (for) an hour.

NOTE: **Pendant**, like *for* in English, may be omitted in the statement.

c. To express how long an action completed in the immediate past lasted, use the **passé composé** with **combien de temps** in a question and **pendant** (which may be omitted) in a statement:

Combien de temps as-tu dormi hier?

How long did you sleep yesterday?

J'ai dormi (pendant) cinq heures.

I slept (for) five hours.

___ ACTIVITÉS _____

A. Au magasin de vêtements. Hidden in the puzzle are 18 clothes-related items. Find and circle the words from left to right, right to left, up or down, or diagonally. Note that hyphenated words are printed as one word in the puzzle:

T	I	U	N	E	D	E	S	I	M	E	H	C	S	A
I	M	P	E	R	M	É	A	B	L	E	S	T	W	F
P	E	Y	A	O	T	E	C	R	M	O	H	N	E	T
C	B	J	Y	N	T	R	I	H	S	T	O	O	A	E
O	O	A	S	N	T	B	T	P	A	A	R	C	T	L
M	R	M	G	M	O	O	A	I	T	R	T	H	S	I
P	L	A	P	E	L	T	U	S	S	J	P	J	H	G
L	L	Y	F	A	S	J	O	F	K	S	A	E	I	R
E	O	N	I	N	I	B	C	C	L	E	U	A	R	M
T	C	N	Y	B	O	T	T	E	S	E	T	N	T	E
R	E	Z	A	L	B	E	V	R	E	R	S	S	E	T

B. **Qu'est-ce que les flics** (*cops*) **disent à M. Chandon**? To find the answer, identify the objects in the pictures. Then write the letters indicated in the blanks below:

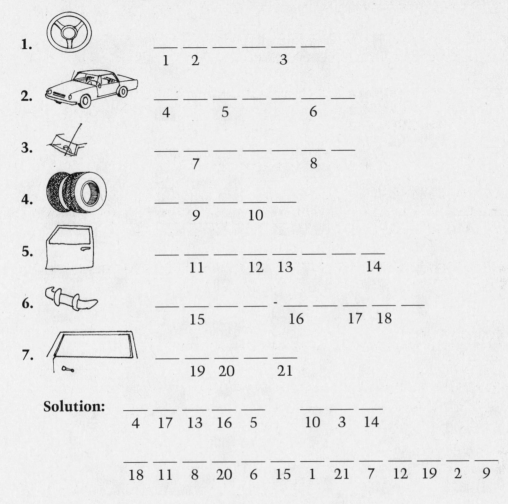

1. ___ ___ ___ ___ ___
     1 2   3

2. ___ ___ ___ ___ ___ ___
    4   5   6

3. ___ ___ ___ ___
      7   8

4. ___ ___ ___ ___
     9   10

5. ___ ___ ___ ___ ___ ___
     11   12 13   14

6. ___ ___ ___ - ___ ___ ___ ___
     15   16   17 18

7. ___ ___ ___ ___
    19 20 21

Solution: ___ ___ ___ ___ ___   ___ ___ ___
   4 17 13 16 5   10 3 14

___ ___ ___ ___ ___ ___ ___ ___ ___ ___ ___ ___ ___
18 11 8 20 6 15 1 21 7 12 19 2 9

C. Your mother asks you to bring in one of the articles hanging on the line. Pick it out from her description. Place an X in the correct circle:

C'est un vêtement de femme.   **Il y a un col.**
C'est à manches longues.   **Le col est à rayures.**
Le tissu est à rayures.

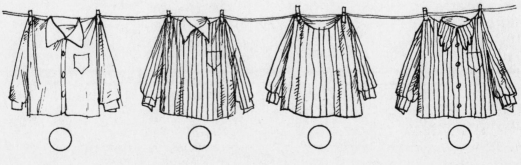

D. Mots Croisés:

HORIZONTALEMENT

1. **(devoir) elle** ____
3. brush
6. tissue
10. no
11. wool
13. **(voir) il** ____
17. steering wheel
19. **(your)** ____ **frère**
20. here
22. gold

23. slippers
24. to snow
25. **(his)** ____ **sœurs**
27. jeans
29. one
31. **(naître) Il est** ____.
34. **(pouvoir) il a** ____
37. suit
39. sleeves
41. **(his)** ____ **frères**

42. friend (f.)
45. (**croire**) **nous avons** _____
47. (your) _____ **maison**
48. dress
50. (**boire**) **nous** _____
52. (**placer**) **Je** _____.
54. (**avoir**) **j'ai** _____
55. (**boire**) **C'est la limonade qu'il a**
   _____.
56. jacket
58. lake
60. and
61. gas

64. they
65. (this) _____ **volant**
66. iron
68. **Je vois la fille. Je** _____ **vois.**
69. here
71. (skate) **vous** _____
73. me
74. to knit
77. (**savoir**) **j'ai** _____
78. (her) _____ **frère**
79. **Je** _____ **vois personne.**
80. (put on) **tu** _____
81. (**croire**) **elles** _____

VERTICALEMENT

1. (**devoir**) **ils** _____
2. he
3. (**boire**) **il** _____
4. (**oser** _to dare_) **elle** _____
5. soap
6. motor
7. one
8. where
9. nothing
10. **Je ne mange** _____ **légumes** _____
   fruits.
11. wide
12. year
14. (**avoir**) **ils** _____
15. vest
16. material
18. law
19. (your) _____ **famille**
21. (this) _____ **veston**
23. pajamas
26. in
28. (**naître**) **elle est** _____
30. bus
32. scarf
33. year
34. comb

35. cat
36. proud
38. there
39. **Je** _____ **lève.**
40. (**avoir**) **tu** _____
41. (**savoir**) **vous avez** _____
43. makeup
44. (to you) **Il** _____ **parle.**
45. collar
46. oil
49. boots
51. on
52. tire
53. key
56. (**voir**) **nous** _____
57. dry
59. (**croire**) **il** _____
62. **Je** _____ **travaille pas.**
63. (**croire**) **tu** _____
67. to say
68. to read
70. one hundred
72. (**avoir**) **nous avons** _____
74. early
75. neck
76. one

E. What does Paul like to do on the weekend? To find out, unscramble the words, then unscramble the letters in the circles:

N W O G B I L   ☐ ☐ ☐ ☐ ☐ ☐ ☐

T N I P X O S I O E   ☐ ☐ ◯ ☐ ☐ ☐ ☐ ☐ ☐ ☐

E R N A I P T   ☐ ◯ ☐ ☐ ☐ ☐ ☐

C R E S U S O   ◯ ☐ ☐ ☐ ☐ ◯ ☐

M A D O P R E E N   ☐ ☐ ☐ ◯ ☐ ☐ ◯ ☐ ☐

Le week-end, Paul aime aller à la _____.

F. Identify the hobbies. Hidden in the picture are ten items that Huguette uses for her hobbies. Circle them in the picture and list the hobbies in the spaces provided:

_____ _____

_____ _____

_____ _____

_____ _____

G. Picture story. Can you read this story? Much of it is in picture form. Whenever you come to a picture, read it as if it were a French word:

Claude va passer le week-end chez son ami Fabrice. Il a déjà fait sa valise. Il y a

mis ses 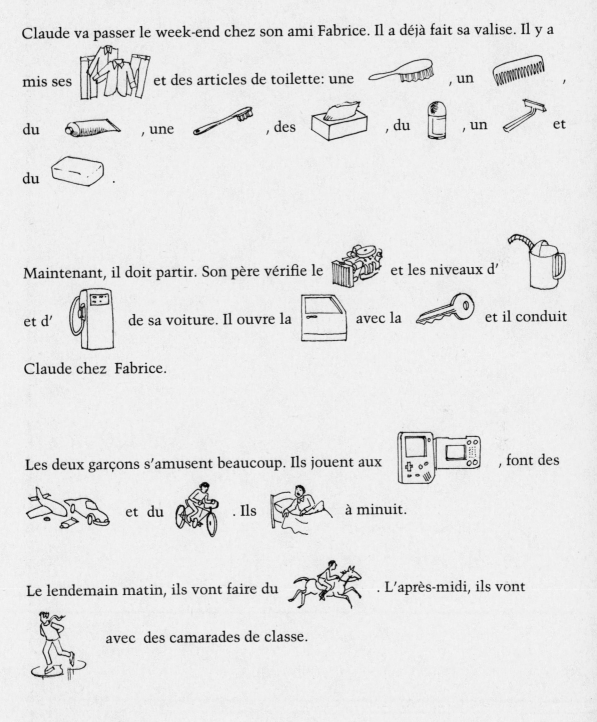 et des articles de toilette: une , un ,

du , une , des , du , un et

du .

Maintenant, il doit partir. Son père vérifie le et les niveaux d'

et d' de sa voiture. Il ouvre la avec la et il conduit

Claude chez Fabrice.

Les deux garçons s'amusent beaucoup. Ils jouent aux , font des

et du . Ils à minuit.

Le lendemain matin, ils vont faire du . L'après-midi, ils vont

avec des camarades de classe.

Quel bon week-end!

Quatrième Partie

16 *Au magasin de meubles*

Cardinal and Ordinal Numbers

☐1 Vocabulaire

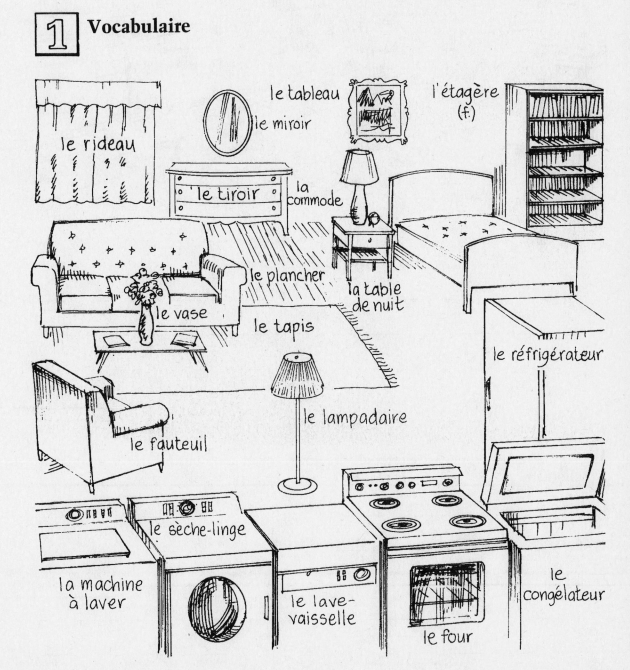

le tableau

le miroir

l'étagère (f.)

le rideau

le tiroir

la commode

le plancher

la table de nuit

le vase

le tapis

le réfrigérateur

le fauteuil

le lampadaire

la machine à laver

le sèche-linge

le lave-vaisselle

le four

le congélateur

___ ACTIVITÉS _____

A. Does this kitchen look all right to you? There are at least eight items you don't normally find in a kitchen. Identify them:

1. _____   5. _____

2. _____   6. _____

3. _____   7. _____

4. _____   8. _____

B. You have just won a prize offered by a furniture and appliance store, and you can choose ten items for your home. Express the ten you would choose:

1. _____   6. _____

2. _____   7. _____

3. _____   8. _____

4. _____   9. _____

5. _____   10. _____

Une bonne affaire

Let's read a story about a couple who goes shopping for furniture. See if you can figure out how much money they spend to furnish their apartment:

Annette et Richard Leduc, jeunes mariés, vont chez un marchand de meubles pour acheter tout ce qu'il faut pour leur nouvel appartement. Richard, un jeune homme très économe, n'a pas envie de gaspiller son argent. Il décide donc d'avance de limiter leurs dépenses à cinq mille dollars. Annette, loin d'être dépensière, est plus flexible. Elle est prête à dépenser un peu plus et acheter vraiment ce qu'elle désire.

gaspiller *to waste*
donc *therefore*
dépenses *expenditures*
  mille *thousand*
dépensière *extravagant*
  prête *ready*

Arrivés au magasin, ils montent au premier étage où il y a tout pour la chambre à coucher.

ANNETTE: Richard, j'adore ces meubles de chambre. Ils sont très modernes.
RICHARD: Mais regarde le prix, ma chérie. Ça coûte trois mille dollars!
ANNETTE: Et alors? Ils sont vraiment parfaits pour nous.

Au deuxième étage, il y a les meubles de salon.

ANNETTE: Prenons ce divan blanc, ces deux fauteuils et cette table en verre.
RICHARD: Mais enfin, ma chérie! Ils coûtent les yeux de la tête! Deux mille six cents dollars!
ANNETTE: Allons, mon amour, nous avons assez d'argent. Ces meubles sont si beaux!

coûter les yeux de la tête *to cost an arm and a leg*

Au troisième étage, ils trouvent les meubles de salle à manger.

ANNETTE: Richard! Regarde cette table et ces six chaises luxueuses. Quelles merveilles!
RICHARD: Mais le prix, le prix . . . Tu ne fais aucune attention au prix, mon chou. L'ensemble coûte deux mille quatre cents dollars!
ANNETTE: Ne sois donc pas si radin, Richard.

luxueuses *luxurious*
  merveilles *marvels*
mon chou *sweetheart*
radin *stingy*

Finalement, Annette fais la liste des meubles de son choix et la remet à un vendeur.

choix *choice*

LE VENDEUR: Très bien, Madame. Voyons . . . Le prix total, y compris les six pour cent de taxe et moins les vingt-cinq pour cent de réduction, revient à six mille trois cent soixante dollars.

y compris *included*
pour cent *percent*
revenir à *to cost, to come to*

RICHARD: Je ne suis pas d'accord. Nous n'allons pas payer autant pour meubler notre appartement. Nous ne sommes pas millionnaires! J'ai dit que notre limite était de cinq mille dollars.

meubler *to furnish*

ANNETTE: Mais Richard, mon amour, j'adore tout ce que j'ai choisi! Ces meubles sont exactement ce que nous cherchions.

LE VENDEUR: Monsieur, nous pouvons sûrement tomber d'accord. J'ai une bonne affaire à vous proposer: donnez-moi maintenant mille cinq cents dollars seulement, puis payez-moi le reste par mensualités.

mensualités *monthly installments*

RICHARD: Évidemment, ça c'est autre chose. Eh bien, d'accord! Donnez-moi ce contrat à signer. Tu vois Annette, il faut toujours réfléchir avant d'acheter. C'est comme ça qu'on épargne de l'argent!

épargner *to save*

Une fois sortis du magasin, Annette lit le contrat: mille cinq cents dollars en liquide et ensuite deux cents dollars par mois pendant deux ans et demi.

en liquide *cash*

ANNETTE: Ah oui, Richard! Quelle bonne affaire en vérité. Fais le calcul. Tu vas voir: nous avons épargné beaucoup d'argent!

___ ACTIVITÉ _____

C. Répondez aux questions par des phrases complètes:

1. Où vont les Leduc?

_____

2. Pourquoi y vont-ils?

_____

3. Qu'est-ce que Richard décide d'avance?

_____

4. Quelle est l'attitude d'Annette?

_____

5. Qu'est-ce qu'il y a au premier étage du magasin?

_____

6. Qu'est-ce qu'ils choisissent au deuxième étage?

_____

7. Qu'est-ce qu'Annette choisit au troisième étage?

_____

8. Quel est le prix total des meubles qu'ils ont choisis?

_____

9. Qu'est-ce que le vendeur propose à Richard?

_____

10. Combien Richard et Annette vont-ils payer en tout pour leurs meubles?

_____

3 You have already learned the numbers to 100. Do you remember them?

1	**un**	13	**treize**	33	**trente-trois**	70	**soixante-dix**
2	**deux**	14	**quatorze**	40	**quarante**	71	**soixante et onze**
3	**trois**	15	**quinze**	41	**quarante et un**	72	**soixante-douze**
4	**quatre**	16	**seize**	44	**quarante-quatre**	77	**soixante-dix-sept**
5	**cinq**	17	**dix-sept**	50	**cinquante**	80	**quatre-vingts**
6	**six**	18	**dix-huit**	51	**cinquante et un**	81	**quatre-vingt-un**
7	**sept**	19	**dix-neuf**	55	**cinquante-cinq**	88	**quatre-vingt-huit**
8	**huit**	20	**vingt**	60	**soixante**	90	**quatre-vingt-dix**
9	**neuf**	21	**vingt et un**	61	**soixante et un**	91	**quatre-vingt-onze**
10	**dix**	22	**vingt-deux**	66	**soixante-six**	93	**quatre-vingt-treize**
11	**onze**	30	**trente**			99	**quatre-vingt-dix-neuf**
12	**douze**	31	**trente et un**			100	**cent**

__ ACTIVITÉ _____

D. Express how much money your friends have available to spend:

EXAMPLE: Robert/26 francs
Robert a vingt-six francs.

1. Sophie/27 francs

_____

2. Patrick/74 francs

_____

3. Claire/6 francs

_____

4. Frédéric/42 francs

_____

5. Odette/80 francs

_____

6. Martine/51 francs

_____

7. François/39 francs

_____

8. Didier/15 francs

_____

9. Madeleine/98 francs

_____

10. Monique/83 francs

_____

4

Now let's learn the numbers over 100. It's very easy:

100 **cent**	500 **cinq cents**	2 000 **deux mille**
101 **cent un**	503 **cinq cent trois**	1 000 000 **un million**
200 **deux cents**	1 000 **mille**	2 000 000 **deux millions**
202 **deux cent deux**	1 004 **mille quatre**	1 000 000 000 **un milliard**

$200 **deux cents dollars** $3.000 **trois mille dollars**

Look carefully at the numbers containing the word **cent**. The plural **-s** of **cent** is dropped when it is followed by another number. The **-s** remains when **cent** is followed by a noun.

Now look at the numbers containing the word **mille**. Does it change in the

plural? _____

Remember: French uses a period where we use a comma and vice versa:

J'ai 2.454 francs.

I have 2,454 francs.

Il a gagné 1.230.225,65 dollars à la loterie.

He won 1,230,225.65 dollars in the lottery.

Some publications use spaces instead of periods to separate digits: **1 230 225.**

___ ACTIVITÉ ___

E. You are a clerk in a large hotel. Several people are checking in. Tell them their room number and then write it in French:

EXAMPLE: Mme Dumas/785
Votre chambre est la sept cent quatre-vingt-cinq.

1. Mme Dupont/649

___

2. M. Durand/813

___

3. Mlle Aimée/592

___

4. Mme Lelouche/281

___

5. M. Rimbaud/436

___

6. Mlle Nalet/999

___

7. Mme Dutronc/374

___

8. M. Lenoir/127

___

9. Mlle Boucher/755

___

10. Mme Xavier/868

___

5 Learn how the following amounts are expressed in French:

cent **voitures**	*a (one) hundred cars*
mille **livres**	*a (one) thousand books*

Unlike English, **cent** and **mille** are not preceded by the indefinite article (**un, une**).

In a date, one thousand is expressed by **mil**:

1993   *mil* **neuf cent quatre-vingt-treize**

NOTE: A date can also be expressed the following way:

1993   *dix*-**neuf cent quatre-vingt-treize**
1865   *dix*-**huit cent soixante-cinq**

million is followed by **de** before another noun:

un *million de* **dollars**	*a (one) million dollars*
sept *millions de* **poissons**	*seven million fishes*

___ ACTIVITÉS _____

F. Write the numerals for the following numbers:

1. cent trois _____

2. quatre cent soixante et onze _____

3. un million vingt _____

4. cent quatre-vingt-quatre _____

5. mille cinq cent cinquante _____

6. huit mille quatre-vingts _____

7. deux cent quatre-vingt-dix-neuf _____

8. quatre-vingt-trois mille _____

9. mille trois cents _____

10. cent vingt mille deux cent quatre-vingt-treize _____

G. Write in French the years in which the following events took place:

EXAMPLE: Christophe Colomb a découvert l'Amérique en 1492.
mil quatre cent quatre-vingt-douze
quatorze cent quatre-vingt-douze

1. L'indépendance des États-Unis a été déclarée en 1776.

_____

2. La révolution française a commencé en 1789.

_____

3. George Washington est né en 1732.

_____

4. Jeanne d'Arc est née en 1412.

_____

5. L'Organisation des Nations Unies a été fondée en 1945.

_____

6. Je suis né(e) en . . .

_____

H. You are the teller in the foreign-exchange division of a bank. Several people need different types of currency. Express what they need:

EXAMPLE: M. Secret/1.120 dollars
M. Secret a besoin de mille cent vingt dollars.

1. M. D'Auvergne/989 francs français

_____

2. M. Chanel/3.795 pesos mexicains

_____

3. Mme Mathieu/8.674 roubles

_____

4. Mme Odette/25.000 pesetas

_____

5. M. Rousseau/350.000 francs belges

_____

6. Mlle Richard/1.750.000 dollars

_____

Do you remember the adjectives **premier** and **deuxième**? Did you notice the numbers for the parts of this book? These numbers are ordinal numbers. Ordinal numbers are used to rank people or things and put them in a certain order:

premier, première	1$^{er, ère}$	*first*
second, seconde	2$^{nd(e)}$	*second* (of two)
deuxième	2^e	*second*
troisième	3^e	*third*
quatrième	4^e	*fourth*
cinquième	5^e	*fifth*
sixième	6^e	*sixth*
septième	7^e	*seventh*
huitième	8^e	*eighth*
neuvième	9^e	*ninth*
dixième	10^e	*tenth*
onzième	11^e	*eleventh*
dix-neuvième	19^e	*nineteenth*
vingt et unième	21^e	*twenty-first*
centième	100^e	*one hundredth*

Except for **premier** and **second**, what suffix is added to the cardinal number to

form an ordinal number? _____

Note that **premier** and **second** are never used with another number:

le *premier* livre	*the first book*
le *trente et unième* livre	*the thirty-first book*
le *second* enfant	*the second child* (of two)
le *vingt-deuxième* enfant	*the twenty-second child*

 The ordinal numbers agree in gender and number with the noun they modify:

le troisième jour	*the third day*
la vingt et unième lettre	*the twenty-first letter*
la seconde fois	*the second time*
les premières années	*the first years*
les deuxièmes rangs	*the second rows*
les cinquièmes places	*the fifth places*

NOTE: **premier** and **second** are the only ordinal numbers to have a feminine form different from the masculine form:

le premier	la première
le second	la seconde

⑧ Look at the following ordinal numbers:

> **la quatrième semaine**
> **le quatorzième jour**
> **les trentièmes anniversaires**

Which silent letter is dropped in the above examples before adding the suffix

-ième? _____

Now look at these ordinal numbers:

> **le cinquième rang**
> **la neuvième semaine**
> **les dix-neuvièmes places**

In the ordinal number **cinquième**, which letter is added before the suffix

-ième? _____

In the ordinal numbers containing **neuf**, what happens to the letter **-f** before

adding **-ième**? _____

Finally, look at the following examples:

> *le* **huitième jour**   *la* **huitième année**
> *le* **onzième étudiant**   *la* **onzième étudiante**

Before an ordinal number beginning with a vowel or a silent **h**, **le** and **la** do not

become _____ .

___ ACTIVITÉS _____

I. Complete the sentences with the appropriate ordinal number:

1. C'est son (100th) _____ anniversaire.

2. C'est la (1st) _____ fois qu'il travaille.

3. C'est son (19th) _____ voyage en France.

4. C'est ma (5th) _____ bonne réponse.

5. Demandez à une (4th) _____ personne.

6. Elle est la (30th) _____ femme à gagner le prix.

7. Il est le (52nd) _____ joueur.

8. Nous sommes au (48th) _____ étage.

J. Express how Antoine compares with the other students in his class:

EXAMPLE: anglais/5ᵉ   Il est cinquième en anglais.

1. français/1ᵉʳ

_____

2. maths/21ᵉ

_____

3. musique/4ᵉ

_____

4. art/12ᵉ

_____

5. biologie/15ᵉ

_____

6. histoire/8ᵉ

_____

7. géographie/10ᵉ

_____

8. algèbre/19ᵉ

_____

QUESTIONS PERSONNELLES

1. Combien de dollars voulez-vous gagner à la loterie?

_____

2. Quand est-ce que vous vous regardez dans un miroir?

_____

3. Depuis quelle année apprenez-vous le français?

_____

4. Que mettez-vous dans les tiroirs de votre bureau?

_____

5. Quelle est la première chose que vous faites quand vous vous levez le matin?

_____

_____ **_VOUS_** _____

Below you will find pictures of items you have around your house. Write out the price tag for each based upon what you believe the cost to be:

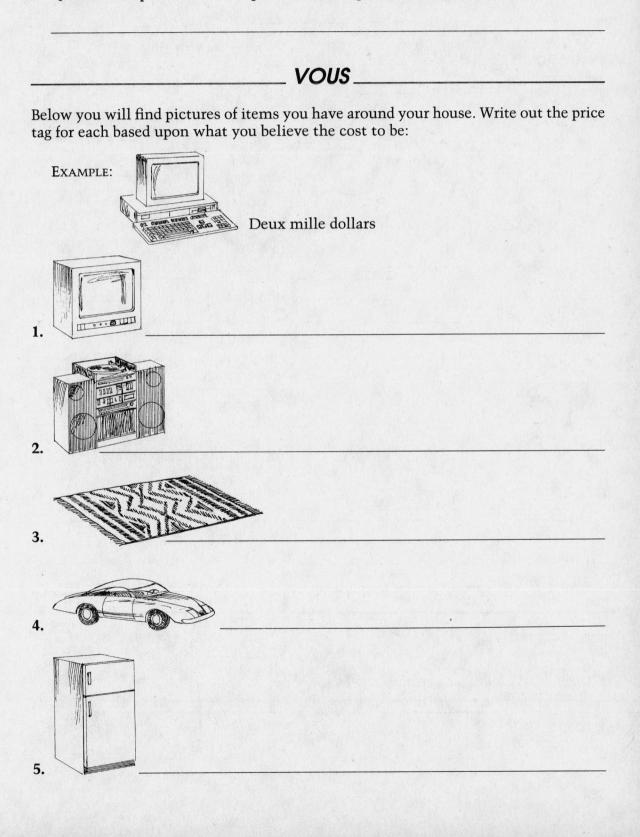

EXAMPLE:

Deux mille dollars

1. _____

2. _____

3. _____

4. _____

5. _____

DIALOGUE

Vous êtes chez le marchand de meubles. Dites au vendeur ce que vous voulez acheter:

COMPOSITION

You have just redecorated your room. Write a note to your friend describing the new look of your room:

_____

_____

_____

_____

_____

Les nombres

Ordinal numbers are used in many ways in the everyday life of a French person:

The first of every month is expressed **le premier**: C'est *le premier* mai.

Trains and planes are divided in two classes: **la première classe**, which is the most expensive, and **la deuxième classe**.

When you watch television, you tune to **la première chaîne** (Channel 1), **la deuxième chaîne** (Channel 2), and so on.

PARIS: ARRONDISSEMENTS

Paris is divided into 20 neighborhoods called **arrondissements**. The number of the **arrondissement** is used in addresses:

> **Musée de l'Armée**
> **Hôtel des Invalides**
> **Paris 7ᵉ**

This museum is in the **septième arrondissement**.

In which **arrondissement** are these places located? Write out the French numbers:

Le Louvre _____

L'Opéra _____

Le Centre Pompidou _____

Le Panthéon _____

Les Invalides _____

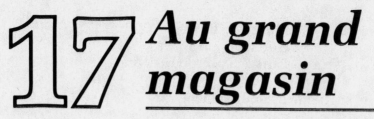

17 Au grand magasin

Verbs with Spelling Changes

1 Vocabulaire

acheter un pantalon

se promener dans les rayons

ranger la marchandise

changer son argent

annoncer les soldes

appeler la vendeuse

s'ennuyer

enlever son manteau

payer à la caisse

essayer des chaussures

préférer une cravate

___ ACTIVITÉ _____

A. Express what these people have just done in the store:

EXAMPLE:

Marie vient de changer son argent.

1. Tu _____.

2. Le vendeur _____.

3. Elle _____.

4. M. et Mme Latour _____.

5. Je _____.

6. Vous _____.

2 Un test psychologique

Quel genre de personnalité avez-vous? Vous enten-dez-vous bien avec vos amis ou vous brouillez-vous souvent avec eux? Êtes-vous timide ou agressif? Avez-vous confiance en vous-même? Pour le savoir, faites le test suivant. Pour chaque situation, choi-sissez la réponse qui correspond le mieux à votre ré-action. Puis additionnez vos points pour découvrir votre caractère.

s'entendre *to get along*
se brouiller *to quarrel*

le mieux *best*
additionner *to add*

1 C'est samedi soir et vous voulez aller au cinéma, mais vos amis préfèrent écouter un genre de musique qui vous ennuie. Que faites-vous?

    (a) Vous allez au cinéma sans eux.   ☐ 5

    (b) Vous allez écouter cette musique avec vos amis.   ☐ 1

    (c) Vous essayez de trouver une alternative qui va plaire à tout le monde.   ☐ 3

plaire *to please*

2 Vous emmenez votre petite amie au restaurant. Le garçon vous apporte l'addition et vous y trouvez une erreur. Il a surestimé la somme. Comment décidez-vous de résoudre ce pro-blème?

surestimer *to overestimate*
résoudre *to solve*

    (a) Vous dites gentiment au garçon qu'il y a une erreur.   ☐ 4

gentiment *kindly*

(b) Vous payez l'addition sans rien dire. ☐ 1

(c) Vous dites au garçon: «Vous ne savez pas compter». ☐ 5

3 Une personne importante vous raconte une blague que vous connaissez déjà. Que faites-vous?

une blague *joke*

(a) Vous l'interrompez et vous lui dites que vous connaissez déjà cette blague. ☐ 5

(b) Vous ne dites rien, vous écoutez la blague, mais vous souriez seulement. ☐ 2

(c) Vous pensez que cette blague est bête mais vous riez quand même à la fin. ☐ 1

riez *laugh*
quand même *anyway*

4 Une amie vient d'acheter une nouvelle robe que vous n'aimez pas. Elle vous demande votre opinion. Vous lui dites:

(a) Si tu n'enlèves pas cette robe horrible, je ne sors pas avec toi. ☐ 5

(b) Je ne sais pas. Je ne suis pas compétent en ces choses. ☐ 3

(c) Elle est très belle. Elle te va très bien. ☐ 1

aller bien *to fit*

5 Vous avez rendez-vous avec quelqu'un à deux heures. Cette personne arrive à deux heures et demie et n'offre aucune explication. Que faites-vous?

(a) Vous regardez votre montre et vous lui demandez ce qui s'est passé. ☐ 4

(b) Vous lui dites bonjour sans mentionner son retard. ☐ 1

(c) Vous vous fâchez et vous lui dites qu'elle est impolie et mal élevée. ☐ 5

impolie *rude*
mal élevée *ill-bred*

6 Vous êtes à une fête. Une personne ennuyeuse vous coince et n'arrête pas de vous parler. Que faites-vous?

coincer *to corner*

(a) Vous lui dites: «Excusez-moi, mais je dois aller aux toilettes». ☐ 5

(b) Vous écoutez ce que cette personne raconte. ☐ 2

raconte *tells*

(c) Vous essayez de changer de sujet de conversation. ☐ 3

7 Quelqu'un vous offre un emploi de bureau. Le travail est intéressant et très bien payé, mais vous n'avez aucune expérience. Que décidez-vous?

un emploi *job*

(a) Vous acceptez l'emploi sans rien dire. ☐ 5

(b) Vous expliquez que vous ne possédez pas la formation nécessaire. ☐ 1

la formation *training*

(c) Vous refusez l'emploi. ☐ 1

8 Vos parents vous disent que vous ne pouvez pas sortir avec vos amis ce week-end. Que faites-vous?

(a) Vous sortez sans leur permission. ☐ 5

(b) Vous essayez de résoudre le problème avec vos parents. ☐ 4

résoudre *to solve*

(c) Vous respectez la décision de vos parents. ☐ 2

9 Un copain d'école vous demande de lui prêter cinq dollars. Vous savez qu'il ne paie jamais ses dettes. Que faites-vous?

prêter *to lend*

dettes *debts*

(a) Vous lui prêtez un dollar et vous lui dites: «C'est tout ce que j'ai.» ☐ 2

(b) Vous lui prêtez les cinq dollars. ☐ 1

(c) Vous ne lui donnez rien. ☐ 5

10 Vous avez rendez-vous ce soir pour aller voir un match de base-ball. Mais quand vous rentrez chez vous, vous vous rappelez soudain que vous avez un examen important le lendemain et que vous devez étudier. Que faites-vous?

se rappeler *to recall*

(a) Vous essayez d'étudier le plus possible avant d'aller au match. ☐ 1

(b) Vous appelez votre ami et vous lui dites que vous êtes malade et que vous ne pouvez pas sortir. ☐ 2

(c) Vous appelez votre ami et vous lui expliquez que vous ne pouvez pas sortir parce que vous devez étudier. ☐ 5

Interprétation des résultats:

39–50 points: Vous êtes indépendant et avez une forte personnalité. Vous êtes sûr de vous. Vous êtes une personne décidée, directe et impulsive. Vous n'êtes pas très diplomatique et vous pouvez froisser les gens. Vous pensez être honnête, mais vous pouvez donner l'impression d'être arrogant et désagréable.

froisser *to offend*

27–38 points: Vous êtes aimable et sympathique. Vous êtes généralement d'accord avec tout le monde. Vous êtes patient et vous savez comment traiter les gens. Vous avez un caractère assez ferme mais vous savez être diplomatique quand il faut.

traiter *to treat*
ferme *strong*

12–26 points: Vous êtes réservé et un peu timide. Vous avez souvent peur de dire la vérité. Essayez d'être plus spontané et d'avoir plus confiance en vous-même.

ACTIVITÉ

B. Répondez aux questions par des phrases complètes:

1. Quelle sorte de test est-ce?

2. Qu'est-ce que ce test vous permet de découvrir?

_____

3. Qu'est-ce que vous devez faire pour chaque situation?

_____

4. Qu'est-ce qu'il faut faire avec les points?

_____

5. Quelle sorte de personnalité possède une personne qui a plus de 39 points?

_____

6. Quels problèmes peut avoir cette personne?

_____

7. Un résultat de 30 points indique quel genre de personnalité?

_____

8. Quel problème peut avoir une personne timide?

_____

9. De quoi une personne timide a-t-elle besoin?

_____

10. Combien de points avez-vous? Est-ce que ce test révèle votre vraie personnalité?

_____

3 Look at the conjugation of the verb **employer** (_to use_):

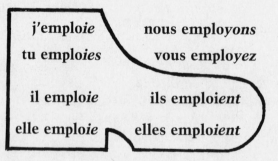

j'emplo_ie_	**nous emplo_yons_**
tu emplo_ies_	**vous emplo_yez_**
il emplo_ie_	**ils emplo_ient_**
elle emplo_ie_	**elles emplo_ient_**

In the present tense, what happens to the **y** of the infinitive in the **je, tu, il/elle, ils/elles** forms? _____

What happens to the **y** in the **nous** and **vous** forms? _____

employer is a "shoe" verb. Why? Look at the conjugation: only the forms inside the shoe change the **y** into an **i**. A "shoe" verb is a verb that undergoes spelling changes for the forms inside the shoe.

Some other "shoe" verbs that end in **-yer** are: **ennuyer** (*to bother*); **essayer** (*to try*); **nettoyer** (*to clean*); **payer** (*to pay*); **s'ennuyer** (*to be bored*).

___ ACTIVITÉS ___

C. Express what the students are using in class:

EXAMPLE: Michel/stylo
Michel emploie un stylo.

1. je/règle

_____

2. nous/livre

_____

3. tu/dictionnaire

_____

4. vous/crayon

_____

5. Paul/cahier

_____

6. les filles/texte

_____

D. Complete the following sentences with the correct form of the verb:

1. (ennuyer) J' _____ le professeur.

2. (essayer) Nous _____ de parler français.

3. (payer) Elle _____ en liquide.

4. (nettoyer) Ils _____ leurs chambres.

5. (employer) Vous _____ ce crayon.

6. (s'ennuyer) Tu _____, n'est-ce pas?

⟨4⟩ Now look at these sentences:

Tu *appelles* ton ami. *You call your friend.*
Tu te *rappelles* l'examen. *You remember the exam.*

The infinitives of these verbs are **appeler** and **se rappeler**. What happened to

the spelling of these verbs? _____

Correct. The **l** of the infinitive doubled to **ll**. The verb **jeter** (*to throw, to throw away*) also undergoes a similar change:

Il *jette* les vieux papiers.

Here is the rule: Verbs ending in **-eler** or **-eter** in the infinitive double the **l** or the **t** before silent **e** in all the singular forms and in the third person plural of the present tense.

appeler and **jeter** are also "shoe" verbs because changes occur for all forms except **nous** and **vous**:

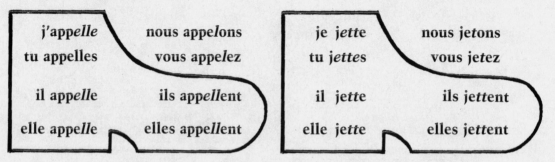

Other "shoe" verbs in **-eler** and **-eter** are: **épousseter** (*to dust*); **feuilleter** (*to leaf through*); **ficeler** (*to tie*); **renouveler** (*to renew*).

___ ACTIVITÉS ___

E. It's the first day of class and you want to know everyone's name. Express what the students say:

> EXAMPLE: il/Jean
> Il s'appelle Jean.

1. il/Georges

_____

2. nous/Marie et Claire

_____

3. tu/Marguerite

_____

4. je/Georgette

_____

5. vous/Laure

_____

6. elles/Dupont

_____

F. Complete the following sentences with the correct form of the verb:

1. (appeler) Nous _____ nos amis.

2. (jeter) Je _____ les papiers.

3. (feuilleter) Vous _____ le magazine.

4. (rappeler) Tu te _____ l'adresse.

5. (ficeler) Il _____ le paquet.

6. (épousseter) Qu'est-ce que vous _____ ?

7. (renouveler) Je _____ mon abonnement (*subscription*).

---

5 Now look at the verb **acheter**:

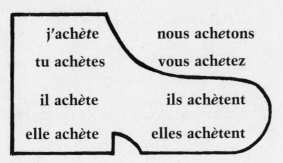

j'ach**è**te   nous ach**e**tons

tu ach**è**tes   vous ach**e**tez

il ach**è**te   ils ach**è**tent

elle ach**è**te   elles ach**è**tent

What spelling change occurs in the "shoe"? _____

_____

Verbs like **acheter** change the silent **e** to **è** in the **je**, **tu**, **il/elle**, **ils/elles** forms in the present tense.

Other "shoe" verbs like **acheter** are: **amener** (*to bring*); **emmener** (*to take along*); **mener** (*to lead*); **promener** (*to walk*); **se lever** (*to rise, to get up*); **se promener** (*to take a walk*).

_ ACTIVITÉS _____

G. Say what you and your friends are doing today:

EXAMPLE: Marie/acheter une robe pour la fête.
          Marie achète une robe pour la fête.

1. ils/se promener dans le parc

_____

2. je/se lever très tôt

_____

3. vous/amener votre frère au cinéma

_____

4. Pierre/acheter des glaces pour tout le monde

_____

5. nous/promener nos chiens

_____

6. tu/emmener Louis au cirque

_____

H. Complete the following sentences with the correct form of the verb:

1. (acheter) Nous _____ un disque.

2. (emmener) J' _____ Jeanne à la montagne.

3. (mener) Elles _____ les animaux à la ferme.

4. (promener) Ils _____ les chiens.

5. (acheter) Elle _____ une blouse.

6. (mener) Tu _____ les affaires du gouvernement.

7. (se lever) Vous _____ tard le dimanche.

8. (se promener) Il _____ .

 There is one more type of "shoe" verb. Look at the conjugation of the verb **posséder** (_to possess_):

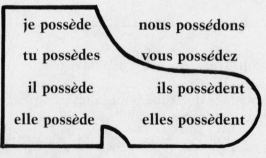

je possède	nous possédons
tu possèdes	vous possédez
il possède	ils possèdent
elle possède	elles possèdent

What spelling changes occur inside the shoe? _____

_____

In the present tense, verbs ending in **é** + consonant + **er** in the infinitive change the **é** to **è** in the **je**, **tu**, **il/elle**, and **ils/elles** forms.

Other "shoe" verbs like **posséder** are: **célébrer** (*to celebrate*); **espérer** (*to hope*); **exagérer** (*to exaggerate*); **préférer** (*to prefer*); **protéger** (*to protect*); **répéter** (*to repeat, to rehearse*).

__ ACTIVITÉS _____

I.   Express what these people prefer to do in their spare time:

EXAMPLE: je/chanter
Je préfère chanter.

1. vous/jouer du piano

_____

2. il/écrire des lettres

_____

3. nous/aller au cinéma

_____

4. tu/dîner au restaurant

_____

5. elles/jouer au tennis

_____

6. je/danser

_____

J.   Complete the following sentences with the correct forms of the verb:

1. (célébrer) Ils _____ le quatre juillet.

2. (posséder) Je _____ cette maison.

3. (préférer) Qu'est-ce que tu _____ ?

4. (répéter) _____ la phrase, s'il vous plaît.

5. (exagérer) Elle _____ toujours.

6. (espérer) Nous _____ aller en France.

7. (protéger) Le chien _____ son maître.

7 Other verbs undergo spelling changes in the present tense to maintain the original sound of the infinitive. Look at these examples:

manger	Vous man**g**ez très peu.	*You eat very little.*
	Nous man**ge**ons à midi.	*We eat at noon.*
commencer	Ils commen**c**ent tôt.	*They begin early.*
	Nous commen**ç**ons tard.	*We begin late.*

What was added to the verb **manger** in the **nous** form? _____

What happened to the **c** in the **nous** form of **commencer**? _____

The rule is easy: Verbs ending in **-ger** in the infinitive keep the **e** before **o** in order to retain the soft **g** sound. Verbs ending in **-cer** in the infinitive change the **c** to **ç** before **o** in order to retain the soft **c** sound.

Now look at **-ger** and **-cer** verbs in the **imparfait**:

Il man*geait* toujours chez Jean.   *He always ate at John's.*
Je commen*çais* à trois heures.   *I used to start at three o'clock.*

How does the spelling of **manger** and **commencer** change in the imperfect?

_____

Right, before the letter **a**, the same rule as in the present tense applies.

Other common **-ger** verbs are: **arranger** (*to arrange*); **changer** (*to change*); **corriger** (*to correct*); **nager** (*to swim*); **voyager** (*to travel*).

Other common **-cer** verbs are: **annoncer** (*to announce*); **effacer** (*to erase*); **placer** (*to place*); **prononcer** (*to pronounce*); **remplacer** (*to replace*).

K. Complete with the correct form in the present tense:

1. (arranger) Nous _____ les fleurs dans le vase.

2. (changer) Vous _____ de livre.

3. (corriger) Je _____ mes devoirs.

4. (nager) Nous _____ bien.

5. (manger) Tu _____ beaucoup.

6. (voyager) Elles _____ en France.

___ ACTIVITÉS _____

L. Your teacher is taking a survey of what foods you and your classmates didn't eat as children. Express the answers she hears:

EXAMPLE: je/légumes
Je ne mangeais pas de légumes.

1. tu/fruits

_____

2. elles/viande

_____

3. nous/salade

_____

4. je/chocolat

_____

5. vous/poisson

_____

6. Paul/bananes

_____

M. Express at what time you and your classmates began your homework when you were younger:

EXAMPLE: je/à 8h
Je commençais à huit heures.

1. ils/à 3h

_____

2. je/à 5h

_____

3. nous/à 7h45

_____

4. Régine/à 4h30

_____

5. vous/à 6h15

_____

6. tu/à 3h10

_____

N. Complete the following sentences with the correct form of the verb in the present tense:

1. (annoncer) J' _____ ma décision.

2. (effacer) Nous _____ le tableau.

3. (commencer) Vous _____ la leçon.

4. (placer) Ils _____ le livre sur le bureau.

5. (prononcer) Nous _____ les mots.

6. (remplacer) Tu _____ le verbe.

_____ **_VOUS_** _____

Choose from the following list of verbs and write five things about yourself, using the present tense:

essayer	nettoyer	s'ennuyer	acheter
se lever	espérer	préférer	exagérer

1. _____

2. _____

3. _____

4. _____

5. _____

DIALOGUE

Vous êtes venu voir votre conseiller parce que vous avez besoin d'aide. Complétez le dialogue:

QUESTIONS PERSONNELLES

1. Qu'est-ce que vous préférez manger?

_____

2. Quel genre de cadeaux achetez-vous pour vos amis?

_____

3. Comment célébrez-vous votre anniversaire?

_____

4. Qu'est-ce que vous faites quand vous vous ennuyez?

_____

5. Où est-ce que vous vous promenez d'habitude?

_____

COMPOSITION

Using five of the verbs provided below, describe a typical shopping day with your friend:

acheter	changer	s'ennuyer
enlever	essayer	appeler
se promener	préférer	payer

1. _____

2. _____

3. _____

4. _____

5. _____

Souvenirs d'Europe

If you travel to Europe, you will certainly want to pick up some souvenirs in countries where French is spoken: France, Switzerland, and Belgium.

Look at the map below and tell what you would buy as gifts for your family and friends in each of the countries:

18 Les merveilles du règne animal

The Verb **courir**;
Comparing People and Things

1 Vocabulaire

la baleine

le cygne

le paon

la girafe

l'ours (m.)

le crocodile

la tortue

la fourmi

le léopard/la panthère

l'écureuil (m.)

le kangourou

le serpent

___ ACTIVITÉS _____

A. Did you ever play "**Qui suis-je**"? This time we are going to play it with animals. See if you can guess the animal by what it says:

1. J'habite en Afrique. J'ai un très long cou et je suis très grande.

   Je suis _____.

2. Je suis un petit insecte, mais je suis très forte et je travaille beaucoup.

   Je suis _____.

3. Je porte ma maison sur le dos et je marche très lentement.

   Je suis _____.

4. Je nage dans l'océan et je suis énorme.

   Je suis _____.

5. Je suis un très bel oiseau blanc et j'habite près des lacs.

   Je suis _____.

6. Je suis gros et brun, je dors pendant tout l'hiver et j'adore le miel (*honey*).

   Je suis _____.

7. On me trouve en Australie. Je protège mon petit qui est dans ma poche (*pocket*).

   Je suis _____.

8. Je n'ai pas de pattes (*legs*) et je suis très long.

   Je suis _____.

B. Here are some cages in a zoo. The names of the animals are missing. Write them in:

  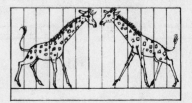

Some of the animals listed above run very quickly. Read the following and see if you can find all the forms of the verb **courir** (*to run*):

Fill in the correct forms of **courir** from the dialog:

je _____   nous _____

tu _____   vous _____

il _____   ils _____

elle _____   elles _____

Past participle: **couru**

— ACTIVITÉS ———————————————

C. Your friend wants to know what places people run to when they are in a hurry. Tell him:

> EXAMPLE: Pierre/à l'école
> Pierre court à l'école.

1. nous/à l'hôpital

———————————————————————————

2. elles/au travail

———————————————————————————

3. tu/à la gare

———————————————————————————

4. je/au lycée

———————————————————————————

5. vous/au magasin

———————————————————————————

6. il/à la pharmacie

———————————————————————————

D. Complete the following sentences with the correct forms of **courir**:

1. Hier, tu ————————————— à la bibliothèque.

2. ————————————— vite, mes enfants.

3. Elles ————————————— rapidement.

4. Il ne ————————————— pas.

5. Nous ————————————— le marathon.

6. Je ————————————— à l'école.

7. Ils ————————————— au lycée.

8. Elle ————————————— vers sa mère.

③ Quelques records du monde

Let's read a story about some world records:

Dans le monde entier, les gens aiment discuter des choses qui sont les plus grandes, les plus petites, les plus hautes, les plus anciennes, etc. N'avez-vous jamais entendu poser de questions telles que: Combien mesure l'homme le plus grand du monde? Quel est l'animal le plus rapide? Quel est l'âge du plus vieil être humain? Les réponses à ces questions et à des milliers d'autres se trouvent dans un livre unique: Le livre Guinness des records.

hautes *high*
telles que *such as*
mesurer *to measure*

milliers *thousands*

Voici quelques intéressants records du monde. La personne la plus grande: un homme qui mesure 8 pieds 11 pouces. La personne la plus petite: une femme qui mesure 23 pouces. La personne la plus grosse: un homme qui pèse 1.069 livres. L'être humain le plus vieux: un Japonais qui est mort à 120 ans. L'animal le plus lourd: une baleine bleue de 11 pieds qui pesait 195 tonnes. L'animal le plus grand: une girafe qui mesurait 20 pieds de haut. L'animal le plus rapide: le léopard qui peut courir de 60 à 63 milles à l'heure. L'animal terrestre le plus gros: un éléphant africain qui mesurait 13 pieds de haut et qui pesait 26.328 livres. Le chien le plus petit: un chihuahua du Mexique qui pesait 10 onces. Le serpent le plus long: un serpent de 27 pieds 9 pouces. Le reptile le plus grand et le plus lourd: un crocodile qui mesurait 27 pieds et qui pesait 1.100 livres. Le poisson marin le plus grand: un requin de 60 pieds 9 pouces qui pesait 90.000 livres. L'arbre le plus haut: un séquoia de Californie qui mesure 366 pieds. L'arbre le plus vieux: un pin des États-Unis qui avait 4.900 ans.

pouces *inches*

peser *to weigh*

lourd *heavy*
tonnes *tons*

terrestre *land*

marin *sea*

un pin *pine tree*

Avez-vous trouvé ces renseignements intéressants? Voici maintenant quelques questions pour vous. Certaines peuvent vous sembler ridicules, mais elles se trouvent pourtant dans le livre officiel des records du monde (les réponses à ces questions sont page 394).

Quel(le) est ou a été
(a)   la pizza la plus grande du monde?
(b)   le poids le plus lourd soulevé par un être hu-   **le poids** *weight*
      main?   **soulever** *to lift*
(c)   le marathon de baisers le plus long?   **baisers** *kisses*
(d)   le parfum le plus cher?
(e)   la perle la plus grosse?
(f)   l'église la plus grande?

___ ACTIVITÉ _____

E.   Répondez par des phrases complètes:

1.   De quoi est-ce que les gens aiment discuter?

_____

2.   Quel genre de question posent-ils?

_____

3.   Où se trouvent les réponses à ces questions?

_____

4.   Selon ce livre, combien mesure l'homme le plus grand du monde?

_____

5.   Combien pèse la personne la plus grosse du monde?

_____

6.   De quelle nationalité était l'homme le plus vieux du monde?

_____

7.   À quelle vitesse un léopard peut-il courir?

_____

8.   De quel pays était le chien le plus petit du monde?

_____

9.   Quel était le reptile le plus grand et le plus lourd du monde?

_____

10.   Où se trouve l'arbre le plus haut du monde?

_____

In order to arrive at the facts you read in the story, people had to make comparisons. Let's look at some examples to see how to form comparisons of adjectives:

Éric est *plus grand que* Michel.	Michel est *moins grand qu'*Éric.
Éric est *plus fort que* Michel.	Michel est *moins fort qu'*Éric.
Éric est *plus âgé que* Michel.	Michel est *moins âgé que* lui.
Éric est *plus lourd que* Michel.	Michel est *moins lourd que* lui.

To form a comparison stating that one is more than another, use _____

before the adjective and _____ after the adjective.

To form a comparison stating less, use _____ before the adjective and

_____ after it.

Note that a stress pronoun (**moi**, **toi**, **lui**, **elle**, **nous**, **vous**, **eux**, **elles**) may be used after **que**:

Janine est plus grande que *moi.*	*Janine is taller than I.*
Marc est plus gentil qu'*eux.*	*Marc is nicer than they.*

___ ACTIVITÉS _____

F. Compare the animals using the clues given:

EXAMPLE: petit

Le chat est plus petit que le cochon.

1. grand

2. lourd

3. rapide

4. intelligent

5. dangereux

6. féroce

7. joli

_____

8. petit

_____

G. What do you find less fun? Give your opinion about the following:

EXAMPLE: le tennis/le base-ball
Le tennis est moins amusant que le base-ball.

1. un film d'amour/un film d'horreur

_____

2. le golf/le football américain

_____

3. un pique-nique/un repas au restaurant

_____

4. nager dans la mer/nager dans une piscine

_____

5. la classe de français/la classe de maths

_____

6. un roman policier/un roman de science-fiction

_____

7. voyager en avion/voyager en bateau

_____

H. Compare the following people:

> EXAMPLE: Il est fort. Luc est plus fort.
> Luc est plus fort que lui.

1. Elle est gentille. Suzanne est plus gentille.

_____

2. Nous sommes calmes. Les filles sont plus calmes.

_____

3. Ils sont nerveux. Elles sont moins nerveuses.

_____

4. Tu es beau. Roger est plus beau.

_____

5. Je suis sympathique. Vous êtes moins sympathique.

_____

6. Il est grand. Jean est moins grand.

_____

 Now look at the following comparison:

> **Un serpent est *aussi dangereux qu*'un crocodile.**
> *A snake is as dangerous as a crocodile.*
>
> **Je suis *aussi grand(e) que* toi.**
> *I am as tall as you.*

To form a comparison of equality (*as . . . as*) in French, use _____

before the adjective and _____ after it.

___ ACTIVITÉ _____

I. You are talking about your two best friends, Paul and Élise. Express that both are equal:

> EXAMPLE: aimable
> Paul est aussi aimable qu'Élise.

1. sérieux

_____

2. charmant

_____

3. amusant

_____

4. intelligent

_____

5. studieux

_____

6. gentil

_____

 What happens if you want to express a superlative — that is, say that something or somebody is the most or the least? Look at these examples:

> **Pierre est _le plus intelligent de la_ classe.**
> _Peter is the most intelligent in the class._

> **André et Margot sont _les plus petits du_ groupe.**
> _Andrew and Margot are the smallest in the group._

> **Rose est _la moins timide des_ filles.**
> _Rose is the least timid of the girls._

> **Louis est _le moins studieux des_ garçons.**
> _Louis is the least studious of the boys._

Which words are used before **plus** and **moins** in the examples? _____,

_____, and _____. Which words are used after the adjectives?

_____, _____, and _____.

In French, the superlative is expressed as follows:

> definite article (**le**, **la**, **les**) + **plus/moins** + adjective + **du**, **de la**, **de l'**, **des**
> the + most/least + adjective + in/of

__ ACTIVITÉS __

J. Using the following adjectives, state who in your family is the most or the least:

EXAMPLE: curieux
Mon père est le plus curieux de la famille.
Ma mère est la moins curieuse de la famille.

1. amusant

_____

_____

2. sévère

_____

_____

3. ambitieux

_____

_____

4. aimable

_____

_____

5. généreux

_____

_____

6. actif

_____

_____

K. Form sentences according to the model:

EXAMPLE: Janine/plus/belle/classe
Janine est la plus belle de la classe.

1. Roger/moins/sérieux/groupe

_____

2. Paulette/plus/heureuse/filles

_____

3. Anne/moins/fière/famille

_____

4. cette voiture/plus/grande/monde

_____

5. ce monument/plus/haut/ville

_____

6. ce musée/moins/intéressant/Paris

_____

7. M. Dupont/plus/amusant/professeurs

_____

8. Mme Renard/plus/gentille/école

_____

_____

 The adjective **bon** has irregular comparative and superlative forms:

ADJECTIVE		COMPARATIVE	SUPERLATIVE
MASC. SING. MASC. PLUR.	**bon** _good_ **bons** _good_	**meilleur** _better_ **meilleurs** _better_	**le meilleur** _the best_ **les meilleurs** _the best_
FEM. SING. FEM. PLUR.	**bonne** _good_ **bonnes** _good_	**meilleure** _better_ **meilleures** _better_	**la meilleure** _the best_ **les meilleures** _the best_

EXAMPLES:

Ce livre est _bon._   _This book is good._
Ce livre est _meilleur que_ le film.   _This book is better than the film._
Ce livre est _le meilleur._   _This book is the best._

Ces histoires sont _bonnes._   _These stories are good._
Ces histoires sont _meilleures_   _These stories are better than the_
  que les films.   _the films._
Ces histoires sont _les meilleures._   _These stories are the best._

— ACTIVITÉ

L. Express what, in your opinion, is the best of the following things:

> EXAMPLE: roman de science-fiction
> Le meilleur roman de science-fiction est «La planète des singes».

1. film de l'année _____

   _____

2. jeu vidéo _____

   _____

3. actrice _____

   _____

4. programme de télévision _____

   _____

5. voiture de sport _____

   _____

6. groupe rock _____

   _____

7. céréales pour le petit déjeuner _____

   _____

 Adverbs are compared in the same way as adjectives. Look at the following examples:

Il marche *plus lentement que* Marie.
He walks more slowly than Marie.

Louise étudie *moins sérieusement que* Roger.
Louise studies less seriously than Roger.

Nous travaillons *aussi rapidement que* vous.
We work as quickly as you.

Elle lit *le plus vite* de la classe.
She reads the fastest in the class.

Élodie et Céline apprennent *le moins facilement* du groupe.
Élodie and Céline learn the least easily of the group.

Since agreement is not made with adverbs, which definite article is always

before **plus** or **moins** in the superlative? _____

Finally, look at the irregular forms of the adverb **bien**:

ADVERB	COMPARATIVE	SUPERLATIVE
bien (*well*)	**mieux** (*better*)	**le mieux** (*the best*)

EXAMPLES:

Elle chante *bien*.   *She sings well.*
Elle chante *mieux que* Marie.   *She sings better than Marie.*
Elle chante *le mieux de la* classe.   *She sings the best in the class.*

Remember: **bon, meilleur(e), le/la meilleur(e)** are used with nouns.
                 bien, mieux, le mieux are used with verbs.

___ ACTIVITÉS ___

M. Compare the following items and tell whether the first is more, less, or as expensive as the second:

EXAMPLE: une radio/une télévision
                  Une radio coûte moins cher qu'une télévision.

1. un fauteuil/une lampe

_____

2. une voiture de sport/une voiture familiale

_____

3. une maison/un château

_____

4. un ballon de football/une balle de base-ball

_____

5. une montre/une bague

_____

6. un bateau/un avion

_____

7. une guitare/un piano

_____

8. un café/un thé

_____

N. Compare the following people to yourself:

EXAMPLE: Anne parle rapidement. (more . . . than)
Anne parle plus rapidement que moi.

1. Pierre parle doucement. (less. . .than)

_____

2. Les garçons jouent calmement. (as. . .as)

_____

3. Elles marchent fièrement. (more. . .than)

_____

4. Marie travaille facilement. (as. . .as)

_____

5. Le professeur parle distinctement. (less. . .than)

_____

6. Tu cours lentement. (more. . .than)

_____

O. Choose the word that best completes the sentence:

1. (bon, bonne, bien) Marie nage _____ .

2. (le meilleur, la meilleure, le mieux) Il est _____ élève.

3. (bons, bonnes, bien) Cette couleur te va _____ .

4. (les meilleurs, les meilleures, le mieux) Ces voitures marchent _____ .

5. (bon, bonne, bien) Cette soupe est très _____ .

6. (le meilleur, la meilleure, le mieux) _____ actrice s'appelle Anne.

7. (bons, bonnes, bien) Les chocolats sont _____ .

8. (les meilleurs, les meilleures, le mieux) Ces fruits sont _____ .

_____ QUESTIONS PERSONNELLES _____

1. Qui est l'étudiant le plus studieux de votre classe de français?

_____

2. Qui est votre meilleur(e) ami(e).

_____

3. Quel chanteur aimez-vous le mieux?

_____

4. Qui est plus grand que vous?

_____

5. Qui danse bien?

_____

_____ VOUS _____

You are a camp counselor and have gone to the zoo with a group of small children. Write some of the questions the children ask you about the animals. For example, they want to know whether the leopard is as strong as the bear; whether the crocodile is as dangerous as the shark; which is the longest snake in the zoo; which is the smallest animal, and so on:

_____

_____

_____

_____

_____

DIALOGUE

Vous participez à une enquête menée par le journal de votre école. Répondez aux questions:

COMPOSITION

You would like a role in the school play. Write a note to the director in which you explain why you think you qualify:

_____

_____

_____

_____

_____

Réponses aux questions de la page 381:
(a) Une pizza de 80 pieds de diamètre et qui pesait 18.664 livres. (b) 6.270 livres. (c) 119 heures et 12 minutes. (d) Une essence de jasmin (*jasmine*) qui coûte plus de 200 dollars l'once. (e) Une perle de 14 livres 1 once. (f) Saint-Pierre de Rome, en Italie, qui couvre 18.110 yards carrés (*square yards*).

INTERVALLE CULTUREL

Expressions animales

Idiomatic expressions using names of animals often help us refer to people or circumstances. Match the French expression with the picture it describes:

Elle a du chien.   Il est fort comme un bœuf.
Elle a une tête de cochon.   Le bébé marche comme un canard.
Il est agile comme un singe.   Il a une langue de vipère.
Il a un appétit d'oiseau.   Il a un cou de girafe.

1. _____   2. _____

3. _____   4. _____

5. _____   6. _____

7. _____   8. _____

19 Les professions et les métiers

Future Tense of Regular Verbs

1 **Vocabulaire**★

le programmeur   l'électricien   le plombier   la vétérinaire

le fermier   l'hôtesse de l'air   la photographe   le boucher

le cordonnier   l'employée de banque   le pilote   la coiffeuse

le mécanicien   le boulanger   la journaliste   la directrice

★In this **Vocabulaire**, we illustrate sometimes male, sometimes female professionals. All those professions, however, have both male and female practitioners. In the vocabulary in the back of your book, see if you can find the male or female counterparts of the professions illustrated on this page.

NOTE: While **plombier** and **pilote** are always masculine in gender, they are also used to designate female practitioners:

Marie-Claire est *un* jeune pilote d'avion.
Lucie est *un* bon plombier.

___ ACTIVITÉ ___

A. Who does the following? Complete the sentences with the appropriate noun:

1. _____ coupe les cheveux des gens.

2. _____ vend de la viande.

3. _____ prépare et vend le pain.

4. _____ est le docteur des animaux malades.

5. _____ répare les chaussures.

6. _____ installe la douche et le lave-vaisselle.

7. _____ prend des photos artistiques.

8. _____ conduit des avions.

9. _____ répare les moteurs de voiture.

10. _____ écrit pour les magazines et les journaux.

11. _____ s'occupe des vaches et fait pousser (*grow*) des céréales.

12. _____ aide les passagers d'un avion.

13. _____ est responsable de la direction d'une société (*company*).

14. _____ écrit des programmes d'ordinateur.

15. _____ est spécialisé dans les installations électriques.

16. _____ travaille dans une banque.

L'horoscope

Do you want to know what will happen in your future? Astrologers say that they can predict the future from the stars. Let's read this story and see what's in the stars for you. Pay attention to the verbs in bold type:

Ne désirez-vous pas savoir ce qui se **passera** dans votre avenir? Les astrologues disent que notre personnalité et notre avenir sont influencés par les étoiles. Chacun de nous naît sous un des douze signes du zodiaque et certaines personnes ne **prendront** jamais de décision importante sans d'abord consulter leur horoscope. Qu'est-ce que demain vous **apportera**? Quelles surprises **révéleront** les astres? Lisez les horoscopes suivants et vous le **découvrirez**.

étoiles *stars*
    chacun *each one*
    naît *is born*

révéler *to reveal*
    astres *stars*

Verseau, du 20 janvier au 18 février
Vous êtes une personne généreuse, compréhensive, romantique et poétique. Vous **recevrez** bientôt une nouvelle de grande importance pour votre bonheur. Vous **réaliserez** votre rêve de faire un grand voyage.

Verseau *Aquarius*

bonheur *happiness*

Poissons, du 19 février au 20 mars
Vous êtes une personne très tendre, idéaliste et sentimentale. Dans les prochains mois, vous **rencontrerez** quelqu'un qui **prendra** une place très importante dans votre vie.

Poissons *Pisces*

Bélier, du 21 mars au 19 avril
Vous êtes une personne courageuse et décidée. Vous **réussirez** à satisfaire tous vos désirs. Vous **recevrez** bientôt des nouvelles d'un ami très cher et vous y **répondrez** avec plaisir.

Bélier *Aries*

réussir *to succeed*

Taureau, du 20 avril au 20 mai
Vous avez beaucoup de bon sens. Vous êtes également une personne pratique et réaliste. Cette année, la fortune vous **sourira**. Un héritage inattendu vous **permettra** de réaliser un de vos plus vieux rêves.

Taureau *Taurus*

pratique *practical*
héritage *inheritance*
    inattendu *unexpected*

Gémeaux, du 21 mai au 21 juin
Vous êtes impatient et impulsif. Vous **mènerez** une vie sociale très active et vous **gagnerez** l'admiration d'une personne qui vous est très chère.

Gémeaux *Gemini*

Cancer, du 22 juin au 22 juillet
Vous êtes une personne sensible et sympathique. Vous aimez aider les autres. Vous **trouverez** bientôt une solution à vos problèmes. Attendez-vous à une année prochaine très intéressante.

sensible *sensitive*

s'attendre à *to expect*

Lion, du 23 juillet au 22 août
Vous êtes une personne sûre d'elle-même et avez des qualités de meneur. Cette semaine, vous **établirez** des contacts avec des gens qui vous **aideront** dans l'avenir.

Lion *Leo*

meneur *leader*
   établir *to establish*

Vierge, du 23 août au 22 septembre
Vous êtes perfectionniste. Avant de faire quelque chose, vous étudiez tous les détails et vous réfléchissez bien. De brillants résultats à un examen vous **ouvriront** de nouvelles perspectives d'avenir.

Vierge *Virgo*

Balance, du 23 septembre au 23 octobre
Vous êtes une personne tranquille et vous recherchez l'harmonie en toutes choses. Vous **gagnerez** beaucoup d'argent cette année, mais faites attention sinon vous le **gaspillerez** vite.

Balance *Libra*

sinon *otherwise*

Scorpion, du 24 octobre au 21 novembre
Vous aimez travailler et vous êtes une personne déterminée qui n'accepte pas l'échec. Vous **essaierez** de changer votre vie cette année, mais les changements que vous **choisirez** de faire vous **apporteront** peu de satisfaction.

échec *failure*

Sagittaire, du 22 novembre au 21 décembre
Vous êtes une personne amusante, sincère et honnête, mais vous devez avoir plus confiance en vous-même. Le nouveau projet que vous **commencerez** bientôt vous **donnera** du prestige.

Sagittaire *Sagittarius*

Capricorne, du 22 décembre au 19 janvier
Vous êtes indépendant et ambitieux, mais aussi mélancolique et pessimiste. Vos problèmes d'argent ne **dureront** pas longtemps. Cette année vous **commencerez** un travail qui **changera** votre situation en mieux.

ACTIVITÉ

B. Répondez aux questions par des phrases complètes:

1. Qu'est-ce que les astrologues disent?

   _____

2. Qu'est-ce que nous avons tous en commun (*in common*)?

   _____

3. Qu'est-ce que certaines personnes font avant de prendre une décision?

   _____

4. Selon cet horoscope, qu'est-ce qu'un Verseau va bientôt recevoir?

   _____

5. Sous quel signe sont nées les personnes tendres, idéalistes et sentimentales?

   _____

6. Quelle sorte de personne est un Cancer?

   _____

7. Quelle sorte de personne est un Lion?

   _____

8. Quel problème a un Sagittaire?

   _____

 Up to now, we have been talking in the present and past tenses. How do we describe actions and events that will happen in the future? The horoscope in the story told you some things that will happen in the future:

Il *gagnera* beaucoup d'argent.	He will earn a lot of money.
Vous *choisirez* de faire des changements.	You will choose to make changes.
Vous y *répondrez* avec plaisir.	You will answer it with pleasure.

Now read this short dialog:

Daniel et Robert **assisteront** à la surprise-partie de Claude. Ils en discutent maintenant:

DANIEL: Avec qui **danseras**-tu à la surprise-partie?
ROBERT: Je **danserai** avec Sylvie, la fille la plus jolie de notre classe de français.
DANIEL: Elle **dansera** avec toi? Mais tu ne sais pas danser!

ROBERT: Mais si (*yes*), je sais danser. Je me suis entraîné hier soir. Je sais que nous **danserons** pendant toute la soirée.

DANIEL: Impossible!

ROBERT: Pas du tout! Et Sylvie **finira** par m'aimer beaucoup.

DANIEL: Qu'est-ce qui se **passera** quand vous **arriverez** chez elle après la surprise-partie?

ROBERT: D'abord je **prendrai** son numéro de téléphone et ensuite je l'**embras-serai**.

DANIEL: Quelle chance!

Look at the verbs in bold type in the story and the dialog and answer these questions: Which form of the verb is the stem of the future tense?

_____ If the verb ends in **-re**, which letter is dropped

from the infinitive before adding the future endings? _____

What endings do you add if the subject is:

je + stem + _____   **nous** + stem + _____

tu + stem + _____   **vous** + stem + _____

il + stem + _____   **ils** + stem + _____

elle + stem + _____   **elles** + stem + _____

Now try to supply the forms of the future tense for these verbs:

	manger	**finir**	**attendre**
je(j')	_____	_____	_____
tu	_____	_____	_____
il/elle	_____	_____	_____
nous	_____	_____	_____
vous	_____	_____	_____
ils/elles	_____	_____	_____

____ ACTIVITÉS _____

C. You are going to spend your vacation at the beach. Express what you will do there:

EXAMPLE: dormir sur la plage
Je dormirai sur la plage.

1. sortir très tôt le matin

_____

2. nager dans la mer

_____

3. prendre des bains de soleil

_____

4. se reposer

_____

5. construire des châteaux de sable

_____

6. jouer avec mes amis

_____

_____

D. Your school is going to have a party. Express how everyone is going to help:

EXAMPLE: nous/chercher des disques
Nous chercherons des disques.

1. Liliane/apporter des sandwiches

_____

2. Georges et Paul/préparer des salades

_____

3. je/choisir des cassettes

_____

4. tu/répondre au téléphone

_____

5. vous/inviter des amis

_____

6. nous/travailler dans la cuisine

_____

7. François/jouer de la guitare

_____

8. les filles/aider à mettre les décorations

_____

E. Next week you are going to the flea market with some friends. Using the elements below, write what each of you will be doing:

je	y arriver tôt
vous	y rester toute la journée
toi et moi, nous	vendre de vieux jouets
Charles et Anne	manger beaucoup
tu	dépenser trop d'argent
Robert	choisir des cadeaux

EXAMPLE: Toi et moi, nous y resterons toute la journée.

1. _____

2. _____

3. _____

4. _____

5. _____

6. _____

F. Change the following sentences from the near future to the future tense:

EXAMPLE: Je vais gagner le match.
Je gagnerai le match.

1. Elle va ouvrir le paquet.

_____

2. Nous allons choisir le cadeau.

_____

3. Il va descendre.

_____

4. Je vais lire un roman.

_____

5. Vous allez aider le professeur.

_____

6. Ils vont boire du thé.

_____

7. Elles vont arriver bientôt.

_____

8. Nous allons nous amuser.

_____

9. Je vais maigrir.

_____

10. Tu vas regarder ce programme.

_____

4 Note the future stem of "shoe" verbs, like **acheter**, **employer**, **appeler**, and **jeter**:

INFINITIVE	FUTURE STEM	FUTURE TENSE	
acheter	achèter-	J'achèterai un pull.	Nous achèterons un pull.
employer	emploier-	Tu emploieras ce stylo.	Vous emploierez ce stylo.
appeler	appeller-	Il m'appellera.	Ils m'appelleront.
jeter	jetter-	Je jetterai la balle.	Vous jetterez la balle.

Unlike the present-tense forms of these verbs, the changes in the future tense occur in the stem of all persons, including the **nous** and **vous** forms.

ACTIVITÉS

G. Complete the following sentences with the correct forms of the future:

1. (acheter) Ils _____ du gâteau.

2. (lever) Nous _____ la main en classe.

3. (mener) Je _____ une vie agréable.

4. (se promener) Elle _____ dans le parc.

5. (amener) Vous _____ votre frère à la bibliothèque.

6. (emmener) Tu _____ ton amie au cinéma.

H. Complete the following sentences with the correct forms of the future:

1. (payer) Je _____ le boucher.

2. (essayer) Il _____ de préparer le dîner.

3. (ennuyer) Vous _____ votre frère.

4. (payer) Elles _____ avant lundi.

5. (employer) Tu _____ un dictionnaire.

6. (nettoyer) Nous _____ avant de partir.

I. Supply the correct future forms:

1. (appeler) Ils _____ Jean.

2. (jeter) Je _____ les papiers.

3. (épousseter) Vous _____ .

4. (ficeler) Elle _____ le cadeau.

5. (rappeler) Tu _____ ta grand-mère.

6. (feuilleter) Nous _____ nos livres.

J. Complete the following sentences with the correct forms of the future:

1. (jeter) Il _____ la balle.

2. (ennuyer) Les garçons _____ toujours les filles.

3. (se lever) Je _____ de bonne heure.

4. (employer) Elle _____ son stylo rouge.

5. (mener) Il _____ le chien chez lui.

6. (acheter) Elles _____ des disques.

7. (essayer) J' _____ de le faire.

8. (appeler) Je les _____ tout de suite.

9. (se promener) Vous _____ avec Josette.

10. (payer) Il _____ la prochaine fois.

---

5 Verbs like **espérer** and **préférer** retain the spelling of the infinitive in all the forms of the future:

> J'*espérerai* toujours.
> Nous *préférerons* aller avec vous.

Verbs ending in **-ger** or **-cer** do not change in the future:

> Nous *mangerons* du gâteau.
> Tu *commenceras* demain.

___ ACTIVITÉ ___

K. Supply the correct forms of the future:

1. (célébrer) Je _____ mon anniversaire demain.

2. (arranger) Nous _____ les chaises.

3. (posséder) Vous _____ une grande maison.

4. (préférer) Elle _____ rester en France.

5. (effacer) Le professeur _____ le tableau.

6. (répéter) Les élèves _____ la phrase en français.

___ QUESTIONS PERSONNELLES ___

1. Quelle est votre date de naissance?

_____

2. Sous quel signe du zodiaque êtes-vous né(e)?

_____

3. Dans quel journal ou magazine pouvez-vous lire votre horoscope?

_____

4. Décrivez votre personnalité.

_____

5. Quelle profession souhaitez-vous exercer à l'avenir?

_____

_____ VOUS _____

How will your life be in fifteen years? Using some of the suggested verbs, write five sentences to describe what you will be doing in fifteen years:

acheter	étudier	parler	vivre (_to live_)
découvrir	gagner	prendre	voyager
écrire	lire	travailler	

1. _____

2. _____

3. _____

4. _____

5. _____

_____ COMPOSITION _____

Your friend would like you to go to the park with him next weekend, but you had to refuse. Tell him/her what you will be doing then:

_____

_____

_____

_____

_____

DIALOGUE

Votre frère et vous discutez de l'avenir. Répondez à ses questions:

INTERVALLE CULTUREL

La population active en France

There are approximately 23 million workers in the French labor force (**la population active**). About two million are agricultural and forestry workers, more than seven million are in construction, mining, and manufacturing, and another fourteen million in banking, transportation, civil service jobs, domestic service, and the various professions.

How do the job benefits of French workers compare to ours? The work week is 39 hours, with overtime paid at a higher rate. French workers are paid by the month and are entitled by law to five weeks of paid vacation. A typical worker will take four weeks in the summer and one week in the winter. In private industry, workers generally receive a yearly bonus equivalent to one month's earnings. Civil servants receive two months' wages as a bonus. The minimum wage in France (called **SMIC**) is now 4,271 francs per month and goes up every July 1st. Look at the following list and figure out in dollars how much these workers earn per month:

Engineer	19,000 F
High school teacher	12,000 F
Civil servant	5,500 F
Secretary	5,000 F
Physician	35,000 F
Hairdresser	7,000 F + tips

20 L'exploration de l'espace

Future Tense of Irregular Verbs

1 Vocabulaire

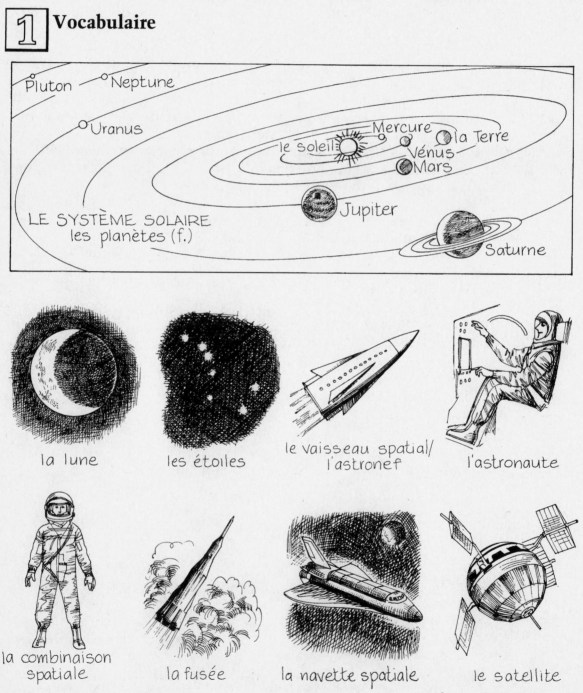

LE SYSTÈME SOLAIRE
les planètes (f.)

Pluton — Neptune

Uranus

le soleil — Mercure — la Terre

Vénus

Mars

Jupiter

Saturne

la lune

les étoiles

le vaisseau spatial/
l'astronef

l'astronaute

la combinaison
spatiale

la fusée

la navette spatiale

le satellite

___ ACTIVITÉS _____

A. Picture story. Can you read this story? Whenever you come to a picture, read it as if it were a French word:

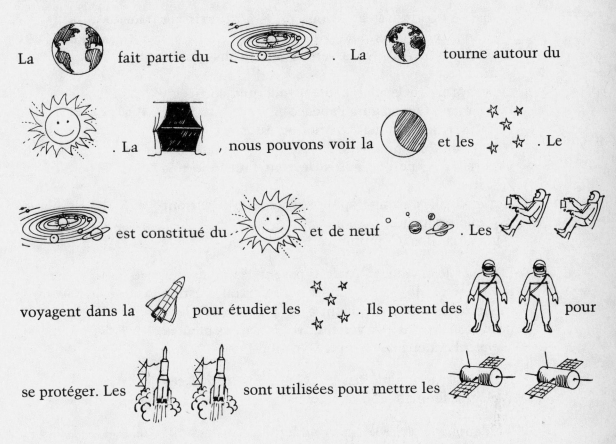

La [🌍] fait partie du [☀planets] . La [🌍] tourne autour du

[☀] . La [⛰], nous pouvons voir la [🌙] et les [⭐] . Le

[☀planets] est constitué du [☀] et de neuf [🪐] . Les [👨‍🚀]

voyagent dans la [🚀] pour étudier les [⭐] . Ils portent des [👨‍🚀] pour

se protéger. Les [🚀🚀] sont utilisées pour mettre les [🛰️]

en orbite autour de la terre.

B. **Humour extraterrestre.** Make up a funny caption for each situation:

_____   _____

Une aventure dans l'espace

l'espace space

Let's read a story about an adventure in space. Pay attention to the verbs in bold type:

TOUR DE CONTRÔLE: Êtes-vous prêts à atterrir sur cette planète inconnue?

atterrir to land
inconnue unknown

L'ASTRONEF ZGR3: Nous **serons** prêts dans quinze minutes.

CONTRÔLE: Quels astronautes **voudront** sortir les premiers? Qui en **aura** l'audace?

l'audace audacity

ASTRONEF: Jean-Paul Rossignol et Audrée Champignon **iront** les premiers.

CONTRÔLE: Qu'est-ce qu'ils **devront** faire une fois sortis?

ASTRONEF: Ils **devront** explorer la planète. Ils **verront** si elle est habitée ou non.

CONTRÔLE: Bon. Communication terminée.

Dès que Jean-Paul et Audrée posent les pieds sur la planète, ils sont entourés d'extraterrestres monstrueux qui ressemblent à des plantes avec leur peau et leurs cheveux verts. Et voilà que ces plantes s'approchent encore plus près d'eux!

dès que as soon as
entourés surrounded

peau skin

JEAN-PAUL: Je n'aime pas ça. Que crois-tu que ces plantes **feront** si nous bougeons?

bouger to move

Soudain l'une d'elle se met à parler:

soudain suddenly
se mettre à to begin

LE CHEF: De quel droit interrompez-vous la paix et la tranquillité de notre planète? Vous êtes des êtres humains, n'est-ce pas? Est-ce que d'autres de votre espèce **viendront** après vous?

droit right   la paix peace

espèce species

JEAN-PAUL ET AUDRÉE: Oui, mais. . .

LE CHEF: Silence! Nous connaissons très bien votre cruauté. Sur la Terre, vous faites de nos frères des salades mixtes. Vous êtes tous des assassins!

cruauté cruelty

JEAN-PAUL: Nous ne sommes pas des assassins! Audrée, qui **viendra** nous sauver maintenant? Comment **pourrons**-nous échapper à ces monstres? **Courrons**-nous au vaisseau? **Recevrons**-nous de l'aide d'un des habitants? Le capitaine du vaisseau **enverra**-t-il du secours? Que **ferons**-nous? C'est incroyable, nous allons être attaqués par des plantes. De simples légumes!

échapper to escape

LE CHEF: De simples légumes? Vous **paierez** cette injure de votre vie! Vous **mourrez** demain à cinq
heures. Vos amis ne **sauront** jamais ce qui vous est
arrivé.

injure *insult*

AUDRÉE: La situation me semble désespérée. Nous
devons accepter l'idée de notre mort prochaine car
je ne vois pas comment nous **pourrons** retourner à
notre vaisseau. Ces plantes nous **mangeront** demain. Quelle mort horrible!

désespérée *hopeless*

LE CHEF: Nous **mettrons** un peu de mayonnaise sur
eux!

JEAN-PAUL: J'ai peur. Au secours! Au secours!

MAMAN: Jean-Paul! Jean-Paul! Il est déjà dix heures
et demie. Éteins la télévision et va te coucher. Tu
finiras par faire des cauchemars à force de regarder
ces films de science-fiction!

éteindre *to turn off*
cauchemars *nightmares*
à force de *as a result of*

__ ACTIVITÉ _____

C. Répondez aux questions par des phrases complètes:

1. Où est-ce que l'astronef ZGR3 atterrira?

   _____

2. Qui ira sur la planète?

   _____

3. Qu'est-ce qu'ils devront y faire?

   _____

4. Comment sont les habitants de cette planète?

   _____

5. Quand est-ce que Jean-Paul et Audrée mourront?

   _____

6. Comment est la situation?

   _____

7. Qu'est-ce qu'ils doivent accepter?

   _____

8. Qu'est-ce qu'ils ne pourront pas faire?

   _____

9. Quelle heure est-il?

_____

10. Qu'est-ce que maman dit à Jean-Paul?

_____

_____

  Did you pay attention to the verbs in bold type in the story? They are all in the future tense. They have regular endings, but their stem is not the infinitive. Can you determine their future stems?

	INFINITIVE	FUTURE STEM
Jean-Paul et Audrée *iront* les premiers.	aller	ir-
Qui en *aura* l'audace?	avoir	_____
Courrons-nous au vaisseau?	courir	_____
Ils *devront* l'explorer.	devoir	_____
Le capitaine *enverra*-t-il du secours?	envoyer	_____
Nous *serons* prêts.	être	_____
Qu'est-ce que ces plantes *feront*?	faire	_____
Vous *mourrez* demain.	mourir	_____
Nous *pourrons* retourner.	pouvoir	_____
Recevrons-nous de l'aide?	recevoir	_____
Vos amis ne *sauront* rien.	savoir	_____
Qui *viendra* vous sauver?	venir	_____
Ils *verront* les habitants.	voir	_____
Quels astronautes *voudront* sortir?	vouloir	_____

__ ACTIVITÉS _____

D. You are preparing a surprise party for your parents' anniversary. Express what everyone will volunteer to do:

> EXAMPLE: je/courir à la boulangerie
> Je courrai à la boulangerie.

1. nous/venir vous aider

_____

2. tu/savoir une chanson

_____

3. ils/vouloir aller à la boucherie

_____

4. je/devoir préparer des plats délicieux

_____

5. vous/avoir des disques à prêter

_____

6. elle/faire une grande salade

_____

7. il/être le chef

_____

8. nous/aller à la boulangerie

_____

9. vous/courir à la pâtisserie

_____

10. ils/recevoir les invités

_____

11. je/pouvoir cuisiner

_____

12. tu/voir que tout/aller bien

_____

13. il/mourir de rire quand il/entendre l'histoire

_____

14. vous/envoyer les invitations

_____

_____

E. Your friends explain what they are doing today. Using the future, say that you will be doing the same things:

> EXAMPLE: Il va à la plage.
>   Moi aussi, j'irai à la plage.

1. Henri reçoit d'excellentes notes en français.

_____

2. Nous allons dîner chez Jacques.

_____

3. Liliane et Marie font un voyage en France.

_____

4. Ses parents doivent acheter une nouvelle voiture.

_____

5. Ma sœur voit un spectacle formidable.

_____

6. Son frère est à l'université.

_____

7. Ma cousine sait sa leçon par cœur.

_____

8. Ma mère vient te voir.

_____

9. J'envoie une lettre à mes grands-parents.

_____

10. Nous courons le marathon.

_____

4 Look carefully at the following sentences:

Quand j'*aurai* assez d'argent, j'*achèterai* une voiture.
When I have enough money, I will buy a car.

Quand je *serai* grand, j'*irai* en France.
When I grow up, I will go to France.

Quand j'*irai* en France, je *parlerai* français.
When I go to France, I will speak French.

Each of the French sentences above contains two verbs. What is the tense of

both verbs? _____ Now look at the English sentences. Are the

same tenses used in English? _____ Which two tenses did you use in those

sentences? _____ and _____ . Which word do

the three French examples have in common? _____ Right. Here is the
simple rule: In French, when **quand** is used to express a future situation, both
the verb after **quand** and the verb of the main clause are in the future tense.

Now look at the following sentences:

Lorsque j'*arriverai* à Paris, je vous *téléphonerai*.
When I arrive in Paris, I will call you.

Je *viendrai* chez toi dès que je *pourrai*.
I will come to your house as soon as I can.

Je *sortirai* avec lui aussitôt qu'il me le *demandera*.
I will go out with him as soon as he asks me.

Which tense is used after **lorsque** (*when*), **dès que** (*as soon as*), and **aussitôt que**

(*as soon as*)? _____ What do these sentences have in common

with the **quand** clauses above? _____
Right. In French, the future tense is also used after **lorsque, dès que,** and
aussitôt que when referring to a situation taking place in the future.

___ ACTIVITÉ _____

F. Express what you and your friends will do in the following situations:

EXAMPLE: Quand j'**aurai** trente ans, je **serai** millionnaire.

1. Lorsque je finirai les cours au lycée, je _____

_____ .

2. Mes parents me donneront leur voiture dès que je _____

_____ .

3. Nous saurons parler français quand nous _____

_____ .

4. Ils rangeront leur chambre aussitôt qu'ils _____

_____ .

5. Dès que j'aurai le temps, je _____

_____ .

6. Je _____
lorsque j'aurai beaucoup d'argent.

7. Vous voterez dès que vous _____

_____ .

8. Lorsque je serai adulte, je _____

_____ .

_____ QUESTIONS PERSONNELLES _____

1. Quel âge aurez-vous en l'an 2000?

_____

2. Vous explorez l'espace. Quelle(s) planète(s) voulez-vous visiter?

_____

3. Quel film de science-fiction préférez-vous?

_____

4. Où irez-vous en vacances cet été?

_____

5. Quand retournerez-vous à l'école?

_____

DIALOGUE

Vous regardez un film de science-fiction avec un ami. Complétez le dialogue:

VOUS

Express what you will do when you graduate from high school:

Quand j'aurai mon diplôme,

1. _____

2. _____

3. _____

4. _____

5. _____

COMPOSITION

Your science assignment is to write a composition about which scientific career you will pursue. State the following:

1. that you will become an astronaut.

_____

2. that you will have many adventures.

_____

3. that you will go to the moon.

_____

4. that you will make a trip to other planets.

_____

5. that you will be famous someday.

_____

INTERVALLE CULTUREL

Concorde

The Concorde is a supersonic plane designed and manufactured as a joint venture by the British and French governments and flown by their subsidized national airlines BOAC and Air France. The plane was built to create goodwill and to impress people with the technological capabilities of the British and French aviation industries. The design of the Concorde is unusual in that the nose tilts from a horizontal to a downward position for takeoff and landing.

The Concorde flies at approximately 800 m.p.h., in excess of the speed of sound, and can fly from New York to Paris in 3 hours 45 minutes, or about half the time of a regular airline flight. The cost of a round-trip ticket is over $4,200, unless there are special promotional fares available.

The Concorde is used almost exclusively by business people. Why do you think this is so? Would you like to fly aboard the Concorde? Explain your reasons.

Révision IV
(Leçons 16–20)

Leçon 16

a. Cardinal numbers:

200 **deux cents**	700 **sept cents**	100.000 **cent mille**
300 **trois cents**	800 **huit cents**	200.000 **deux cent mille**
400 **quatre cents**	900 **neuf cents**	1.000.000 **un million**
500 **cinq cents**	1.000 **mille**	2.000.000 **deux millions**
600 **six cents**	2.000 **deux mille**	1.000.000.000 **un milliard**

(1) **cent** does not take an **s** when followed by another number:

cinq cents   **cinq cent dix**   **deux cent mille**

(2) **cent** keeps the **s** when followed by a noun:

deux cents dollars   **six cents personnes**

(3) **mille** does not take an **s** in the plural:

trois mille   **cinq cent mille dollars**

(4) **cent** and **mille** are not preceded by the indefinite article (**un, une**):

cent pages   *a hundred pages*
mille fois   *a thousand times*

(5) In a date, 1000 is expressed by **mil** or **dix**:

mil **neuf cent quatre-vingt-treize**   *1993*
dix-**neuf cent quatre-vingt-treize**   *1993*

(6) **million** is followed by **de** before another noun:

un million *de* **dollars**
quatre millions *d'*élèves

b. Ordinal numbers:

1er, 1ère	**premier, première**	6^e	**sixième**
2^{nd(e)}	**second(e)** (of two)	7^e	**septième**
2^e	**deuxième**	8^e	**huitième**
3^e	**troisième**	9^e	**neuvième**
4^e	**quatrième**	10^e	**dixième**
5^e	**cinquième**		

The ordinal numbers agree in gender and number with the nouns they modify, **premier** and **second** are the only ordinal numbers to have a feminine form different from the masculine form:

> **Voilà les *premières* pages du *troisième* chapitre.**
> **Elle est la *seconde* fille des Roland.**
> **Ils sont les *cinquièmes* à me poser cette question.**

Leçon 17

Some French verbs change their spelling in certain forms to maintain the original sound of the infinitive:

a. Verbs ending in **-yer** change the **y** to **i** in the singular forms and the third person plural of the present tense:

nettoyer:	**Je nettoie ma chambre.**
employer:	**Il emploie son stylo.**
payer:	**Nous payons à la caisse.**
s'ennuyer:	**Vous vous ennuyez.**
	Ils s'ennuient sans toi.

b. Verbs ending in **-eler** and **-eter** normally double the **l** or the **t** in the singular forms and the third person plural of the present tense:

appeler:	**J'appelle mon frère.**
	Nous appelons Jean.
	Ils l'appellent au téléphone.
jeter:	**Tu jettes le livre.**
	Vous jetez les papiers.
	Elles jettent leurs vieux vêtements.

c. Verbs ending in **-e** + consonant + **er** change the silent **e** to **è** in the singular forms and the third person plural of the present tense:

acheter:	**J'achète des fruits.**
amener:	**Tu amènes les enfants au cinéma.**
promener:	**Il promène le chien.**
mener:	**Nous menons la danse.**
lever:	**Vous levez la main.**
se promener:	**Elles se promènent au parc.**

d. Verbs ending in **é** + consonant + **er** change the **é** to **è** in the singular forms and the third person plural of the present tense:

exagérer:	Tu exagères toujours.
préférer:	Jean préfère la viande.
répéter:	Nous répétons la question.
célébrer:	Je célèbre mon anniversaire.
espérer:	Vous espérez gagner.
posséder:	Elles possèdent beaucoup de tableaux.

e. Verbs ending in **-cer** change **c** to **ç** before **a** and **o** in all forms and tenses:

commencer:	Nous commençons à midi.	Ils commençaient à s'ennuyer.
effacer:	Nous effaçons le tableau.	Il n'effaçait jamais le tableau.

f. Verbs ending in **-ger** keep their **e** before the letter **a** and **o** in all forms and tenses:

manger:	Nous mangeons tard.	Il mangeait trop.
voyager:	Nous voyageons ensemble.	Ils voyageaient souvent.

Leçon 18

a. Present-tense forms of the verb **courir** (*to run*):

je cours	nous courons
tu cours	vous courez
il court	ils courent
elle court	elles courent

b. **plus** + adjective + **que** are used to form a comparison stating that one is more than another:

Janine est *plus* grande *que* Christine.

moins + adjective + **que** are used to form a comparison stating that one is less than another:

Cet exercice est *moins* difficile *que* l'autre.

aussi + adjective + **que** are used to form a comparison of equality:

Le poulet est *aussi* bon *que* le poisson.

c. A stress pronoun (**moi, toi, lui, elle, nous, vous, eux, elles**) may be used after **que**:

Jean est plus grand que *moi*.
Je suis aussi fort que *lui*.
Elle est moins fière qu'*elles*.

d. In French, the superlative is expressed as follows:

definite article (**le**, **la**, **les**) + **plus/moins** + adjective + **du**, **de la**, **de l'**, **des**

> **Marie est *la plus* belle *de la* classe.**

e. The comparative of adverbs in French is formed in the same way as that of adjectives:

> **Il court *plus vite que* Pierre.**
> **Marie apprend *moins rapidement que* Léon.**
> **Il marche *aussi lentement que* moi.**

For the superlative of adverbs, since no agreement is necessary, only the definite article **le** is used:

> **Paul joue *le* mieux de tous.**
> **Anne chante *le* mieux de toutes les filles.**

f. The adjective **bon** and the adverb **bien** have irregular comparative and superlative forms:

	COMPARATIVE	SUPERLATIVE
bon(s) (**bonne**)(s) *good*	**meilleur**(e)(s) *better*	**le/la/les meilleur**(e)(s) *the best*
bien *well*	**mieux** *better*	**le mieux** *the best*

Leçon 19

a. The future tense of regular **-er** and **-ir** verbs is formed by adding the future endings to the infinitive; **-re** verbs drop the **e** before the future endings:

je (j')		-ai
tu		-as
il/elle	étudier	-a
nous	finir	-ons
vous	vendr	-ez
ils/elles		-ont

b. Verbs ending in **e** + consonant + **er** change the silent **e** to **è** in all forms of the future:

> **J'achèterai des fruits.**
> **Tu amèneras les filles au cinéma.**
> **Il promènera le chien.**
> **Nous mènerons la danse.**
> **Vous vous lèverez tôt.**
> **Elles se promènent au parc.**

c. Verbs ending in **-yer** change the **y** to **i** in all forms of the future:

> Je netto*i*erai la voiture.
> Il emplo*i*era son stylo.
> Nous pa*i*erons plus tard.
> Vous essa*i*erez encore une fois.

d. Verbs ending in **-eler** and **-eter** double the **l** or the **t** in all forms of the future:

> J'appe*ll*erai mon frère.
> Nous appe*ll*erons Jean.
> Tu je*tt*eras le livre.
> Vous je*tt*erez les papiers.

e. Verbs ending in **-cer**, **-ger**, and **é** + consonant + **er** use the infinitive with no change in the future tense:

> Nous commencerons à midi.
> J'effacerai le tableau.
>
> Nous mangerons tard.
> Ils voyageront ensemble.
>
> Ils exagéreront toujours.
> Je répéterai la question.

Leçon 20

a. To form the future of irregular verbs, add the future endings to the irregular future stem:

aller	*ir-*	être	*ser-*	savoir	*saur-*
avoir	*aur-*	faire	*fer-*	venir	*viendr-*
courir	*courr-*	mourir	*mourr-*	voir	*verr-*
devoir	*devr-*	pouvoir	*pourr-*	vouloir	*voudr-*
envoyer	*enverr-*	recevoir	*recevr-*		

b. The future is used after **quand** (*when*), **lorsque** (*when*), **dès que** (*as soon as*), and **aussitôt que** (*as soon as*) when referring to a situation taking place in the future:

> Quand tu *seras* grand, tu *seras* pilote d'avion.
> Lorsque j'*irai* à l'université, j'*apprendrai* l'électronique.
> Dès qu'il *aura* le temps, il *viendra* te voir.
> Aussitôt que nous *pourrons*, nous *ferons* un pique-nique.

___ ACTIVITÉS _____

A. **Où est-ce qu'Alain garde son argent**? To find the answer, identify the objects in the pictures, then write the letters indicated in the blanks below:

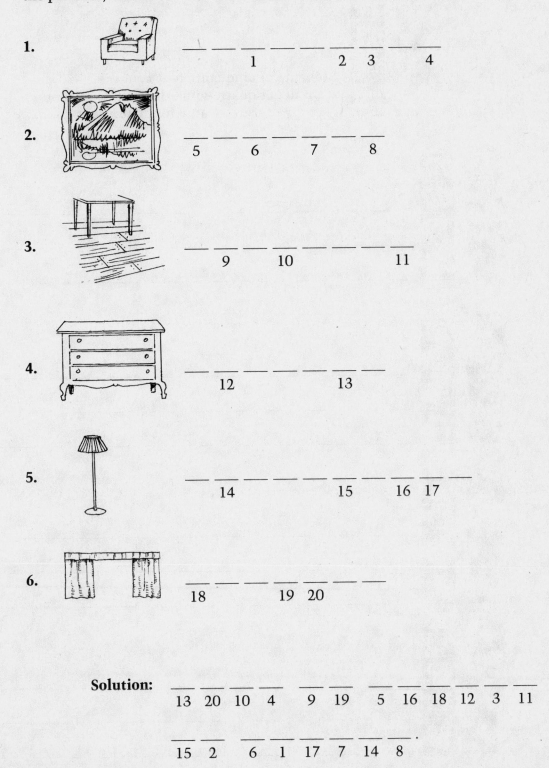

1. ___ ___ ___ ___ ___ ___ ___
       1   2 3   4

2. ___ ___ ___ ___ ___
  5   6   7   8

3. ___ ___ ___ ___
    9   10   11

4. ___ ___ ___ ___ ___
   12   13

5. ___ ___ ___ ___ ___ ___
  14   15   16 17

6. ___ ___ ___ ___
  18   19 20

Solution: ___ ___ ___ ___ ___ ___ ___ ___ ___ ___ ___ ___
    13 20 10 4   9 19   5 16 18 12 3   11

___ ___ ___ ___ ___ ___ ___ ___ .
  15 2   6 1 17 7 14 8

B. Add the column in stages from top to bottom:

EXAMPLE:

Soixante et cinquante font cent dix.
Cent dix et quatre-vingt-dix font deux cents.
Deux cents et quarante font deux cent quarante.

1.

_____

_____

_____

2.

_____

_____

_____

3.

_____

_____

_____

4.

_____

_____

_____

C. Complete the sentences with the correct form of a verb chosen from the following list:

acheter	appeler	ranger	payer
emmener	commencer	nettoyer	préférer

1. J' _____ mon frère au grand magasin.

2. Il _____ la vendeuse.

3. Elles _____ les soldes.

4. Ils _____ les rayons.

5. Tu _____ de jolies robes.

6. Nous _____ nos courses.

7. Vous _____ à la caisse.

8. Nous _____ la marchandise.

D. Look at the pictures and compare the objects in them with the clues. The answer depends sometimes on your point of view:

1. rapide: _____.

2. important: _____.

3. petit: _____.

4. intéressant: _____.

5. grand: _____.

6. élégant: _____.

7. âgé: _____.

8. amusant: _____.

E. How many of these words do you remember? Fill in the French words, then read down the boxed column to find the answer to this question: **Qui est M. Raspail?**

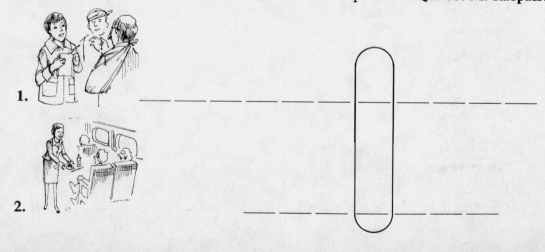

1. __ __ __ __ __ __ __ __ __

2. __ __ __ __ __ __ __ __

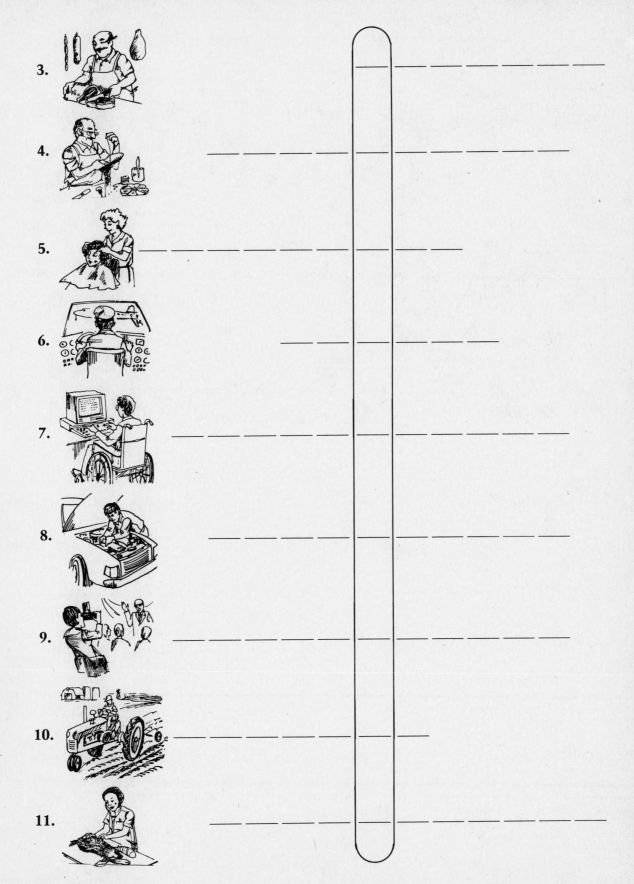

F. Find the hidden animals. There are 10 animals hidden in the picture. List them below:

_____   _____

_____   _____

_____   _____

_____   _____

_____   _____

G. It's the year 3000 and you, an inspector in the Earth's Department of Immigration, are interviewing newcomers from outer space. You have just received word to keep on the lookout for a particular creature that reproduces itself every 24 hours. You can see what a problem that would create. Spot this creature from the information given:

Il porte des chaussures.
Il n'a pas de barbe mais des moustaches.
Il a des antennes au lieu d'oreilles.
Il paraît toujours heureux.
Il a de très petits pieds.
Il a des yeux très près l'un de l'autre.

H. Mots croisés:

HORIZONTALEMENT

2. (appeler) vous ____
8. (avoir) tu ____
9. (emmener) Demain tu l'____.
12. (lire) C'est la lettre qu'il a ____.
15. (voir) demain vous ____
18. here
20. you
21. (oser) j'ai ____
22. bicycle
23. (amener) j'____
24. or
25. to you
26. (our) ____ lits
30. (vouloir) demain il ____
32. (envoyer) Nous l' ____ demain.
35. and
36. (manger) nous ____
38. (être) Demain elle ____ là.
39. (aller) J' ____ demain.
41. (peas) petits ____

42. (devoir) demain il ____
43. (aller) Nous ____ demain.
45. year
46. (appeler) nous ____
49. (servir) tu ____
52. (herself) Elle ____ peigne.
54. (mener) tu ____
55. to him
56. (neither . . nor) ne . . ____
57. (his) ____ voiture
60. (se lever) Demain il se ____ tôt.
63. some
65. (courir) je ____
66. some
67. on
68. of
69. (être) elle ____
71. (aller) demain tu ____
72. (falloir) il ____

VERTICALEMENT

1. (croire) il a ____
2. (acheter) j' ____
3. (not) Il ne chante ____.
4. (être) tu ____
5. (avoir) j'ai ____
6. this
7. enough
10. to me
11. king
12. (lire) demain elle ____
13. (espérer) elle ____
14. (your) ____ parents
15. (vouloir) demain tu ____
16. (répondre) il ____
17. (être) elle ____
18. he
19. condition
27. gold
28. (savoir) demain tu ____
29. I
30. (voyager — imparfait) vous ____

31. (commencer) nous ____
33. (venir) demain je ____
34. (faire) demain nous ____
37. (nager — imparfait) je ____
40. (rire) je ____
41. (posséder) je ____
44. (posséder) tu ____
45. (s'asseoir to sit) il s'____
47. (pouvoir) demain tu ____
48. (not) Je ____ danse pas.
50. in
51. (rendre) elle le ____
53. (partir) je ____
58. (aimer) j'____
59. in order to
61. (voir) j'ai ____
62. (avoir) demain elle ____
64. (sentir) tu ____
69. and
70. (your) ____ mère

I.   L'exploration de l'espace. Hidden in the puzzle are 14 items floating in space. Find and circle the words from left to right, right to left, up or down, or diagonally:

```
E  S  T  E  N  R  U  T  A  S  P  J
R  L  P  L  O  M  A  R  S  E  L  U
F  E  L  U  A  N  O  R  T  S  A  P
E  É  U  N  V  O  R  I  A  E  N  I
N  S  T  E  P  R  L  S  S  N  È  T
O  U  O  E  I  L  T  S  E  E  T  E
R  F  N  L  E  R  I  L  T  R  E  R
T  U  L  T  E  A  G  E  U  R  S  C
S  S  A  E  V  I  N  U  S  E  E  E
A  S  É  T  O  I  L  E  S  T  O  I
```

Proficiency Test

1. Speaking

a. Your teacher will award up to 10 points for your oral performance in the classroom.

b. Oral Communication Tasks (20 points)

Your teacher will administer a series of communication tasks in four categories. Each task prescribes a simulated conversation in which you play yourself and the teacher assumes the role indicated in the task. Each task requires at least four utterances on your part, for which you can earn up to 5 points of credit. An utterance is any spoken statement that leads to accomplishing the stated task. Assume that in each situation you are speaking with a person who speaks French.

2. Listening Comprehension

a. Multiple Choice (English) (20 points)

Part 2a consists of 10 questions. For each question, you will hear some background information in English. Then you will hear a passage in French *twice*, followed by a question in English. After you have heard the question, look at the question and the four suggested answers in your book. Choose the best suggested answer and write its number in the space provided.

1 What is Charles' problem? _____

    1. He didn't do his homework.
    2. He was late to school.
    3. He'll be absent tomorrow.
    4. He left his homework at home.

2 What did your sister buy? _____

    1. A dress.   3. A robe.
    2. A nightgown.   4. Pajamas.

3 What will you have to study for the test? _____

    1. The verb endings.   3. The structures.
    2. The past tense.   4. The vocabulary.

4 Which meal is Thomas eating? _____

    1. Breakfast.   3. Supper.
    2. Lunch.   4. Afternoon snack.

5 In which season of the year are we? _____

    1. Spring.   3. Fall.
    2. Summer.   4. Winter.

6 Why can't you take the scheduled bus? _____

    1. None of the buses is running today.
    2. Your bus has just left.
    3. There is a problem on the highway.
    4. Your ticket is no longer valid.

7 What is your friend's suggestion? _____

    1. To go to the movies.   3. To go to a concert.
    3. To go to a dance.   4. To go to the beach.

8 Where can these items be bought? _____

    1. In a restaurant.   3. In a butcher shop.
    2. In a drugstore.   4. In a supermarket.

9 What's the good news? _____

    1. You have been invited to spend your vacation in France.
    2. Your friend has received excellent marks this term.
    3. Your friend's father got a job in Paris.
    4. Your friend might spend the summer in France.

10 What does your friend want you to do? _____

    1. Listen to a certain radio station.
    2. Go out and buy a record.
    3. Buy her a radio.
    4. Send her the words of a song.

b. Multiple Choice (French) (10 points)

Part 2b consists of 5 questions. For each question, you will hear some background information in English. Then you will hear a passage in French *twice*, followed by a question in French. After you have heard the question, look at the question and the four suggested answers in your book. Choose the best suggested answer and write its number in the space provided.

11 Que font les enfants? _____

    1. Ils nagent dans la mer.
    2. Ils se promènent.
    3. Ils jouent sur la plage.
    4. Ils cherchent des coquillages.

12 Où vont aller les jeunes gens?   _____

    1. Au lycée.   3. À la montagne.
    2. Sur une île tropicale.   4. En France.

13 De quoi ces jeunes gens parlent-ils?   _____

    1. De la difficulté des cours.
    2. De la nécessité de gagner de l'argent.
    3. De différentes professions.
    4. Du grand nombre d'universités.

14 Que savez-vous de cette jeune fille?   _____

    1. Elle est paresseuse.
    2. Elle a plus de vingt ans.
    3. Elle veut devenir professeur.
    4. Elle est ambitieuse.

15 Qu'est-ce que Thérèse n'aime pas?   _____

    1. Son salaire.
    2. Ses conditions de travail.
    3. L'attitude de la directrice.
    4. Le lieu où elle travaille.

c. Multiple Choice (Visual) (10 points)

Part 2c consists of 5 questions. For each question, you will hear some background information in English. Then you will hear a passage in French *twice*, followed by a question in English. After you have heard the question, look at the question and four pictures in your book. Choose the picture that best answers the question and circle its number.

16 Which picture best describes Jean's occupation?

       1   2   3   4

17 What are some of the things bought by the customer?

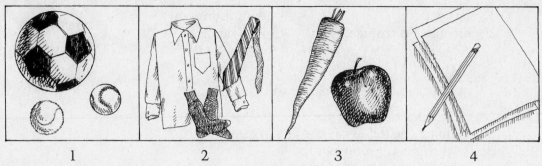

1   2   3   4

18 Where is Louise going?

1   2   3   4

19 What is being described?

1   2   3   4

20 What did the policeman do?

1   2   3   4

3. Reading

a. Multiple Choice (English) (12 points)

Part 3a consists of 6 questions or completions in English, each based on a reading selection in French. Choose the best answer to each question. Base your choice on the content of the selection. Write the number of your answer in the space provided.

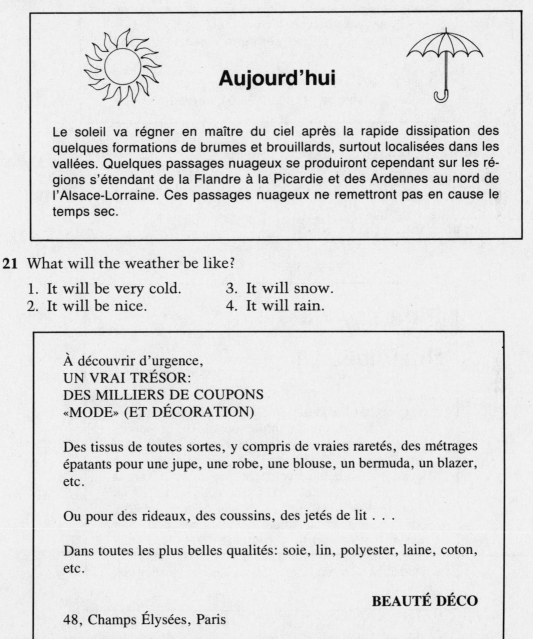

Aujourd'hui

Le soleil va régner en maître du ciel après la rapide dissipation des quelques formations de brumes et brouillards, surtout localisées dans les vallées. Quelques passages nuageux se produiront cependant sur les régions s'étendant de la Flandre à la Picardie et des Ardennes au nord de l'Alsace-Lorraine. Ces passages nuageux ne remettront pas en cause le temps sec.

21 What will the weather be like?

1. It will be very cold.
2. It will be nice.
3. It will snow.
4. It will rain.

À découvrir d'urgence,
UN VRAI TRÉSOR:
DES MILLIERS DE COUPONS
«MODE» (ET DÉCORATION)

Des tissus de toutes sortes, y compris de vraies raretés, des métrages épatants pour une jupe, une robe, une blouse, un bermuda, un blazer, etc.

Ou pour des rideaux, des coussins, des jetés de lit . . .

Dans toutes les plus belles qualités: soie, lin, polyester, laine, coton, etc.

BEAUTÉ DÉCO

48, Champs Élysées, Paris

22 Why would you go to this store?

1. To learn how to sew.
2. To decorate your house.
3. To buy clothing.
4. To purchase material.

ON RECHERCHE

Charles Lambert, né le 28 octobre 1973 à Cherbourg, demeurant à Nanterre, n'a pas reparu à son domicile depuis le 5 mai 1988.

SIGNALEMENT: 1,74 m, cheveux châtain clair, yeux bleus. Ses parents, très inquiets, souhaitent recevoir de ses nouvelles et remercient toute personne susceptible de leur fournir des renseignements à son sujet.

Téléphoner au (1) 49.36.48.29 ou au commissariat de police de Nanterre: (1) 49.83.98.04, bureau 469.

---

23 This ad was placed to

1. find a missing person.
2. ask for help in locating a criminal.
3. attract a girlfriend.
4. announce the birth of a child.

Bon Voyage

International

vous offre la plus large sélection de yachts de qualité en vente sur le marché international. Un personnel polyglotte qualifié est à votre disposition pour vous conseiller sur l'achat ou la vente de votre yacht. Le Département Location vous propose un grand choix de yachts à moteur et à voile que vous trouverez en Méditerranée, aux Caraïbes et dans le Pacifique. Ces yachts sont soigneusement sélectionnés pour leur qualité, leur confort et la compétence de leur équipage. Bon Voyage International met également à la disposition de sa clientèle un service de gestion expérimenté.

24 According to this ad, why should you shop in this store?

1. They employ a competent, multilingual staff.
2. Their prices are the best.
3. They have stores on all continents.
4. They give the best guarantee.

Instructions pour régler la combinaison de la serrure

La mallette est livrée avec la combinaison 000. Vous pouvez garder cette composition ou former votre combinaison personnelle à l'aide des instructions suivantes:

Opération No. 1
Réglez les chiffres sur la combinaison d'ouverture. (La combinaison d'ouverture est réglée sur 000 quand vous achetez votre nouvelle mallette.)

Opération No. 2
Poussez le bouton vers le cadran avec le pouce, sans lâcher prise.

Opération No. 3
Maintenant tournez les chiffres selon votre combinaison secrète en les notant ailleurs pour les avoir comme référence en cas d'oubli. Utilisez des numéros qui vous sont familiers comme par exemple une partie de votre numéro de téléphone, date de naissance, adresse, sécurité sociale, etc.

Opération No. 4
Lâchez prise et faites revenir le bouton en position normale. La combinaison sera enregistrée.

Ouvrez encore une fois la serrure pour contrôler.

---

25 What do these instructions tell you?

1. How to tape a record.
2. How to prepare a special dish.
3. How to play a game.
4. How to set a combination lock.

Cette carte doit être remplie par le détaillant au moment de l'achat et elle doit être présentée par l'acheteur pour toute réparation sous garantie.

No. du modèle _____   Article _____

Nom du client _____

Adresse _____
30712734
Indiquer ce numéro sur toute correspondance se rapportant à la garantie.

---

26 This form is used

1. as identification.
2. to order a magazine.
3. as a proof of purchase.
4. to enter a contest.

b. Multiple Choice (French) (8 points)

Part 3b consists of 4 questions or completions in French, each based on a reading selection in French. Choose the best answer to each question. Base your choice on the content of the reading selection. Write the number of your answer in the space provided.

Bijoux Brillants
Le plus formidable choix. «Rien que des affaires exceptionnelles!» écrit le guide «Paris pas cher». Alliances, brillants, solitaires, bagues, rubis, saphirs, émeraudes, bijoux, or, argenterie, etc.

QUATORZE CARATS
Angle bd des Français
15, Chaussée d'Antin

Achat tous bijoux ou échanges. Autre magasin, autre grand choix: **Étoile**, 85, rue de l'Opéra.

---

27 Vous répondrez à cette annonce si vous

1. cherchez du travail.
2. voulez acheter un cadeau.
3. vendez votre maison.
4. changez de domicile.

L'AUBERGE DE LA VILLE

Dans une auberge aux murs centenaires, re-découvrez la saveur du terroir et le charme de l'hospitalité. Les serveurs, Jean-Luc et Jean-Claude, savent vous guider avec gen-tillesse, humour et compétence pour le mariage d'une carte des vins exception-nelle et d'une cuisine généreuse. Chaque repas est une fête, une fête entre amis.

---

28 Cet article parle

1. d'un bon restaurant.
2. d'un hôtel moderne.
3. d'une fête de mariage récente.
4. d'un nouveau magasin.

Vierge (23 août – 22 septembre)

1er décan: Tout est calme, en famille aussi: ça germe pour tout projet, et anciens comme enfants vous donneront appui et satisfactions.
2e décan: Vacances? Tout doux, tout calme entre moments suspendus, voyages agréables et douceurs qui s'écoulent sans contretemps.
3e décan: Ne signez rien sans relecture (contrats, cartes de crédit, chèques) et soyez vigilant.

29 Qu'est-ce que cet horoscope vous prédit?

1. Vous tomberez malade.
2. Il ne faut pas voyager.
3. Votre vie sera très tranquille.
4. Il faut chercher un avocat.

Canal 2

Voyage autour du monde

*6.30 Télématin. Présenté par Suzie Duprès *8.30 «Amoureuse-ment vôtre» *8.55 «Éric et compagnie» *11.35 «Quoi de neuf, doc-teur?» *12.00 Météo 1.2.3. Soleil *12.03 Flash d'informations *12.05 Les mariés de Canal 2 *12.30 Dessinez: c'est gagné!

13.00 Journal
Présenté par Jean Dupont et Lucie Arnoux.
13.35 Météo 1.2.3. Soleil
13.40 Tour de France
Col de Vars.

14.15 Aventures—voyages
Voyage autour du monde en famille
(Première partie)
Réalisé par Louis Duchamp.
Après des préparatifs de plusieurs années, un architecte, Louis Duchamp, sa femme et leurs trois enfants ont vendu leur maison et sont partis pour un tour du monde de plusieurs années.

15.10 Tour de France
Présenté par Roger Chenet, Olivier Marquette et François Latour.
*L'étape du jour en direct (15e étape): Gap – Briançon *Le Tour de France féminin. Commentaires: Sylvie Bonnet *À chacun son tour, par Jacques Rémy, Robert Moreau et Michel Lebois.

17.55 Trivial Pursuit
Jeu présenté par Marc et Marie Noëlle.

30 À quelle heure pourrez-vous regarder un reportage sportif?

1. À 11.35   3. À 14.15
2. À 13.35   4. À 15.10

4. Writing

a. Notes (6 points)

Write 2 notes in French as directed below. Each note must consist of at least 12 words.

1. You have received a birthday present from a cousin. Write a note in French expressing your thanks.

   _____

   _____

   _____

   _____

2. You are spending two weeks in Fort-de-France, Martinique, during your vacation. Write a note in French to a friend telling how you are.

   _____

   _____

   _____

   _____

b. Lists (4 points)

Write 2 lists in French as directed below. Each list must contain 4 items. One-word items must not be proper names.

1. Your class is planning a party. In French, list 4 things you might want to bring to the party.

   _____

   _____

   _____

   _____

2. You need clothing for the new school year. In French, list 4 articles of clothing you could buy.

_____

_____

_____

_____

French-English Vocabulary

A

à to, at; **à carreaux** checkered; **à côté de** next to; **à force de** as a result of; **à l'heure** on time; **à nouveau** again; **à propos** by the way; **à rayures** striped; **à vrai dire** to tell the truth
abeille f. bee
abonnement m. subscription
absolu absolute
absolument absolutely
absorber to absorb
accompagner to accompany
accordéon m. accordion
accusé m. defendant
achat m. purchase
acheter to buy
acheteur m. buyer
acier m. steel
addition f. check
additionner to add
affaire f. deal, bargain
affreux (f. **affreuse**) terrible, awful
afin de in order to
agité agitated
agneau m. lamb
agréable pleasant
aide f. help
aider to help
ailleurs elsewhere
aimable kind, pleasant
aller to go, to feel, to fit
alliance f. wedding ring
allumer to light, to switch on
ambitieux (f. **ambitieuse**) ambitious
amener to bring
amer (f. **amère**) bitter
amoureux (f. **amoureuse**) in love
amusant fun
amuser to amuse; **s'amuser** to have fun, to have a good time
an m. year
ancien (f. **ancienne**) old, former

anneau m. ring
annonce f. announcement; **annonce publicitaire** advertisement; **petite annonce** classified ad
annoncer to announce
anonyme anonymous
antenne f. antenna
apercevoir to notice
appeler to call; **s'appeler** to be called
apporter to bring
apprendre to learn, to teach
approcher to approach; **s'approcher** to come near
appui m. support
après-demain day after tomorrow
arbre m. tree
argent m. money, silver
argenterie f. silverware
arrêter to stop, to arrest; **s'arrêter (de)** to stop
arriver to arrive, to happen
article m. article
aspirine f. aspirin
assassiner to assassinate
asseoir to seat; **s'asseoir** to sit down
assez rather, enough
assis seated
assurance f. insurance
astre m. star
astronaute m. & f. astronaut
astronef m. spaceship
attendre to wait (for); **s'attendre à** to expect
attentivement attentively
atterrir to land
auberge f. inn
aucun none
audace f. audacity
aujourd'hui today
au lieu de instead of
au secours! help!
aussitôt que as soon as
au sujet de about

autant (de) so much, as many
autour de around
autre other; **un/une autre** another
autrement otherwise
avance: en avance early
avantage m. advantage
avant-hier the day before yesterday
avenir m. future
avocat m. (f. **avocate**) lawyer; **avocat de la défense** defense lawyer
avoir to have; **avoir besoin de** to need; **avoir envie de** to feel like; **avoir honte de** to be ashamed of; **avoir mal à** to have an ache; **avoir raison** to be right

B

bague f. ring
baiser m. kiss
Balance f. Libra
baleine f. whale
bande f. band; **bande dessinée** comic strip
banque f. bank
barbe f. beard
bas low
baskets f. pl. sneakers
bataille f. battle
bateau m. boat
batterie f. drums
bavard talkative
beau (f. **belle**) handsome, beautiful
beaucoup a lot, many; **beaucoup de** a lot of, many
Bélier m. Aries
bête stupid
bêtise f. nonsense
bien well; **bien sûr** of course

bientôt soon; **à bientôt** see you soon

bienvenue f. welcome; **soyez le bienvenu** welcome

bijou m. (pl. **bijoux**) jewel

bijouterie f. jewelry store

bijoutier m. (f. **bijoutière**) jeweler

billet m. ticket; **billet doux** love note

blague f. joke

blazer m. blazer jacket

blesser to hurt; **se blesser** to hurt oneself

boire to drink

boisson f. drink

boîte f. box; **boîte aux lettres** mailbox

bon (f. **bonne**) good; **bon sens** common sense

bonbon m. candy

bonheur m. happiness

bord m. border; **au bord de la mer** at the seashore

botte f. boot

boucher m. (f. **bouchère**) butcher

boucle f. buckle, loop; **boucle d'oreille** earring

bouger to move

boulanger m. (f. **boulangère**) baker

bouteille f. bottle

bouton m. button

brillant shiny, outstanding

briller to shine

broche f. pin, brooch

brosse f. brush; **brosse à dents** toothbrush

brosser to brush; **se brosser les cheveux** to brush one's hair; **se brosser les dents** to brush one's teeth

brouillard m. fog

brouiller to mix up; **se brouiller** to quarrel

bruit m. noise

brume f. mist

bureau m. desk, office

C

ça that

cacher to hide; **se cacher** to hide oneself

cadeau m. gift

cadran m. dial

caillou m. (pl. **cailloux**) pebble

caisse f. cashier's, cash register

caissier m. (f. **caissière**) cashier

calculer to calculate

calvitie f. baldness

camarade m. & f. comrade, friend

campagne f. country

canard m. duck

cantine f. cafeteria

capitaine m. captain

capot m. hood (of a car)

Capricorne m. Capricorn

car because

carré square

carrière f. career

carte f. card, map; **carte postale** postcard

cas m. case; **en cas de** in case of

casser to break; **se casser (un bras)** to break (one's arm)

cauchemar m. nightmare

ce this, that; **ce que** what; **ce qui** what

cela that, it

célèbre famous

célébrer to celebrate

celle f. the one; **celles** f. those

cent hundred; **pour cent** percent

centenaire one hundred years old

centre commercial m. shopping mall

cependant however

ceux m. pl. these, those

chacun each one

chaîne f. chain

chance f. luck; **bonne chance** good luck

changer to change

chanson f. song

chanter to sing

chapeau m. hat

chapitre m. chapter

chaque each, every

charmant charming

châtain chestnut-brown

château m. castle; **château de sable** sand castle

chaussure f. shoe

chauve bald

chemin m. way

chemise f. shirt; **chemise de nuit** nightgown

chèque m. check

cher (f. **chère**) dear, expensive

chercher to look for

chic stylish

chiffre m. number

choisir to choose

choix m. choice

chose f. thing; **quelque chose** something

chou m. (pl. **choux**) cabbage, puff pastry; **mon chou** sweetheart

chouette! great!

ciel m. (pl. **cieux**) sky

ciseaux m. pl. scissors

citron m. lemon

clarinette f. clarinet

clef f. key

clou m. nail

code postal m. zip code

cœur m. heart; **par cœur** by heart

coffre m. chest, trunk (of a car); **coffre-fort** safe

coiffeur m. (f. **coiffeuse**) hairdresser

coin m. corner

coincer to corner

col m. collar, mountain pass

colère f. anger; **se mettre en colère** to become angry

collectionner to collect

collier m. necklace

combien how many, how much

combinaison f. combination; **combinaison spatiale** space suit

commander to order

comme like, as

commencer to begin

commentaire m. commentary

commissariat de police m. police station

commode f. chest of drawers

commun common

compagnie f. company

compétence f. competence

compétiteur (f. **compétitrice**) competitor

complet complete

complet m. man's suit

complice m. accomplice

composition f. composition

compréhensif (f. **compréhensive**) understanding

comprendre to understand; to include

compter to count

concerner to concern
conducteur m. (f. **conductrice**) driver
conduire to drive, to conduct
conduite f. conduct; **leçon de conduite** f. driving lesson
confiance f. confidence
confort m. comfort
congélateur m. freezer
connaître to know, to be acquainted with
conseil m. advice
conseiller m. (f. **conseillère**) counselor, advisor
conseiller to counsel, to advise
construire to build
consulter to consult
conte m. short story; **conte de fées** fairy tale
content glad
continuer to continue
contraire: au contraire on the contrary
contrat m. contract
contravention f. parking ticket, fine
contre against
contretemps m. mishap, delay
copain m. (f. **copine**) friend, pal
coquillage m. shell
cordialement cordially
cordonnier m. (f. **cordonnière**) shoemaker
corriger to correct
Corse f. Corsica
coton m. cotton
coucher to put to bed; **se coucher** to go to bed
couper to cut
coupon m. remnant (of material)
coureur m. (f. **coureuse**) racer; **coureur à pied** runner
courir to run
cours m. course
course f. race
court short
coussin m. cushion
coûter to cost; **coûter les yeux de la tête** to cost an arm and a leg
couvert m. place setting (at table); **mettre le couvert** to set the table
couvert covered
couvrir to cover
cravate f. tie

crevette f. shrimp
crier to scream
crocodile m. crocodile
croire to believe
croisière f. cruise
croix f. cross
cruauté f. cruelty
cuir m. leather
cuisiner to cook
cuivre m. brass; m. pl. brass instruments
curieux (f. **curieuse**) curious
cyclisme m. cycling
cycliste m. & f. cyclist
cygne m. swan

D

d'abord at first
d'accord O.K., I agree
d'habitude usually
de of, from
debout standing
début m. beginning
décan m. subdivision of a zodiacal sign
découvrir to discover
décrire to describe
dedans inside
dehors outside
déjà already
demain tomorrow
demande f. order
demander to ask (for); **se demander** to wonder
démarrer to start
demeurer to live
dentifrice m. toothpaste
déodorant m. deodorant
dépêcher: se dépêcher to hurry
dépense f. expenditure
dépensier (f. **dépensière**) extravagant
depuis since, for; **depuis quand** since when
dernier (f. **dernière**) last
derrière behind
dès que as soon as
désagréable unpleasant
descendre to descend, to go down
désespéré hopeless
déshabiller to undress; **se déshabiller** to undress oneself
désolé sorry
désordre m. disorder

dessiner to draw
destructif (f. **destructive**) destructive
détaillant m. retailer
détester to hate
dette f. debt
deuxième second
devant in front of
devenir to become
devoir to have to, must; to owe
diamant m. diamond
diamètre m. diameter
dinde f. turkey
diplôme m. diploma
dire to say, to tell
direct direct; **en direct** live (radio, T.V.)
directeur m. (f. **directrice**) director, manager
discuter to discuss
domestique m. & f. servant
donc therefore
donner to give; **donner sur** to face
dormir to sleep
dos m. back
doucement softly, gently
douceur f. sweetness
douche f. shower
doux (f. **douce**) soft
drapeau m. flag
droit m. right
durer to last

E

échapper to escape; **s'échapper de** to escape from
écharpe f. scarf
échec m. failure
économe thrifty
écouler: s'écouler to flow
écouter to listen (to)
écraser to crush
écrire to write
écureuil m. squirrel
éditorial m. editorial
effacer to erase
efficace efficient
égal equal
également equally
électricien m. (f. **électricienne**) electrician
éliminer to eliminate
embarrassant embarrassing
embrasser to kiss

émeraude *f.* emerald
emmener to take along
empêcher to prevent
emploi *m.* job
employé *m.* (*f.* **employée**) employee
employer to use
empreinte *f.* print; **empreinte de pas** footprint; **empreinte digitale** fingerprint
en in, some, of it, about it, from it
enchanter to delight
encore yet, still; **encore une fois** again
endormir to put to sleep; **s'endormir** to fall asleep
endroit *m.* place
enfance *f.* childhood
enfin finally
enlever to take off, to remove
ennuyer to bore; **s'ennuyer** to be bored
ennuyeux (*f.* **ennuyeuse**) boring
enregistrer to record
enseigner to teach
ensemble together
ensemble *m.* outfit
ensuite next, then
entendre to hear; **s'entendre avec** to get along with
entier (*f.* **entière**) entire
entourer to surround
entraîner to train; **s'entraîner** to train oneself
entrevue *f.* interview
enveloppe *f.* envelope
environ about
envoyer to send
épais (*f.* **épaisse**) thick
épargner to save
épatant swell, great
épousseter to dust
époux *m.* (*f.* **épouse**) spouse
épuisé exhausted
équipage *m.* crew
erreur *f.* mistake
espace *m.* space
espèce *f.* species, type
espérer to hope
essayer to try, to try on
essence *f.* gas
établir to establish
étage *m.* floor
étagère *f.* bookshelf
étape *f.* lap, stage
éteindre to turn off (*lights*)

étendre to spread out; **s'étendre** to spread out
éternité *f.* eternity
étoile *f.* star
étonnement *m.* surprise
étonner to surprise, to astonish
étranger (*f.* **étrangère**) foreign
être to be; **être à** to belong to; **être en train de** to be in the middle of; **être sur le point de** to be on the verge of
être humain *m.* human being
étroit narrow
eux them, they
événement *m.* event
évidemment obviously
évident obvious
éviter to avoid
exagérer to exaggerate
exclamer: s'exclamer to exclaim
exercer, s'exercer to exercise, to practice
explication *f.* explanation
expliquer to explain
exploration *f.* exploration
exposition *f.* exhibit
extraterrestre *m. & f.* extraterrestrial

F

face: en face de facing
fâcher to anger; **se fâcher** to become angry
facile easy
façon *f.* fashion, manner
faire to do, to make; **faire attention** to pay attention; **faire de la planche à voile** to go windsurfing; **faire des courses** to go shopping; **faire du cheval** to go horseback riding; **faire du patin à glace** to go ice-skating; **faire du patin à roulettes** to go roller-skating; **faire du ski (alpin)** to go skiing; **faire du ski nautique** to go water-skiing; **faire du vélo** to go biking; **faire partie de** to be part of; **faire une croisière** to go on a cruise; **faire une promenade** to go for a walk, a ride; **faire une randonnée** to go hiking; **s'en faire** to worry; **ne vous en faites pas!** don't worry!

fait: en fait as a matter of fact
falloir to be necessary
familier (*f.* **familière**) familiar
fatigué tired
fauteuil *m.* armchair
faux (*f.* **fausse**) false, wrong
félicitations *f. pl.* congratulations
fermer to close
fermier *m.* (*f.* **fermière**) farmer
fête *f.* feast, party, holiday
feu *m.* fire; **feu rouge** red light
feuilleter to leaf through
ficeler to tie
fier (*f.* **fière**) proud
fièrement proudly
fin *f.* end
finalement finally
finir to finish
flûte *f.* flute
fois *f.* time; **une fois** once
fonder to found
formation *f.* training
forme *f.* shape
former to form
fort strong, loud
four *m.* oven
fourmi *f.* ant
fournir to supply
frais *m. pl.* expenses
franc (*f.* **franche**) frank
franchement frankly
frapper to hit, to knock
frein *m.* brake
fréquenter to frequent
frit fried
froisser to offend
fusée *f.* rocket

G

gagnant *m.* winner
garantie *f.* guarantee
garantir to guarantee
gaspiller to waste
Gémeaux *m. pl.* Gemini
généralement generally
genou *m.* (*pl.* **genoux**) knee
gens *m. or f. pl.* people
gentil (*f.* **gentille**) nice, kind
gentiment gently, softly, nicely
germer to germinate
gestion *f.* administration, management
gilet *m.* vest
girafe *f.* giraffe

goûter to taste
grâce à thanks to
grand big, tall; **grand magasin** *m.* department store
gros (*f.* **grosse**) fat, big
guichet *m.* booth
guitare *f.* guitar

H

habiller to dress; **s'habiller** to dress oneself, to get dressed
habitant *m.* inhabitant
habité inhabited
habiter to live in
haleine *f.* breath
haut high; **haut les mains!** hands up!
héritage *m.* inheritance
heure *f.* hour; **de bonne heure** early
heureusement luckily, fortunately
heureux (*f.* **heureuse**) happy
hibou *m.* (*pl.* **hiboux**) owl
hier yesterday
histoire *f.* story
historique historical
honnête honest
hors-d'œuvre *m.* (*pl.* **hors-d'œuvre**) appetizer
hôtesse *f.* hostess; **hôtesse de l'air** flight attendant, stewardess
huile *f.* oil
humour *m.* humor

I

ignorer to ignore
il y a there is, there are; **il y a +** *time* ago
île *f.* island
immobile motionless
imperméable *m.* raincoat
implantation *f.* implantation
impoli rude
impressionner to impress
inattendu unexpected
inconnu unknown
incroyable incredible, unbelievable
indiquer to indicate
ingénieur *m.* engineer
injure *f.* insult
inquiet (*f.* **inquiète**) worried

inspecteur *m.* inspector; **inspecteur de police** detective
installation *f.* equipment, installation
instrument *m.* instrument; **instrument à cordes** string instrument; **instrument à percussion** percussion; **instrument à vent** wind instrument
intéresser to interest; **s'intéresser à** to be interested in
intérêt *m.* interest
intérieur *m.* interior; **à l'intérieur de** inside
interrompre to interrupt
interview *f.* interview
invité *m.* guest

J

jaloux (*f.* **jalouse**) jealous
jasmin *m.* jasmine
jauni yellowed
jean *m.* jeans
jeté de lit *m.* bedspread
jeter to throw, to throw away
jeu *m.* game
jeune young; **jeune marié** *m.* (*f.* **jeune mariée**) newlywed
jouer to play; **jouer à** to play (*sport*); **jouer au bowling** to go bowling; **jouer de** to play (*musical instrument*)
joujou *m.* (*pl.* **joujoux**) toy
jour *m.* day
journal *m.* newspaper
journaliste *m. & f.* journalist
journée *f.* day
juge *m.* judge
Jupiter Jupiter
jus *m.* juice
jusqu'à until
juste fair

K

kangourou *m.* kangaroo
klaxon *m.* horn

L

lâcher to let go
laine *f.* wool
laisser to leave, to allow

lampadaire *m.* floor lamp
large wide
larme *f.* tear
lave-vaisselle *m.* dishwasher
laver to wash; **se laver** to wash oneself
léger (*f.* **légère**) light
lendemain *m.* next day
lentement slowly
léopard *m.* leopard
leur their, to them
lever to raise; **se lever** to get up
lieu *m.* place
limiter to limit
lin *m.* linen
Lion *m.* Leo
liquide liquid; **en liquide** cash
lire to read
livre *f.* pound
livrer to deliver
location *f.* rental
loin (**de**) far (from)
longtemps a long time
lorsque when
loterie *f.* lottery
lourd heavy
lui him, to him, to her
lune *f.* moon
lunettes *f. pl.* eyeglasses
luxueux (*f.* **luxueuse**) luxurious

M

machine à laver *f.* washing machine
magicien *m.* (*f.* **magicienne**) magician
magie *f.* magic
maigrir to lose weight
maintenant now
mais but
maïs *m.* corn
maître *m.* *master*
maître-nageur *m.* lifeguard
mal bad, badly; **mal élevé** ill-bred
malheureusement unfortunately
malheureux (*f.* **malheureuse**) unhappy
malin (*f.* **maligne**) clever
mallette *f.* attaché case
manche *f.* sleeve; **à manches courtes** short-sleeved; **à manches longues** long-sleeved; **sans manches** sleeveless

manger to eat
mannequin *m.* fashion model
manquer to miss
manteau *m.* coat
maquillage *m.* makeup
maquiller: se maquiller to apply makeup
marchand *m.* merchant
marchandise *f.* merchandise
marché *m.* market
marcher to walk; to work, to function
mari *m.* husband
mariage *m.* wedding
marier to wed; se marier to get married
marin sea
marocain Moroccan
Mars Mars
matin *m.* morning
mauvais wrong, bad
me me, to me
mécanicien *m.* (*f.* mécanicienne) mechanic
méchant naughty
médicament *m.* medicine
meilleur better; le meilleur the best
même same, even
mener to lead
meneur *m.* (*f.* meneuse) leader
mensonge *m.* lie
mensualité *f.* monthly installment
menteur *m.* (*f.* menteuse) liar
mentir to lie
mer *f.* sea; au bord de la mer at the seashore
Mercure Mercury
merveille *f.* marvel
merveilleux (*f.* merveilleuse) marvelous
mesurer to measure
météo *f.* weather forecast
métier *m.* trade
métrage *m.* length in meter
mettre to put, to put on; mettre le couvert to set the table; se mettre à to begin; se mettre à table to sit at the table (to eat); se mettre en colère to become angry
meuble *m.* piece of furniture
meubler to furnish
Mexique *m.* Mexico
midi *m.* southern region (of a country)

miel *m.* honey
mieux better; le mieux the best
mille thousand
milliard *m.* billion
millier *m.* thousand, about a thousand
miroir *m.* mirror
moins less; moins . . . que less . . . than
mois *m.* month
modèle *m.* model, pattern
monde *m.* world
monnaie *f.* money, change
monstrueux (*f.* monstrueuse) monstrous
montagne *f.* mountain
monter to go up
montre *f.* watch; montre-bracelet *f.* wristwatch
montrer to show
moquer to mock; se moquer de to make fun of
mort *f.* death
mot *m.* word
moteur *m.* engine
mouche *f.* fly
mouchoir *m.* handkerchief; mouchoir en papier tissue
mourir to die; mourir de rire to die laughing
moustache *f.* mustache
moustique *m.* mosquito
mouvementé eventful
mur *m.* wall

N

nager to swim
naissance *f.* birth
naître to be born
naturel (*f.* naturelle) natural
navette *f.* shuttle; navette spatiale space shuttle
ne . . . aucun not any
ne . . . jamais never
ne . . . ni . . . ni neither . . . nor
ne . . . personne nobody, no one
ne . . . plus no longer
ne . . . que only
ne . . . rien nothing
neiger to snow
Neptune Neptune
nerf *m.* nerve
nettoyer to clean
neuf (*f.* neuve) new
neveu *m.* nephew

niveau *m.* level
nom *m.* name
nord *m.* north
note *f.* grade, note
nourriture *f.* food
nous we, us, to us
nouveau (*f.* nouvelle) new; de nouveau again
nouvelle *f.* news item; *f. pl.* news
nuageux cloudy
numéro *m.* number

O

obéir to obey
objet *m.* object
occupé busy
offert offered
offrir to offer
omelette *f.* omelet
once *f.* ounce
or *m.* gold
orangeade *f.* orangeade
ordonner to order
oubli *m.* omission
oublier to forget
ours *m.* bear
ouvert opened
ouverture *f.* opening
ouvrir to open

P

paix *f.* peace
palais *m.* palace
panier *m.* basket
panneau *m.* sign, billboard; panneau de signalisation road sign
pansement *m.* bandage
pantalon *m.* pants
panthère *f.* panther
pantoufle *f.* slipper
papier *m.* paper; papier hygiénique toilet paper
paquet *m.* package
par by, per
paraître to appear, to seem
parasol *m.* beach umbrella
pare-chocs *m.* bumper
pareil (*f.* pareille) similar
paresseux (*f.* paresseuse) lazy
parfait perfect
parfum *m.* perfume, flavor
partir to leave

partout everywhere
passager *m.* (*f.* **passagère**) passenger
passe-temps *m.* hobby
passé last, past
passer to pass, to spend (*time*); **se passer** to happen
pâtes *f. pl.* pasta
patin *m.* skate; **patins à roulettes** roller skates
patiner to skate
pâtisserie *f.* pastry, pastry shop
patte *f.* animal leg *or* foot, paw
pauvre poor
payer to pay
peau *f.* skin
pêcher to fish
peigne *m.* comb
peigner to comb; **se peigner** to comb oneself
pelle *f.* shovel
pendant during, while
pendant d'oreille *m.* drop earring
penser to think
perdre to lose
perfectionniste perfectionist
perle *f.* pearl
permettre to permit, to allow
personnel *m.* personnel
perte *f.* loss
peser to weigh
peu few, little
peur *f.* fear
peureux (*f.* **peureuse**) fearful
phare *m.* headlight
pharmacie *f.* pharmacy, drugstore
pharmacien *m.* (*f.* **pharmacienne**) pharmacist
photographe *m. & f.* photographer
pièce *f.* piece, room; **pièce de monnaie** coin; **pièce de théâtre** play
piéton *m.* (*f.* **piétonne**) pedestrian
pilote *m.* pilot
pin *m.* pine tree
pistolet *m.* gun
placer to place, to put
plaire to please
plaisanterie *f.* joke
plaisir *m.* pleasure
planche à voile *f.* windsurfer
plancher *m.* floor
planète *f.* planet

plaque *f.* plate; **plaque d'immatriculation** license plate
plat *m.* dish
pleurer to cry
plombier *m.* plumber
plus more; **plus ou moins** more or less; **plus . . . que** more . . . than; **plus tard** later
plusieurs several
pneu *m.* tire
poche *f.* pocket
pochette *f.* envelope, sleeve
poème *m.* poem
poids *m.* weight
Poissons *m. pl.* Pisces
poli polite
policier *m.* police officer
poliment politely
polyglotte multilingual
porter to wear
portière *f.* car door
poser to put; **poser une question** to ask a question
posséder to possess, to own
poste *f.* post office
poste *m.* job
poterie *f.* pottery
pou *m.* (*pl.* **poux**) louse
pouce *m.* inch, thumb
pour for, in order to
poursuivre to pursue
pourtant still, nevertheless
pousser to push, to grow; **pousser un cri** to scream out; **pousser un soupir de soulagement** to utter a sigh of relief
pouvoir to be able to, can
pratique practical
précédent preceding
précieux (*f.* **précieuse**) precious
précipiter to rush; **se précipiter sur** to jump on
prédire to predict
préférer to prefer
premier (*f.* **première**) first
prendre to take; **prendre une douche** to take a shower
préparatif *m.* preparation
près (**de**) near
présenter to introduce; **se présenter** to introduce oneself
presque almost
prêt ready
prêter to lend

prise *f.* grasp
prison *f.* jail
prix *m.* price, prize
prochain next
procureur *m.* prosecutor
programmeur *m.* (*f.* **programmeuse**) programmer
projet *m.* plan, project
promenade *f.* walk, ride
promener to walk; **se promener** to take a walk
promettre to promise
prononcer to pronounce
propriétaire *m. & f.* owner
protéger to protect
provisions *f. pl.* provision
puis then
pyjama *m.* pajamas

Q

qualité *f.* quality
quand when; **quand même** anyway
quel (*f.* **quelle**) which
quelque chose something
quelqu'un someone
quitter to leave
quotidien (*f.* **quotidienne**) daily

R

raconter to tell
radin stingy
radis *m.* radish
raffiné refined
ragoût *m.* stew
raison *f.* reason; **avoir raison** to be right
raisonnable reasonable
ralentir to slow down
randonnée *f.* hike
rang *m.* row
ranger to put in order
rapide fast
rappeler to call back; **se rappeler** to recall
rapporter: se rapporter à to refer to
rareté *f.* rarity
raser to shave; **se raser** to shave oneself
rasoir *m.* razor
rater to fail
rationnel (*f.* **rationnelle**) rational

rayon *m.* department (of a department store)
réagir to react
réaliser to direct (*film*)
récemment recently
recevoir to receive
réclamer to claim
recommander to recommend
récréation *f.* recess
réduit reduced
réfléchir to think
réfrigérateur *m.* refrigerator
règle *f.* rule, ruler
régler to set
règne *m.* kingdom
régner to reign
regretter to regret, to be sorry
relecture *f.* rereading
remède *m.* remedy
remercier to thank
remettre to put back; **remettre en cause** to question
remplacer to replace
remplir to fill
rencontrer to meet
rendre to return; **se rendre compte** to realize
renouveler to renew
renseignement *m.* piece of information
rentrer to return
renvoyer to fire
reparaître to reappear
réparation *f.* repair
réparer to repair
repas *m.* meal
répéter to repeat, to rehearse
répondre to answer
réponse *f.* answer
reportage *m.* reporting; **reportage sportif** sports report
repos *m.* rest
reposer: se reposer to relax, to rest
reprendre to take back
requin *m.* shark
réservoir *m.* tank; **réservoir d'essence** gas tank
résoudre to resolve
ressembler to look like
rester to remain, to stay
retour *m.* return; **de retour** back (*home*)
retourner to go back; to return
réussir to succeed
rêve *m.* dream
réveil *m.* alarm clock

réveiller to wake (up); **se réveiller** to wake up
révéler to reveal
revenant *m.* ghost
revenir to come back; **revenir à** to cost, to come to
revoir to see again
revue *f.* magazine
rideau *m.* curtain
ridicule ridiculous
rien nothing
rigoler to joke
rire to laugh
rivière *f.* river
riz *m.* rice
robe *f.* dress; **robe de chambre** robe; **robe du soir** gown
roi *m.* king
roman *m.* novel
rosbif *m.* roast beef
rôti roasted; **rôti de bœuf** roast beef
roue *f.* wheel
rougir to blush
rouler to drive, to roll; **rouler à bicyclette** to ride a bicycle
route *f.* road
rubrique *f.* section (*newspaper, magazine*); **rubrique sentimentale** advice to the lovelorn
rue *f.* street

S

sable *m.* sand
sage wise, quiet
Sagittaire *m.* Sagittarius
sain sound, healthy; **sain et sauf** safe and sound
salle *f.* room; **salle d'attente** waiting room
salut! Hi!
sans without
satellite *m.* satellite
satisfaire to satisfy
Saturne Saturn
saucisse *f.* sausage
sauver to save; **se sauver** to run away
saveur *f.* flavor, taste
savoir to know (how to)
savon *m.* soap
scolaire school
Scorpion *m.* Scorpio
seau *m.* pail

sec (*f.* **sèche**) dry
sèche-linge *m.* dryer
secours *m.* help; **au secours!** help!
sélectionner to select
selon according to
semaine *f.* week
sens *m.* sense; **bon sens** common sense
sensible sensitive
sentir to feel, to smell
serpent *m.* snake
serrure *f.* lock
serveur *m.* (*f.* **serveuse**) waiter
servir to serve
sévère strict
seul alone, only
seulement only
short *m.* shorts
si so, yes, if
siècle *m.* century
sinon otherwise
sirène *f.* siren
ski nautique *m.* waterskiing
société *f.* society, company
soie *f.* silk
soigneusement carefully
soir *m.* evening
soirée *f.* evening; party
solaire solar; **système solaire** *m.* solar system
soldes *m. pl.* clearance sale
soleil *m.* sun
solitaire *m.* diamond ring
sonner to ring
sortir to go out
soudain suddenly
souffrir to suffer
souhaiter to wish
soulever to lift
sourire to smile
souvenir: se souvenir de to remember
souvent often
spatial spatial; **navette spatiale** *f.* space shuttle
spécialiser: se spécialiser to specialize in
studieux (*f.* **studieuse**) studious
stupéfié astounded
succès *m.* success
sucer to suck
sud *m.* South
suggérer to suggest
suisse Swiss
suivant following
suivre to follow

sujet *m.* subject
sûr sure
surestimer to overestimate
surtout especially
sympathique nice

T

table *f.* table; **table de nuit** night table
tableau *m.* painting
taille *f.* size
tambour *m.* drum
tandis que while
tant (de) so much, so many; **tant pis** too bad
tapis *m.* rug
tard late
tarte *f.* pie
tas *m.* pile
Taureau *m.* Taurus
te you, to you
tel que (*f.* **telle**) such as
tellement so
témoin *m.* witness
tempête *f.* storm
temps *m.* time, weather; **de temps en temps** from time to time
terminer to end
terre *f.* earth, ground; **par terre** on the ground
terrestre land
terroir *m.* soil
thé *m.* tea; **thé glacé** iced tea
timbre *m.* stamp
tiroir *m.* drawer
tissu *m.* material, fabric
titre *m.* title
tomber to fall; **tomber d'accord** to come to an agreement; **tomber malade** to fall sick
tonne *f.* ton
tortue *f.* turtle
tôt early
toujours always
tour *f.* tower; *m.* turn; **tour du monde** trip around the world
tout all, every; **tout de suite** immediately; **tout d'un coup** suddenly; **tout le monde** everybody; **tout le temps** all

the time; **tous les deux** both; **tout seul** all alone
train *m.* train; **en train de** in the middle of
traiter to treat
tranquilité *f.* tranquility
tranquille tranquil, calm
travailler to work
traverser to cross
très very
trésor *m.* treasure
tribunal *m.* court of justice
tricot *m.* knitting
tricoter to knit
triste sad
trombone *m.* trombone
tromper: se tromper to make a mistake
trompette *f.* trumpet
trop too much, too many
trou *m.* hole
trouver to find; **se trouver** to be located
truc *m.* trick
type *m.* guy
typique typical

U

Uranus Uranus
urgence *f.* emergency
utiliser to use

V

vacances *f. pl.* vacation
vague *f.* wave
vaisseau *m.* vessel; **vaisseau spatial** spaceship
vaisselle *f.* dishes
valeur *f.* value
valise *f.* suitcase
vallée *f.* valley
vase *m.* vase
veau *m.* veal
vendeur *m.* (*f.* **vendeuse**) salesclerk
vendre to sell
venir to come; **venir de** to have just
vente *f.* sale

ventre *m.* abdomen, belly
Vénus Venus
vérifier to check
vérité *f.* truth
vers toward, at about
Verseau *m.* Aquarius
verser to pour
vêtements *m. pl.* clothes
vétérinaire *m. & f.* veterinarian
victime *f.* victim
vide empty
vie *f.* life; **vie de château** life of ease
Vierge *f.* Virgo
vieux (*f.* **vieille**) old
vif (*f.* **vive**) bright, lively
village *m.* village
violemment violently
violon *m.* violin
vipère *f.* viper
visage *m.* face
vitamine *f.* vitamin
vite quickly
vitesse *f.* speed
vitre *f.* pane of glass; car window
vivre to live
voici here is, here are
voilà there is, there are
voile *f.* sail
voir to see
voisin *m.* neighbor
voiture *f.* car
voix *f.* voice
vol *m.* flight, robbery
volant *m.* steering wheel
voler to steal
voleur *m.* (*f.* **voleuse**) thief
voter to vote
vouloir to want, to wish
vous you, to you; **vous-même** yourself
voyager to travel
voyant *m.* fortune teller
vrai true, real; **à vrai dire** truly, really
vraiment really

Y

y there, it, them
yeux *m. pl.* eyes

English-French Vocabulary

A

able: be able pouvoir
accomplice complice *m.*
accordion accordéon *m.*
acquainted: be acquainted with connaître
active actif (*f.* active)
actively activement
advertisement annonce publicitaire *f.*
ago il y a + *time*
allow permettre, laisser
angry fâché; **become angry** se fâcher
announce annoncer
ant fourmi *f.*
antenna antenne *f.*
armchair fauteuil *m.*
arrange arranger
article article *m.*
as . . . as aussi . . . que
asleep endormi; **fall asleep** s'endormir
aspirin aspirine *f.*
astronaut astronaute *m. & f.*
attentive attentif (*f.* attentive)
attentively attentivement

B

baker boulanger *m.* (*f.* boulangère)
bandage pansement *m.*
bank banque *f.*; **bank employee** employé de banque *m.* (*f.* employée)
basket panier *m.*
be être; **be able** pouvoir; **be well** aller bien
beach plage *f.*; **beach umbrella** parasol *m.*
bear ours *m.*
beautiful beau (*f.* belle)
become devenir
believe croire
best meilleur, mieux
better meilleur, mieux

bicycle, bike vélo *m.*
billion milliard *m.*
blazer blazer *m.*
boat bateau *m.*; **go boating** faire une promenade en bateau
bookshelf étagère *f.*
boot botte *f.*
bore ennuyer; **be bored** s'ennuyer
bowling bowling *m.*; **go bowling** jouer au bowling
brake frein *m.*
brass cuivre *m.*; **brass instruments** cuivres *m. pl.*
break casser; se casser (*an arm*)
bring apporter; amener
brooch broche *f.*
brush brosse *f.*; **brush one's hair** se brosser les cheveux; **brush one's teeth** se brosser les dents
bumper pare-chocs *m.*
butcher boucher *m.* (*f.* bouchère)
buy acheter

C

call appeler; téléphoner; **be called** s'appeler
car voiture *f.*; **car door** portière *f.*
cash register caisse *f.*
cashier caissier (*f.* caissière)
cashier's caisse *f.*
castle château *m.*; **sand castle** château de sable
century siècle *m.*
chain chaîne *f.*
change changer
checkered à carreaux
chest of drawers commode *f.*
choose choisir
clarinet clarinette *f.*
classified ad petite annonce *f.*
clean nettoyer
clothes vêtements *m. pl.*
coat manteau *m.*

coin pièce (de monnaie) *f.*
collar col *m.*
collect collectionner
comb peigne *m.*
comb (one's hair) se peigner
come venir; **come back** revenir
comic strip bande dessinée *f.*
cook cuisiner
corn maïs *m.*
cotton coton *m.*
country campagne *f.*
court (of justice) tribunal *m.*
cover couvrir
crocodile crocodile *m.*
cruel cruel (*f.* cruelle)
cruise croisière *f.*; **go on a cruise** faire une croisière
curtain rideau *m.*

D

day jour *m.*, journée *f.*; **day after tomorrow** après-demain; **day before yesterday** avant-hier; **next day** lendemain *m.*
defendant accusé *m.*
defense lawyer avocat de la défense *m.*
deodorant déodorant *m.*
department (*of a department store*) rayon *m.*
department store grand magasin *m.*
destructive destructif (*f.* destructive)
diamond diamant *m.*
discover découvrir
discuss discuter
dish plat *m.*
dishwasher lave-vaisselle *m.*
disorder désordre *m.*
do faire
draw dessiner
drawer tiroir *m.*
dress robe *f.*; **get dressed** s'habiller
drink boire; boisson *f.*

drive conduire
drugstore pharmacie *f.*
drum tambour *m.*
drums batterie *f.*
dry sec (*f.* sèche)
dryer sèche-linge *m.*
duck canard *m.*

E

early tôt, de bonne heure
earring boucle d'oreille *f.*; **drop earring** pendant d'oreille *m.*
earth terre *f.*
easily facilement
editorial éditorial *m.*
electrician électricien *m.* (*f.* électricienne)
emerald émeraude *f.*
employee employé *m.* (*f.* employée)
engine moteur *m.*
enough assez (de)
envelope enveloppe *f.*
eternity éternité *f.*
every chaque
except sauf
exhibit exposition *f.*
expensive cher (*f.* chère)
exploration exploration *f.*
eye œil *m.* (*pl.* yeux);
  eyeglasses lunettes *f. pl.*

F

famous célèbre
farmer fermier *m.* (*f.* fermière)
feel sentir; **feel well** aller bien
festival fête *f.*
few peu (de)
find trouver
fingerprint empreinte digitale *f.*
finish finir, terminer
first premier *m.* (*f.* première)
fish pêcher
flight attendant hôtesse de l'air *f.*; steward *m.*
floor plancher *m.*
flute flûte *f.*
follow suivre
food nourriture *f.*
freezer congélateur *m.*
frequently fréquemment
friend ami *m.*, copain *m.* (*f.* copine); camarade *m. & f.*
fun amusement *m.*; **have fun** s'amuser; **make fun of** se moquer de

furniture meubles *m. pl.*; **piece of furniture** meuble *m.*

G

gas essence *f.*; **gas tank** réservoir d'essence *m.*
get up se lever
gift cadeau *m.*
giraffe *f.* girafe
go aller; **go bicycling** faire du vélo; **go out** sortir; **go to bed** se coucher
gold or *m.*
good bon (*f.* bonne)
guitar guitare *f.*
gun pistolet *m.*

H

hair cheveux *m. pl.*
hairdresser coiffeur *m.* (*f.* coiffeuse)
happy heureux (*f.* heureuse)
have avoir; **have a good time** s'amuser; **have to** devoir
headlight phare *m.*
hide cacher; (**oneself**) se cacher
hike faire une randonnée; randonnée *f.*
hobby passe-temps *m.*
hole trou *m.*
hood (*of a car*) capot *m.*
hope espérer
horn klaxon *m.*
horseback riding faire du cheval
how many, how much combien
hurry se dépêcher
hurt (**oneself**) se blesser

I

instrument instrument *m.*; **string instrument** instrument à cordes; **wind instrument** instrument à vent
interesting intéressant
iron fer *m.*

J

jail prison *f.*
jeans jean *m.*
jewel bijou *m.* (*pl.* bijoux)

jeweler bijoutier *m.* (*f.* bijoutière)
jewelry store bijouterie *f.*
job métier *m.*; poste *m.*
journalist journaliste *m. & f.*
judge juge *m.*
juice jus *m.*
Jupiter Jupiter
just: have just venir de

K

kangaroo kangourou *m.*
key clef *f.*
king roi *m.*
kingdom règne *m.*, royaume *m.*
knit tricoter
know savoir, connaître

L

lamb agneau *m.*
lamp lampe *f.*; **floor lamp** lampadaire *m.*
last dernier (*f.* dernière)
late tard, en retard
laugh rire
law loi *f.*
lead mener
leather cuir *m.*
leave laisser, partir, quitter
lemon citron *m.*
leopard léopard *m.*
less moins; **less . . . than** moins que
license plate plaque d'immatriculation *f.*
lifeguard maître-nageur *m.*
little peu (de), petit
lively vif (*f.* vive)
look regarder; **look at oneself** se regarder
look for chercher
lot beaucoup; **a lot of** beaucoup de
low bas (*f.* basse)

M

magazine revue *f.*, magazine *m.*
mailbox boîte aux lettres *f.*
make faire
makeup maquillage *m.*; **apply makeup** se maquiller
manager directeur *m.* (*f.* directrice)

many beaucoup (de)
map carte *f.*
Mars Mars
marvel merveille *f.*
material tissu *m.*
mechanic mécanicien *m.* (*f.* mécanicienne)
merchandise marchandise *f.*
merchant marchand *m.*
Mercury Mercure
million million *m.*
mirror miroir *m.*
mistake faute *f.*; **make a mistake** se tromper
mock se moquer de
model mannequin *m.*; modèle réduit *m.*
money argent *m.*
month mois *m.*; **last month** le mois dernier; **next month** le mois prochain
moon lune *f.*
more plus; **more than** plus que
mountain montagne *f.*
much beaucoup (de)
must devoir

N

narrow étroit
necessary nécessaire; **be necessary** falloir
necklace collier *m.*
neither . . . nor ne . . . ni . . . ni
Neptune Neptune
never ne . . . jamais
new neuf (*f.* neuve), nouveau (*f.* nouvelle)
news nouvelles *f. pl.*
newspaper journal *m.*
nice gentil (*f.* gentille), sympathique
nightgown chemise de nuit *f.*
night table table de nuit *f.*
nobody ne . . . personne
no longer ne . . . plus
no one ne . . . personne
not ne . . . pas
nothing ne . . . rien
novel roman *m.*
now maintenant
number numéro *m.*; **telephone number** numéro de téléphone

O

oil huile *f.*
omelet omelette *f.*

only seul, seulement
open ouvrir, ouvert
other autre
oven four *m.*

P

pail seau *m.*
painting tableau *m.*
pajamas pyjama *m.*
panther panthère *f.*
pants pantalon *m.*
paper papier *m.*; **toilet paper** papier hygiénique
pasta pâtes *f. pl.*
past passé
pay payer
pearl perle *f.*
pebble caillou *m.* (*pl.* cailloux)
percussion instrument à percussion *m.*
perfectly parfaitement
permit permettre, laisser
pharmacist pharmacien *m.* (*f.* pharmacienne)
photographer photographe *m. & f.*
pie tarte *f.*
pilot pilote *m.*
pin broche *f.*
planet planète *f.*
play pièce de théâtre *f.*
play jouer; (*an instrument*) jouer de; (*a sport*) jouer à
plumber plombier *m.*
Pluto Pluton
poem poème *m.*
police officer policier *m.*; **police detective** inspecteur de police; **police station** commissariat de police *m.*
post office poste *f.*
postcard carte postale *f.*
pottery poterie *f.*
prefer préférer
price prix *m.*
programmer programmeur *m.* (*f.* programmeuse)
promise promettre
prosecutor procureur *m.*
proud fier (*f.* fière)
put, put on mettre; **put back** remettre; **put in order** ranger

R

raincoat imperméable *m.*
razor rasoir *m.*

read lire
really vraiment
reasonable raisonnable
receive recevoir
refrigerator réfrigérateur *m.*
relax se reposer
remember se souvenir de
remove enlever
reporting reportage *m.*
rest se reposer
return rentrer, retourner
rice riz *m.*
ring anneau *m.*, bague *f.*
river rivière *f.*
roast beef rosbif *m.*, rôti de bœuf *m.*
robbery vol *m.*
robe robe de chambre *f.*
rocket fusée *f.*
rug tapis *m.*
run courir; **run away** se sauver

S

sale vente *f.*; **clearance sale** soldes *m. pl.*
salesclerk vendeur *m.* (*f.* vendeuse)
sand sable *m.*
satellite satellite *m.*
Saturn Saturne
sausage saucisse *f.*
say dire
scarf écharpe *f.*
sea mer *f.*
see voir
sell vendre
seriously sérieusement
serve servir
shark requin *m.*
shave raser; **shave oneself** se raser
shell coquillage *m.*
shoemaker cordonnier *m.* (*f.* cordonnière)
shop faire des courses
shorts short *m.*
shovel pelle *f.*
shrimp crevette *f.*
silver argent *m.*
silverware argenterie *f.*
since depuis
sit s'asseoir
skate patiner; **ice-skate** faire du patin à glace; **roller-skate** faire du patin à roulettes
ski ski *m.*; faire du ski alpin
sky ciel *m.* (*pl.* cieux)
sleep dormir

sleeve manche *f.*; **long-sleeved** à manches longues; **short-sleeved** à manches courtes; **sleeveless** sans manches
slipper pantoufle *f.*
slowly lentement
smell sentir
snake serpent *m.*
sneakers baskets *f. pl.*
snow neiger
so si, tellement; **so much** tant de
soap savon *m.*
solar solaire; **solar system** système solaire *m.*
soon bientôt
space espace *m.*; **spaceship** astronef *m.*, vaisseau spatial *m.*; **space suit** combinaison spatiale *f.*
sports report reportage sportif *m.*
squirrel écureuil *m.*
stamp timbre *m.*
star étoile *f.*, astre *m.*
start démarrer
steering wheel volant *m.*
stew ragoût *m.*
stewardess hôtesse de l'air *f.*
stop arrêter, s'arrêter de
story histoire *f.*; **short story** conte *m.*
street rue *f.*
striped à rayures
strong fort
study étudier
suit complet *m.* (*for men*)
sun soleil *m.*
swan cygne *m.*
swim nager

T

take prendre; **take along** emmener
tale conte *m.*; **fairy tale** conte de fées *m.*

tea thé *m.*; **iced tea** thé glacé *m.*
tell dire
thank remercier
theft vol *m.*
there y; **there is, are** il y a
thick épais (*f.* épaisse)
thief voleur *m.* (*f.* voleuse)
thousand mille, millier
through par
tie cravate *f.*
tire pneu *m.*
tissue mouchoir en papier *m.*
today aujourd'hui
tomorrow demain
too many, too much trop (de)
toothbrush brosse à dents *f.*
toothpaste dentifrice *m.*
toy joujou *m.* (*pl.* joujoux), jouet *m.*
trade métier *m.*
travel voyager
tree arbre *m.*
trip voyage *m.*
trombone trombone *m.*
trumpet trompette *f.*
trunk coffre *m.*
try, try on essayer
turkey dinde *f.*
turtle tortue *f.*
typical typique

U

undress oneself se déshabiller
Uranus Uranus

V

vacation vacances *f. pl.*
vase vase *m.*
veal veau *m.*
Venus Vénus
very très
vest gilet *m.*
veterinarian vétérinaire *m. & f.*
victim victime *f.*

violin violon *m.*
vitamin vitamine *f.*

W

wake up se réveiller
walk marcher, promener (*a dog*); **take a walk** se promener
wash oneself se laver
washing machine machine à laver *f.*
watch montre *f.*
water-ski faire du ski nautique
wave vague *f.*
wear porter
week semaine *f.*; **last week** la semaine dernière; **next week** la semaine prochaine
weekend fin de semaine *f.*, week-end *m.*
whale baleine *f.*
wheel roue *f.*; **steering wheel** volant *m.*
wide large
window fenêtre *f.*; **car window** vitre *f.*
windsurfer planche à voile *f.*
with avec
without sans
witness témoin *m.*
wool laine *f.*
work marcher, travailler
wristwatch montre-bracelet *f.*
write écrire

Y

year an *m.*, année *f.*; **last year** l'année passée; **next year** l'année prochaine
yesterday hier
young jeune

Z

zip code code postal *m.*

Grammatical Index

Topical Index